llor

3

Like a Sponge Thrown into Water

Francis Lieber

Washington July 9th 1841

68.

author of Political Ethics

Francis Lieber

Like a Sponge Thrown into Water

Francis Lieber's European Travel Journal of 1844–1845

A Lively Tour Through England, France,
Belgium, Holland, Germany, Austria, and Bohemia

WITH

Observations on Politics, the Visual and Performing Arts,
Economics, Religion, Penology, Technology, History,
Literature, Social Customs, Travel, Geography, Jurisprudence,
Linguistics, Personalities, and Numerous Other Matters

BY

One of the Nineteenth-Century's Most Influential Minds
Transcribed from the Autograph Manuscript
Preserved in the Collections of the South Caroliniana Library
at the University of South Carolina

Edited with an introduction and commentary by

Charles R. Mack and Ilona S. Mack

UNIVERSITY OF SOUTH CAROLINA PRESS

Published by the University of South Carolina Press for the South Caroliniana Library
with the assistance of the University of South Carolina Bicentennial Commission,
the Caroline McKissick Dial Publication Fund, and the South Caroliniana Society

UNIVERSITY OF SOUTH CAROLINA *BICENTENNIAL*

© 2002 University of South Carolina

Published in Columbia, South Carolina, by the
University of South Carolina Press

Manufactured in the United States of America

06 05 04 03 02   5 4 3 2 1

Library of Congress Cataloging-in-Publication Data

Lieber, Francis, 1800–1872.
  Like a sponge thrown into water : Francis Lieber's European travel journal of
1844–1845 : a lively tour through England, France, Belgium, Holland, Germany,
Austria, and Bohemia : with observations on politics, the visual and performing
arts, economics, religion, penology, technology, history, literature, social customs,
travel, geography, jurisprudence, linguistics, personalities, and numerous other
matters / by one of the nineteenth-century's most influential minds ; edited by
Charles R. Mack and Ilona S. Mack.
     p. cm.
"Transcribed from the autograph manuscript preserved in the Collections of the
South Caroliniana Library at the University of South Carolina."
  Includes bibliographical references and index.
  ISBN 1-57003-447-8 (cloth : alk. paper)
    1. Lieber, Francis, 1800–1872—Journeys—Europe. 2. Europe—
Description and travel. 3. Political scientists—United States—Biography.
4. German Americans—Biography. I. Mack, Charles R., 1940–
II. Mack, Ilona S. (Ilona Schulze), 1943– III. Title.
E415.9.L7 L54 2002
914.04'283—dc21

                                                        2001007379

This publication is dedicated
with deep appreciation
to the memory of

Dr. Oswald F. Schuette
1922–2000

Professor and chair of
the Department of Physics
University of South Carolina
and
devoted Lieber scholar

Contents

Illustrations

NOTE TO THE FRONTISPIECE: This silhouette portrait (S/NPG.91.126.72.A) of Francis Lieber was included in an album of Edouart silhouettes given to the National Portrait Gallery of the Smithsonian Institution in Washington, D.C. in 1991 by Robert L. McNeil, Jr. That album was published by Andrew Oliver as *Auguste Edouart's Silhouettes of Eminent Americans, 1839–1844* (Charlottesville: University of Virginia Press for the National Portrait Gallery, 1977), with the Lieber portrait appearing as no. 185. Edouart's full-length silhouette of Francis Lieber was cut from black paper, with a white paper insert at the collar, affixed to a paper ground, measuring 11¹⁄₁₆ × 8¼ in. Lieber's jaunty profile is set against a lithograph background of imaginary Roman ruins and antique fragments, likely chosen as an allusion to the subject's tastes and to the republican character of his adopted country. Appearing at the top of the sheet is the handwritten inscription: "Francis Lieber, Washington, July 7, 1841," followed by the identifying comment (in another hand): "author of Political Ethics." At the bottom right, Lieber's name appears again, together with the comment "author of Political Ethics" written in the same hand as that above. The artist, Auguste Amant Constant Fidele Edouart, was born in Dunkerque, France, in 1789 and died in 1861 in the town of Guisnes, near Calais. He made a successful career as a silhouettist, establishing a studio in London in 1813, where he exhibited at the Royal Academy in 1815–16. He also worked in Ireland and in America for ten years beginning in 1839. It was Edouart's custom to create duplicate portraits of his subjects; the whereabouts of the one given to Lieber is unknown while the present copy was included in the artist's personal album which he entitled "American Characters." The silhouette was executed while Lieber was in Washington enlisting the aid of the Prussian Minister to the United States, the Baron Friedrich Ludwig von Roenne, who he hoped would work on his behalf in securing a pardon from King Friedrich Wilhelm IV. Since the pardon (for the crime of leaving Prussia without permission) was prerequisite to a return to his homeland and a general European tour, this silhouette portrait is the appropriate prelude to our publication of Francis Lieber's *European Travel Journal.*

Heretofore unpublished in a Lieber connection, Edouart's silhouette now joins a small list of nine currently known Lieber portraits: (1) the drawing by Theodore von Hildebrandt showing Lieber, ca. 1824–26, among the members of Pentadelphia Society of Berlin (reproduced in the Special Section of the *National-Zeitung,* Berlin, 13 December 1896 and discovered by the late Mike Schuette and brought to our attention by John Catalano); (2) the Edouart silhouette of 1841; (3) William Harrison Scarborough's oil portrait of 1848–49, commissioned by the Euphradian Society of South Carolina College (present location unknown; formerly in the possession of Francis Lieber III, Bryn Mawr, Pa. and reproduced in Helen Hennig, *William Harrison Scarborough: A Parade of the Living Past,* Columbia, S.C.: R. L. Bryan, 1937, no. 225a), and here used as illus. no. 2; (4) a marble portrait also commissioned by the Euphradian Society but tossed from its window and smashed at the start of the Civil War; (5) a photographic portrait commissioned by the senior class at Columbia University in 1858 and given to each member (this likeness is probably to be associated with a wet plate, albumen *carte de visite* photograph mounted on a 2⅜ × 4 inch card bearing the backmark of D. Appleton & Co., N.Y. sold in November

2001 as item # cdv2969 by War Between the States Memorabilia of Gettysburg, Pa.; (6) an engraving, evidently based upon a different photographic source, first used in 1882 as the frontispiece to Thomas Sergeant Perry's *The Life and Letters of Francis Lieber* (Boston: James R. Osgood, 1882); (7) a photograph preserved in the Library of Congress, Washington, D.C., LCBH82-4591 (we again are indebted to John Catalano for calling this to our attention); (8) a standing, three-quarter length photograph of Lieber striking a "Napoleonic" pose at Columbia University (brought to our attention by Dr. Ronald Hyatt of the University of North Carolina–Chapel Hill); and (9) the posthumous bronze portrait by John Quincy Adams Ward set up in 1895 over his grave on New York City's Woodlawn Cemetery, located in the Bronx at Jerome and Bainbridge Avenues (plaster cast in the South Caroliniana Library of the University of South Carolina donated in 1935 by Miss Mary Lieber).

Preface and Acknowledgments

During its two-hundred-year history, the University of South Carolina (until 1906 known as South Carolina College) has laid claim to its share of distinguished faculty members. But perhaps none has achieved greater renown than the author of the journal presented here. Francis Lieber was one of the most celebrated and influential intellectual figures of the nineteenth century, on either side of the Atlantic. Interestingly, Lieber's twenty-one years of service at South Carolina College, from 1835 to 1856, were the most productive of his career. Unfortunately, as is so often the case with the passing of the years, memory of his many accomplishments (and their lasting impact) has begun to fade.

I had spent almost two decades teaching at the University of South Carolina before I actually became aware of the historical presence of Francis Lieber. Yes, I knew that the original "Horseshoe" of the old campus boasted a handsome brick building of Federal character named Lieber College and that the man after whom it was named (I later learned that he and his wife were its first residential occupants) had once been an illustrious member of the faculty, but it was only a few years ago, when a university colleague of mine, Oswald (Mike) Schuette, dragged me into the South Caroliniana Library to look at this journal, that I truly discovered Francis Lieber. Mike, a distinguished member and long-time chair of the Department of Physics, was a man of many interests and had long been our campus's chief custodian of Francis Lieber's memory (and that of his scientist son, Oscar). Mike thought that I, as an historian of Italian Renaissance art, might be appreciative of an eloquent passage in the journal describing Lieber's reaction to Raphael's *Madonna del Sisto* in the Dresden Gallery. He was absolutely right; I found it to be a beautifully worded description of an evocative encounter with a work of great art. I promised Mike that I would use it as the basis for a paper or even an article. I never did. But I was now aware of Lieber and I even read through Frank Freidel's 1947 biography and the earlier, slender volume by Lewis Harley. Lieber proved to be a fascinating character. That was more than a decade ago and my focus soon shifted back to other projects more related to my own fields of specialization.

My interest in Francis Lieber and his journal was revived in conjunction with preparations for the University of South Carolina's 2001 bicentennial year. At Mike Schuette's urging, an ad hoc committee, chaired by Dr. Harry Lesesne, associate director of the USC Bicentennial Commission, was established to organize an international symposium dealing with Francis Lieber. I was pleased to be invited to serve on the Lieber Committee and, as we laid our plans, I realized that this would be the perfect occasion to do what should have been done long ago—to publish Francis Lieber's *European Travel Journal.*

In acknowledging all those who have made the publication of this volume possible, I must give first place to Mike Schuette, whose dogged determination was really responsible for this effort. While Mike was active in the organizational stages of the USC bicentennial year's recognition of Francis Lieber, he sadly did not live to participate in the University's Francis Lieber Symposium, held in November 2001, or to witness the publication of this journal. He did, however, have the satisfaction of knowing that both would take place and of how appreciative his colleagues were of his leadership in the Lieber projects. His seminal role has been gratefully acknowledged in both the dedication of this volume and of the 2001 symposium. He knew of the former and could have guessed the latter.

When I suggested publishing the journal to Dr. George Terry, Vice Provost and Dean of Libraries and Information Systems at the University of South Carolina, he was immediately enthusiastic and supportive, as was the journal's present custodian, the Director of the South Caroliniana Library, Dr. Allen Stokes. Dr. Stokes and his staff assisted in every way and kindly made available a photocopy of the journal, which greatly accelerated the process of transcription. It is unfortunate that neither the man who inspired it nor the one who made its publication possible were able to witness the appearance of this volume. Dr. George Terry died unexpectedly in October 2001.

I am additionally appreciative of the assistance of Henry Fuller and Tom Johnson at the South Caroliniana Library. Dr. Lesesne and other members of the USC Bicentennial Office facilitated this project in many ways. My colleagues on the Lieber Symposium committee, especially John Catalano (who called my attention to the Lieber photograph in the Library of Congress), were helpful sources of information. Professors Catherine Castner and Buford Norman of my university's Department of French and Classics rendered assistance with some of the French and Latin passages. Externally, I am indebted to Sandra Levinson (a former graduate student of mine), at the National Museum of American Art in Washington, D.C., who assisted in some important archival matters and who introduced me to the handsome silhouette portrait of Francis Lieber which serves as the frontispiece to this volume. I am additionally indebted to Ann Prentice Wagner, the Assistant Curator of Prints and Drawings at the National Portrait Gallery, for providing further information concerning this remarkable portrait and its artist. Dr. Ronald W. Hyatt of the Department of Exercise and Sport Science of the University of North Carolina-Chapel Hill also contributed an additional photograph to be added to our list of Lieber likenesses which he had discovered in the possession of Columbia University.

The University of South Carolina Press greeted the publication proposal with much encouragement. Alexander Moore at the Press provided constant and useful guidance and his colleague, Scott Evan Burgess, did a superb job of editing. Their assistance was most beneficial. Financial support which made the publication of the journal possible came from several institutional sources and from the USC Bicentennial Commission, as acknowledged at the beginning of this volume. During my work on the project in Berlin in the summer of 2000, the hospitality and assistance of Brigitte Bonsack and Karl Heinz Mayer were greatly appreciated. Much of the transcription, research, and writing was carried out during a sabbatical leave in the fall of 2000.

My wife's collaboration in this editorial effort has been essential. A native Berliner like Lieber, she not only provided a second set of interpretive eyes to correct many a potential error in the transcription of Lieber's sometimes difficult and, occasionally faint, handwriting, but she also translated those passages written in German and was particularly sensitive to the Germanic nuances in Lieber's use of English in the rest of the entries. Her involvement in the preparation of the entry commentaries was also intimate. This was a project of spousal cooperation in the fullest sense.

CHARLES R. MACK

William Harrison Scarborough, *Portrait of Francis Lieber* (1848), commissioned by The Euphradian Society of South Carolina College in 1848 (Present location unknown; formerly Francis Lieber III, Bryn Mawr, Pa.)

Francis Lieber and His Journal

"I live the life of a long dried sponge thrown into water," enthused Professor Francis Lieber in a letter written from Paris in September of 1844 to his friend and later prominent senator from Massachusetts, Charles Sumner.[1] Such words expressed Lieber's emotions on his first trip back to Europe since his flight to America some seventeen years earlier. For ten months, he gloried in the people, places, art, theater, and diversity of his European wanderings. Presented here is the journal that Francis Lieber kept during his purposeful travels through England and much of the European continent north of the Alps and in which he recorded his daily experiences. As such, it offers us a window through which we can view the Europe of the 1840s, between the Age of Napoleon and the tumultuous revolutionary days of 1848. But such travel journals are not unusual, in and of themselves. Many a nineteenth-century voyager kept similar records and a number of them were even published at the time. This particular journal, however, is more than an ordinary daily itinerary or guidebook. Its real value lies in the importance of the person who kept it and what he had to say about whom he met and what he saw and experienced.

It is no great exaggeration to say that Francis (Franz) Lieber was a "household name" on both sides of the Atlantic throughout much of the nineteenth century. With a breadth of genius and far-ranging vision comparable to that of Thomas Jefferson (whose confidence in a broad-based democracy the Whiggish German did not share), Lieber was a true "Renaissance man." Living as he did at the beginning of the Industrial and Information Ages, he was among the last for whom it was practical to assimilate and contribute to such a broad spectrum of knowledge.

Born in Berlin on 18 March 1798, Francis Lieber lived a life of adventure, achievement, fame, some considerable frustration, and, ultimately, lasting significance.[2] As a child he was horrified by the Napoleonic humiliation of his native Prussia, a memory which turned him into a forceful nationalist, whether championing the dream of a unified Germany or defending the constitutional federalism of his adopted country of America. As a youth he came under the instructional influence and shared the patriotic fervor of Friedrich Jahn (known as "Turnvater Jahn," the father of gymnastic sport), a man who promoted sound minds and bodies devoted to German union and liberty. Fired by Jahn's pronouncements and his revolutionary zeal, the young Franz Lieber joined the German troops who helped rout Napoleon at Waterloo. He almost died in that campaign and boasted of his wounds throughout the remainder his life.

In the subsequent era of restoration, Lieber found himself at odds with the conservatism of the Prussian regime and his position as a chief lieutenant of Jahn soon brought the unwanted attention of the police; his liberal views and supposed association with student agitators ultimately even caused his interrogation and detention. In effect driven from Berlin, Lieber took a doctoral degree (in Mathematics) at the University of Jena before setting off to join an international band of young idealists on the crusade to liberate Greece from Turkish domination. Disillusioned by that quixotic experience, Lieber landed in Italy in 1822 and took the position of tutor to the son of the Prussian minister to Rome, the great classical scholar Barthold Niebuhr. Really more Niebuhr's secretary and protégé, Lieber absorbed much from that impressive mind including a more moderating and conservative political outlook. The lessons of the ancient Roman Republic, so much admired by Niebuhr, comprised a major aspect of Lieber's revised political outlook —"No right without its duties; no duty without its rights" became his guiding principle.

Having returned to Berlin in 1823, Lieber seems to have decided to work within the political system in order to achieve his goals of German unification and institutional republicanism. His youthful enthusiasm abated, he had also become interested in finding a position in keeping with his education and ambitions. The Prussian police remained suspicious, however, and twice arrested him. Lieber actually spent a total of twelve months in Berlin jails, an experience which helped to determine his abiding interest in legal procedures and penal reform. Finally, in 1826, realizing that he would never be above suspicion and that all German doors to civil or university employment would be closed to him, Lieber fled to England. His admiration for English institutions was emphatic and he probably hoped to remain in that country. He quickly made influential friends and began to refine his command of the new language. He found employment as a tutor with the family of a German businessman in London; soon love between the young teacher and his pupil, Matilda Oppenheimer, blossomed. Ever hopeful of attaining a worthy position in England, Lieber eventually yielded to an adventuresome prospect as director of a newly founded, German-style gymnasium in Boston and set sail for what he may have anticipated as only a temporary interlude in America.

In Boston he managed the city's popular gymnasium and opened a swimming pool which counted among its visitors the American president, John Quincy Adams, as well as the naturalist John James Audubon. Soon Matilda Oppenheimer joined Lieber in America and the two were married. The couple began a family, eventually giving birth to three sons, Oscar Montgomery, Hamilton (whose name attests to his father's political and economic persuasions) and Guido Norman. Francis Lieber rejoiced in the American experience, which seemed to offer so much opportunity both politically and personally. He rejected on principle both absolute monarchies and, remembering the earlier French experience, pure democracies as being dangerously autocratic; for him, American republicanism and representative government offered a tempered balance. Despite its rawness, America became for Lieber, as it did for so many other immigrants, the land of promising refuge. Mindful of Germany's failure to achieve national unification, he extolled the American union of states and became one of its greatest champions. Putting his European origins behind him, Lieber became not only an American resident but a citizen.

Constantly on the hunt for professional opportunities and a prestigious position from which to display his diverse talents, Lieber proposed the compilation of an *Encyclopedia Americana,* an idea which was accepted by the Philadelphia publisher John Carey. That publication took as its model not the English *Encyclopedia Britannica* but the celebrated Brockhaus *Conversations-Lexikon* of Germany; Lieber served as the organizing editor and primary author of the new endeavor. Although the publication of the *Encyclopedia,* beginning in 1829, was an enormous success, it brought little financial reward to Lieber. It did, however, earn him a wide-spread reputation and intellectual acceptance. Lieber became an intimate with some of America's greatest figures of scholarship and politics and a correspondent with their counterparts in Europe. From his now prolific pen flowed treatise upon treatise and essay upon essay, dealing with subjects from statecraft to linguistics, from penitentiary reform to economics. He could count among his friends and admirers such figures as Henry Wadsworth Longfellow, Charles Sumner, Alexis de Tocqueville, Daniel Webster, Judge Joseph Story, Julia Ward Howe, etc. He maintained a literary friendship with Edgar Allan Poe, who solicited a manuscript from him for the *Southern Literary Messenger* in 1836, and with Washington Irving to whom he dedicated his *The Stranger in America* in 1835. Seemingly, his career had been launched, but his search for a permanent position of stature was a series of "might-have-beens." While he largely devised the program for Philadelphia's Gerard College and advised on the creation of New York City University, much to his disappointment he never was offered a position on either faculty; nor were his desires for a Harvard invitation ever realized.

It was not until 1835, when he was recruited by the recently reorganized South Carolina College as its new professor of history and political economics, that he partially accomplished his objective. His arrival in Columbia, however, must have been a shock. Boston, New York, and Philadelphia were no European centers of culture, and tiny Columbia was even less so. Although the College was a solid and respected institution, it did not have the cachet of its Northern counterparts and, worst of all, the economy of his new home was based upon a system he despised. He could agree with his Southern hosts on the issue of Free Trade but not upon the matter of States' Rights or their "peculiar institution." He suppressed his unionist and abolitionist views as long as he could but they would eventually, two decades later, prove his undoing. Each summer, as soon as the semester came to a close, Lieber fled to his friends in the North and his hope of finding some sort of teaching position there. Many times he came close to achieving his desire but it all came to naught. Yet, in exile in South Carolina as he may have felt, the time spent in Columbia proved to be the most productive of his career. From this period came his major publications: the *Legal and Political Hermeneutics* (1837), the *Manual of Political Ethics* (1838–39), the *Essays on Property and Labour* (1841), and *On Civil Liberty and Self-Government* (1853). These were the works that solidified his reputation as one of the most productive and influential minds of the age. And as a thinker, Francis Lieber can be seen today as both an eclectic synthesizer and as an innovative and, ofttimes, uncanny visionary. Alarmed, for instance, by what he had heard of the extreme Czarist despotism in Russia, he predicted to his friend George Hillard in 1851 that "this will create ultimately a convulsive explosion and give for a time, fearful power to Communism, Socialism and all other sorts of French democratic absolutism."[3] Even Karl Marx hardly proved a better prophet.

After nine years in his South Carolina "exile" and with an ever-widening circle of influential friends and admirers, Lieber turned his attention to escape and a European "sabbatical" for 1844–45. Already in the early 1830s Lieber had written to a friend in Germany that he had "castles in the air about Europe. Oh, that they might become realities."[4] It was not that he yearned for a permanent return to his native land; he had become quite Americanized but he was starved for the world of intellectual energy, for stimulating conversation, and for the sights and sounds of cultural activity. In the same letter, Lieber noted that "I cannot say I have homesickness for Germany—but for Europe, for science and art." In another letter, written in 1837 to a friend who intended to go to Europe, he complained: "Your letter has made me sad. I cannot hear that someone is going to Europe without feeling how my heart is breaking."[5] Clearly, he was eager to re-familiarize himself with what he had sacrificed in coming to America. Lieber had finally received, in 1842, an official pardon from the Prussian government (for having left its jurisdiction without permission) and this made the trip feasible and prompted his decision. Then, too, the more progressive climate initiated with the reign of the new king of Prussia, Friedrich Wilhelm IV, promised a favorable official reception and—just possibly—some prospect of employment. The trip seems to have been specifically occasioned by a sort of Oppenheimer family reunion which brought back the far-flung members of this prosperous mercantile family to their seat in Hamburg, Germany. The extended Oppenheimer clan included the Liebers from the United States as well as Matilda's sister and her children from Puerto Rico. The Liebers apparently traveled separately, Matilda departing earlier, with Norman and Hamilton, directly for Hamburg; Oscar was already in school there under the supervision of his mother's German relatives.[6]

Francis Lieber himself sailed later and, despite feeling (his frequently expressed) pangs of separation, with the intent of turning the Oppenheimer family gathering into a "business trip" which would take him first to London, Paris, and the battlefields of Waterloo before joining his family in Hamburg. Matilda and the boys, we gather from the journal, stayed put in Hamburg while Lieber kept mostly on the move, visiting with them on two lengthy occasions. His own journey allowed him to make and renew contacts (as well as see the sights and sample the pleasures) in England, France, the Low Countries, and Austria, as well as in Germany and his native Berlin (where he visited with his brothers and sisters).

In many ways Lieber's European Tour was a resounding success. Evidently his fame had proceeded him and, if his name was not familiar enough, he was armed with letters of introduction from his many friends in the high circles of American politics and intellectual life. He was wined, dined, and otherwise entertained wherever he went in both England and on the continent, in large and small towns alike. Politicians, diplomats, scholars, the literati, and the nobility seem to have demanded his presence. However, once the trip was over he must have returned to America disappointed for, yet again, desired appointments seemed just beyond his grasp and the one actually offered (from Prussia) he could not afford to accept.

Back in South Carolina, the presidency of the College eluded him as well, whether due to his temperament, his foreign origin, his liberal Episcopalianism, or his suspected anti-slavery sentiments.[7] It was an opportune moment when he left South Carolina in disgust in 1856; the Civil War was looming and, happily, a position on the faculty of Columbia College (now University) in New York City soon came his way. He remained at Columbia College until his death in 1872, although often on leave to serve his government in a number of official and unofficial capacities. Among his many far-sighted contributions were ideas for an international copyright law, the organization of the captured Confederate archives, the International Red Cross, the American adoption of the postal message card, a proposal for a U.S. Department of Statistics (made as early as 1834 and based upon Prussian, French, and British models) and, most significantly, the first ever code of warfare (U.S. Military Orders No. 100), which formed the basis for the later

Hague (and Geneva) Conventions (and the underpinnings for both the Nuremberg Trials and the more recent Yugoslavian war crimes tribunal). Along the way, Lieber introduced into the American vocabulary the terms and concepts of "publicist," "penology," "individualism," "interdependence," "city-state," "commonwealth of nations," "Pan-American," "nationalism," "internationalism" and "bureaucracy."[8]

~

When Francis Lieber and his wife left South Carolina in the winter of 1856, his notes, manuscripts, letters, and journals went North with them. Those that have survived are now, for the most part, in the collections of the Henry E. Huntington Library in Pasadena, the Library of Congress, and the university libraries at Johns Hopkins in Baltimore, Columbia in New York, and Harvard in Boston. His journal, however, was returned to Columbia, South Carolina, in 1966 as part of a gift of Lieber family papers and other materials presented to the South Caroliniana Library of the University of South Carolina by Francis Lieber III, the grandson of Guido Norman Lieber. There it has since remained, unpublished and little consulted.[9]

Francis Lieber's *European Travel Journal of 1844–1845* is part tourist compendium (including accounts of conveyances used, miles traveled, prices charged, meals taken, and hotels slept in), cultural commentary (on the people, places, and, above all, art works encountered), record of conversations (with royalty and nobles, statesmen and scholars, common laborers, etc.), and notation of impressions and ideas, many of which had or would surface in his separate publications and proposals. It also offers a fascinating insight into his family life and personal beliefs, observations, and idiosyncracies. And there is some vanity. Lieber is quick to express his delight when recognized and is flattered when his work is appreciated or his advice sought. How he must have enjoyed it when he chanced to be on the scene as an unknown lawyer appeared in a London office and asked for one of his publications!

Francis Lieber's habit of name-dropping, particularly if the person was a member of the nobility, seems oddly sycophantic today, coming as it did from the pen of a proclaimed republican; it is an initially annoying aspect, but somehow in the end seems endearing. With all his many letters of introduction, visitations, and invitations, one comes away almost surprised that he did not meet Charles Dickens at an English breakfast or sup with Heinrich Heine in Düsseldorf; and he only missed George Sand in Paris because she was out of town. On the other hand, he did bump, quite literally, into the elderly Duke of Wellington at a London street corner and, of course, he renewed his acquaintance with Alexis de Tocqueville in Paris. His two lengthy conversations with King Friedrich Wilhelm IV of Prussia are especially interesting, as is his interview with the great geographer and naturalist, Alexander von Humboldt. Lieber's inclusion of his transcription of a particularly poignant letter from Julia Ward Howe (written in fluent German) provides an extra reward for the reader.

Throughout the journal, Lieber emerges as an astute and objective observer of minute details, whether they be linguistic, social, or artistic (in respect to the last, he has a fine eye for sculptural shapes, physical features, hues of color, etc.). His curiosity is boundless. His discussions are serious and informative, whether over political systems or prison reform, yet his capacity for pure enjoyment is refreshing. He is a frequent theatergoer, storing up such opportunities in London, Paris, Munich, Berlin, and Vienna against the relatively barren Carolina semesters to come. At the London Zoo, he rides an elephant and expresses amazement that it was not until then that he actually saw a living American beaver and otter. Lieber provides sharp analyses of human nature and he also displays quite an eye for the ladies. In the era of the "science of phrenology," he pays close attention to physiognomy, describing at some length the portrait features of great leaders. He often allows his emotions to run and his reaction to painting, sculpture, and dance can be enraptured, even ekphrastic. But he does not lose objectivity; he can even be sharply critical of his beloved Raphael or of a new artistic discovery, the contemporary German sculptor Johann Dannecker. If there are thematic constants in the journal (aside from his quest for employment and his admiration for the dancing siren of the day, Fanny Elssler), they are his interests in judicial reform and prison conditions and his belief in the concept of nationhood. In many respects, of course, Lieber is a product of his times; as such, he provides much historical insight. Lieber, for instance, displays a love/hate relationship (shared by many in his day) for the figure of Napoleon Bonaparte, as well as an Anglo-German anxiety regarding latent French militarism. In a number of other ways he would seem to offer much of more enduring profit; his notions of the state, of penal reform, of interpretive artistic criticism, and of civic responsibility, for example, might well be considered for modern reapplication. His negative views on the Austrian public lottery are an added note of interest.

Francis Lieber's journal consists of 216 pages of day-to-day entries, written in ink on lined pages measuring $7\frac{7}{8}$ x $6\frac{3}{8}$ inches sewn on tapes within a thin leather-on-board cover, typical for such personal ledgers. The end papers and the edges are marbled. A small label, affixed to the inside of the front cover, tells us that it was sold by Love & Barton Booksellers of 12 Market Street of Manchester. Whether this volume was bought in America by Lieber and begun at the start of his journey or purchased in England with the American phase of the trip filled in later is not clear. The daily entries, for the most part, seem to have been set down on a day-to-day basis, although the author does indicate that some were written after the fact. On his second trip to Berlin (October-November 1844), for whatever reason, Lieber decided not to make journal entries (his explanation indicates that he felt his conversation with the King of too delicate a nature to set down while in Prussia) and, instead, inserted three letters that he had written to his wife, detailing the events. Also added to the journal are several newspaper clippings, a copy of an English postal letter, a train schedule, a blank bank check, a letter from an official of a Hamburg poor house, an engraving of the Houses of Parliament, and other materials which caught his attention. Particularly delightful is the inserted block-lettered note written in pencil by the Lieber's middle son, Norman, containing his Christmas "wish list."

In the course of transcribing and editing the journal, we have tried to preserve the full flavor of the original. We have thought it advisable, however, to introduce some corrections and modifications into the transcription. Where mistakes in spelling appear to have been unintentional and where simple lapses in grammar and spelling occur, we have made the appropriate changes in order to produce a more "reader friendly" text. The same is true for general sentence structure. Lieber's practice of punctuation, for instance, echoes a latent German usage but is, essentially, idiosyncratic. Commas, for example, are scattered about in a seemingly indiscriminate fashion; the same is true for semicolons. In preparing this edition, we have eliminated many of both in the cause of readability. Lieber also employed the dash with great frequency, particularly as an indication that he was switching subjects. We have found this "system" useful and, in many instances, have retained it, both for its utility and because it suggests the character of Lieber's writing. We have italicized recognized titles of works of art and literature. We also have attempted to clarify his abbreviations—for names, places, titles, and even persons—when his intentions are clear and have, accordingly, completed some of his words for him. To facilitate publication, Lieber's marginal notations and insertions have been integrated into the text at the appropriate juncture and are denoted by parenthetical enclosure. Our editorial comments within the text are enclosed in brackets.

Rather than interrupt the flow of the entries through the use of footnotes, an appendix of commentary keyed to the date of each entry will attempt to clarify Lieber's account. In several places in his text, Lieber made mention of his use of the celebrated guidebook series published by John Murray of London.[10] Accordingly, in our commentary to the individual entries, we have followed Lieber's own advice and have made extensive use of the Murray guides (attempting to use editions as close to the time of Lieber's journey as were available), comparing Lieber's descriptions and touristic information with those in the guides. This has proved most helpful in reconstructing the specific details of our author's itinerary and in interpreting his sometimes cryptic meanings. Where the page numbers in the original guides included an asterisk, we have retained the original marking.

Lieber recorded his two conversations with the king of Prussia and the comments of Alexander von Humboldt largely in the German language of those interviews. In the body of the journal's text we have chosen to translate these lengthy passages into English but, in order to illustrate the ease with which Lieber switched between languages, we have presented the original German texts in an appendix. The same was done for the letter from Julia Ward Howe which Lieber transcribed into his journal. Shorter passages in the entries in either French or German are included within the text followed by their English translations in brackets.

Many of the personages whom Lieber encountered are of historical interest, and another appendix provides a brief biographical sketch of identifiable individuals, arranged in alphabetical order. Lieber's journal has numerous leitmotifs (penal reform, political economy, art criticism, etc.); therefore yet another appendix is arranged by major themes with references to entry dates. A concluding index of names and places will further serve as a guide to the journal. It is hoped that these annotations, together with this brief essay on the author's life and contributions, will be found useful to the reader in tracing Francis Lieber's path across the Europe of the 1840s.

Notes

1. Frank Freidel, *Francis Lieber: Nineteenth-Century Liberal* (Baton Rouge: Louisiana State University Press, 1947), p. 216.

2. The year of Francis Lieber's birth is disputed, some preferring 1800, following Lieber's own usage. Freidel (Ibid., p. 3n. 4), however, claims to have found definitive evidence for the year 1798. That date is now accepted by most authorities.

3. Ibid., p. 268.

4. Ibid., p. 112.

5. Hugo Preuss, *Franz Lieber, ein Bürger zweier Welten* (Hamburg: J. F. Richter, 1888), p. 33.

6. In a diary entry of 24 February 1844, given in Perry, *The Life and Letters of Francis Lieber* (Boston: James R. Osgood, 1882, p. 179), Lieber noted the receipt of a "Letter from Hamburg. Great joy at our coming. Oscar writes: 'I never wrote nor do I think I shall ever write a happier letter. What glorious news your last brought me.'" On 3 March, Lieber wrote in the same diary: "Getting ready fast. The days of my solitude are over."

7. South Carolina College faculty meeting records do show that Lieber served as President pro tem of the institution in 1851 and, in that capacity, he is listed among the past presidents of the university.

8. Freidel, *Francis Lieber*, p. 101 and Steven Alan Samson, "Francis Lieber on the Sources of Civil Liberty," *Humanitas*, 9, 2 (1996). See Lieber's own essay "What I have Done" of 1861, noted in Freidel (*Francis Lieber*, p. 179), in which are listed words he thought he originated.

9. While still in the possession of Matilda Lieber, this journal was used by Thomas Sergeant Perry for his *The Life and Letters of Francis Lieber*. Perry selected only a few of the entries to use in his book (pp. 180–93) and used them in much abbreviated and amended form. He offered no commentary as to events or persons discussed.

10. Much of the library holdings of the old South Carolina College survived the Civil War to be incorporated into that of the new University of South Carolina. While the present Thomas Cooper Library of the University possesses several volumes of the nineteenth-century *Murray Guides*, it is curious that those very volumes cited and used by Lieber on his trip are missing. One cannot help but wonder if he took them with him on his European sabbatical and neglected to return them to the College Library.

Like a Sponge Thrown into Water

A Visit to Europe
from April 14, 1844 to January 16, 1845

FRANCIS LIEBER

Columbia and American Departure

6 March. Rebecca comes yet. All professors take leave. Henry not. Students no blessing. Simmons, Senior, wants yet preparatory course of study for law.

7 March, Thursday. Baskin sends 3 partridges for breakfast. From Columbia to Charleston, 106 miles railway $6.50. First regular singing of mockingbird at Branchville. I delight in it whenever I hear it, however often. At 3 o'clock at Charleston. Alston Hague at the depot, with Aston's snuffbox of Court Oak for Preston and the drawing of a live oak by Mary McCord from Savannah. To Weldon 130 miles $13. From the sea we saw a forest in fire, which is an every day's occurance.

8 March, Friday. Smithfield in the morning. Forests of stiff utility (pitch pines) labeled by the sapping or rather tapping axe. The little prairie about 20 miles from Smithfield. Dinner of course at Goldsborough. Perfectly straight line of 52 miles between Goldsborough and Weldon. $12.

9 March, Saturday. 2 morning at Petersburgh. 5 Richmond. 10 Fredricksburg and Potomac bay. Snug steamer and beautiful bay. Canvasback duck, but I [had] headache. ½ past 2 o'clock at Washington. Choate, Markoe and Ingersoll. Markoe says Webster's correspondence with Ashburton and others written by chief clerk chiefly; that he drinks very badly.

10 March, Sunday. To Markoe. Long talk on the Institute. Upshur would have made me bearer of dispatches. Captain Stockton, of the *Princeton*, on the sofa, talks much of the disaster. Judge Story. With Choate to Webster, who says: "You may have letters to any of my friends." Long and interesting talk on climate and vegetable geography. I ask "Have you seen *Orpheus*?" Answer "No."

11 March, Monday. After breakfast to Choate. At 9 in Alexandria steamboat to see the *Princeton*, steam frigate, not more than fr. 6 to 700 tons. Ericson English engineer, refused by English government engaged by cpt. Stockton. Contract. made for $220,000 (?) built for $180,000. Perfect sailing ship. Propeller, under the water, like wings of windmill, with the difference that wind, surrounding element propels and will [wheel?] stationary, but here steam engine propels acting on the surrounding element, and ship moveable. No piston but a large surface which produces motion like two pair of hands turning a handmill. Easy disconnection of propeller. Nothing whatever can be seen, not even smoke stack, which is like an opera glass, screwed out. Elegant cabin far more roomy than usual, with curtains. The burst gun; round the ring at the trunnion all granulated, is the break of <u>welded</u> wrought iron always so. The English one is rent a little opposite to touch hole. The burst one American make. 3 boilers, all of which can be separately cleaned whilst the others are used. Stockton had given me introduction to first lieutenant. He escaped miraculously; So Davis (Jack Downing). At 12 return to Markoe. Upshur meant to do much for me. Congressional Library. Picture of Columbus presented by Mr. Middleton. Cannot find it so beautiful as Preston says. My *Ethics* well read. Write there to Story. Senate does not sit, because artillery had just practiced near it, and broken all windows. American! And that immediately after *Princeton*. In the Baltimore car meet Gevers, Dutch Chargé d'Affaires, who offers letters. Baltimore Mon. Harper. What a confiding Catholic. With Gevers about.

12 March, Tuesday. With Gevers to railway cars for Philadelphia; introduced me to Mrs. Johnson (Norris) whom I had known as a little child. In Philadelphia saw J. J. Barclay, talk prison, and Mrs. Wilcox (Miss Waln) and him! An old man, who cannot easily keep open his eye-lids, with mustachios!

13 March. To New York arrive by two. Arrange matters, etc.

14 March, Thursday. In the afternoon to Boston. Arrive at Boston, late — about ½ past 9. Go to Betsy.

15 March. To Aston Audley, hair cut; Thayer, and show him Judge Story's affectionate letter; to Hillard & Sumner, where I find the bouquet letter from Fanny Appleton with letters from Longfellow to Freiligrath, etc., from Ticknor to several people. To Mary Sumner working at a purse for me. The Inglis; as she expected us to go so soon; Jane at a purse and Lydia at slippers for me. With Hillard to Crawford's *Orpheus*. Not so fine as one might expect from engraving yet it shows genius undoubtedly. The head and right arm are a fine poem, but there is too little rest in the whole; looks as looking down a precipice; right arm and lyre too hard, wooden, drapery heavy, face, I think too young, left hand too large, [word illegible] the thumb, but still head, arm, upper position very fine. Saw Ticknor; Sumner writes hastily yet letters. None had expected me, because the letter indicating my approaching departure arrives only the day with me. Start for New York.

16 March. Arrive at New York for Montezuma cannot sail on account of weather and on the wharf going to Boston, I had written to Marshall, who now owns chief part of the blackball line, and was the Captain who commanded the Britannia which brought me out, and wished me much to go in his Montezuma, that I would go if he could give me separate room. I found all was right.

17 March, Sunday. Dine at Heckscher's, take tea at Oakey's, and supper at Ward's. Heckscher gives me letters, Oakeys do so Ward. Medorer gives me a box of cigars and large bottle of eau de Cologne.

18 March, Monday. Get purse from Mary. Sail at 12 o'clock. These packets, the flowers of the ocean. Capt. Lowber, a fine fellow.

[After an apparently uneventful crossing, Francis Lieber resumes his Journal entries]

Francis Lieber's European itinerary (from M. Malte-Brun, *New General Atlas,* Philadelphia: Grigg & Elliot, 1837)

England

14 April, Sunday. Old English comfort-bed. The strongest character of substantial comfort, cleanliness, sufficiency, fresh, a little stiffness. Mary strikes me as the cleverest, pretty. Frederic, a graceful pratter — reminds me of Norman. Fine old church, old elms — very long service. Visit Union House. Woodhouse had never been there — nor did he know who Hallam is! Union clean, ventilated yet very cheerless. Children look very well — even those born there. Took a walk [with] Woodhouse — my eyes feast on the green — how sweet, how civilized! Many poor, very old, tottering houses in Leominster, yet a certain trimness about of all of these even very different however from American pipe clay cleanliness. Town house must be very old.

15 April, Monday. Ride with Joseph to Croft Ambrey (fine hill) about 7 mile from Leominster; pass Croft Castle, fine old trees, Lucter School; Berrington, Lord Rodney's seat, pass through park. —I often know more about England than [the] people here. Drive with James Woodhouse to his house in the Hill 8 miles from Leominster. He is an excellent fellow and somewhat of the Yankee in business. The country is glorious. Hereford is truly all I ever dreamt in childhood of meadows, and valleys — what roads, vales, little gardens, lawns, trees, gentle rivers, hedges, orchards, wheatfields — it is like poetry. People bow here and curtsey to passers by.

16 April. Walk with Augusta and the girls — oh how delicious! I hear the first sky lark. I could have cried. Wheat a foot high. Cherries in blossom. It must look like a paradise when all the orchards are in blossom. Drink the finest cider I ever drank at James', kiss them all through and start at 1 for Worcester. Fine country through Tenbury; becomes more and more plain toward Worcester. Pass Lord Ward's seat where the Queen Dowager was residing, see Marvin Hill, arrive by 6 at West Severn, old church on passing the bridge. Shilling here, shilling there, everyone wants something, and the worst is one's self comes to consider a shilling nothing. Start for Oxford.

Oxford

17 April. Talkative coachman. By two in the morning we arrive. I had gone inside [the coach], the rattling woke me, and the first thing I beheld, rapidly passing was University College — this old, solemn building! Good room at the Angel, of course will be dear like thunder. When I went out was struck with the mass of Gothic building. James Woodhouse had given me 3 letters to College people, and not one here — vexation. Went into bookseller's shop. The man advised me what I should see for so short a time. Radcliffe Library; thence Bodleian Library; everything is old, Gothic — Book with Albert's, Wellington's and Everett's signatures, some show Mss. e.g., Saxon Bible, Pictures: the following interest me. William I of Orange, strong mouth, but I had imagined him very different; Sarpi, keen face; Oxenstierna, strange large face, strong; Friedrich I of Prussia like a bad corporal, as he always looks; Columbus, very bad; Philip II, as he always looks,

William III and Mary, strong faces; Charles II, very big nose; James II, coarse feature; Strafford, fine expression, somber, thinking, the melancholy of grasping minds with slight irony around his mouth; Land very different, high arched eyebrows, but otherwise strong features not course, but not intellectual either. Montaigne, like a modern gentleman, and very decidedly English as his father was an Englishman; Mary of Scots by Zucchero shows fine traits; Grotius, not very peculiar; Elizabeth, shocking; Henry VIII, as always. A chair which he often used; Clarendon, round face with blond hair, if his. —To New College. There is a walk between New College, All Souls, etc., and one between Baliol, Corpus & Christ, where a man can hardly fancy himself in 1844, surrounded as he is only by old Gothic buildings. Gothicism <u>lives</u> here yet. Fine chapel at New College; so at Magdelan (pron. Moddlen) — repaired yet in the ancient Gothic style, with great taste and consistency. (Fine Altarpiece by Morales, as supposed, *Christ Carrying the Cross.*) Broadway, i.e. a grand alley of ancient elms such as there are probably nowhere else, and what walks along the brooks and between the large green meadows. Christ Church Chapel dining hall. I cannot see what Huebner, in his book on English Universities says that all the pictures have a tory look. But Germans will always find something out of the hidden. How strange it sounds when the porter says here lives Dr. Posey, there Dr. Backland, there Dr. Hampdon; and again you have seen Brazen Nose, Baliol, Christ Church, etc. so often. Fine ground connected with Magdelan — consisting only of one walk around an immense turf. How fond the English are of grass, and well they may. Bookseller tells me that German books sell no longer as well as they did, except German editions of classics — Much bell ringing the whole day. Since I have [left] Florence, nothing has had such a transporting effect upon me. I mean transported me to other times, as Oxford. It is a strange feeling of its own to behold an old edifice. It tells a tale. Oh, chase not history! Give her time to trace a few footsteps! I forget the monument of Cranmer (whom I do not reverence) Latimer and Ridley where they were burnt. I knew nothing but read the inscription. How it fell upon me. —All this makes me feel my loneliness. See the Guide to Oxford. A man dressed in the most perfect gentleman's style drives the bus to Steventon, Great Western Railway, yet arrived there asks for the "coachman;" he looked so, that I felt like giving him a shilling yet the fare had been but 2 shillings. Expenses are enormous! Start at 20 minutes before 8, and arrive at Paddington (56¼ miles) at ½ past 9 with I should think at least ½ an hour stoppages. Magnificent cars, high, for four abreast. Easy rolling. 4 shillings for cab to Brunswick Hôtel Jermyn Street about 4 miles from Paddington. Mass of servants.

[Lieber inserted a Great Western Railway timetable at this point]

London

18 April. Deliver letters, (without, of course, seeing anyone) to Dr. Ferguson, John Kenyon, Mr. Everett, Richard Monkton Milnes, MP, Henry Hallam. Viscount Morpeth is not in town but at York Castle; I am sorry. Lord Brougham not in town. Mary Mackintosh not in town. Belgrave Square and all that part is I am sure unique in the World. "Magnificent Distances" in reality; palace upon palace. Now and then a red pair of breeches moving along. Drawing room today; so all the white calves of coachmen & footmen out. Thence in Bus to City — old "City Road" ah, I knew thee well, all the different parts. <u>City</u> two things cannot be more different than the character of Belgrave etc. and City — all bustle, business. Old Hambro receives me uncommonly well, calls me Liebert, no doubt thinks me a Jew. Two letters from my beloved Matilda. I read them there; happy, happy. I can hardly resist going over. What shall I do? —See London Bridge; through King William Street — all new. Police man politely shows me a good chop house. They are like guides kept for me by Great Britain. Walked where I walked so often! Saw Thanet Place — how I felt when standing there in all the din and bustle. Saw Putnam. Meant to go to the Opera but no ticket to be had. Many <u>ladies</u> to gallery. —The girls in the street behave much better but how plain and badly dressed compared to New York public girls. All women here I have seen dress badly; met two French ladies in Hyde Park. I knew at a distance that they must be French or American. In Cheapside a cheese shop with "Fine American Cheese." English drink far less porter now — all ale. Clumpsy [*sic*] large 4–wheel vehicles for one horse with coachman, footman, and four people often inside; looks very bad. All vehicles look clumpsy compared to American. Try to go to Opera; not possible.

19 April. Again letters; receive invitations. To the City. Again a sweet letter from Matilda. Oh love is better than all things, London with all the red and yellow breeches included. See the Tunnel going by steamboat down (4°). See description. Solemn impression; the beautiful arch, gaslight; stalls between them where all sorts of things are sold, and prints of the Tunnel printed. Music, two women playing horn and clarinet, at the other end singing and exhibition of Swiss cottage — all under river Thames. I have no doubt the company [word unclear] left those stalls. Now, it is odd to create room for trafficking under a river. Police everywhere; shows me politely to a chop house, having learned it, when asking, when do you really want.

20 April, Saturday. Take rooms 3 Boston Street £1.10s a week; but pray gentle reader look at the annexed bill [missing]. Had I dined there or supped! Miles and members call. Breakfasted at Dr. Ferguson and meet Lord [left blank] — ordinary enough. Ferguson, a distinguished man, said, when I observed how curious a fact it was that all American women look so genteel & refined — even the lowest [born] — small head, thin silky hair, delicate eyebrows yet thick set ones — "Oh, that is easy to be accounted for. The superabundance of public women, who are always rather good looking were sent over in former times." Well done. Opera, <u>Semiramide</u> by Rossini. I dislike the music; it reminds you all the time of the composer — no natural flow of genius, but Grisi seems to me to have the most birdlike voice and intonation I have ever heard. Favanti, no; Lablache yes; Fornasari, know him from America. Carlotta Grisi, the dancer, not to be compared to Fanny Elssler, though graceful enough.

21 April, Sunday. Breakfast at John Kenyon's, 40 York Terrace. Good pictures, fine marbles and granite of Scotland. Mrs. Macrady, wife of actor, there. She invites me to see her — preaches against modern stage dancing. Kenyon told me the other day that Corn Law League paid £500 to Rev. Mr. Fox, Unitarian, to speak against Corn Law. I meant to hear him but cannot. Lunch at one at Joseph Parker, 21 Great George Street, close to Westminster — great parliament lawyer and solicitor of the Charity Commission. He has read, and I find carefully, my *Ethics;* a radical, but <u>not</u> for universal suffrage; well informed about U.S. His wife, granddaughter of Priestly; says repudiation has had the worst possible effect on the English working classes. They say, that's right, that's republicanism, so we will do, when we have the power. <u>Luxe</u>, high rooms, pictures, splendor. Another lawyer, Mr. Blunt came in. We, Mrs. Parker and two ladies, [went] over [the] bridge to South West Railroad, on it to Kingston Station; coach to Hampton Court, Parkes & I outside, smoking; we soon understood each other; does not like Sumner's brother — Yankee <u>zudringlich</u> [obtrusive] — but likes Sumner much. How beautiful the Thames. Palace [of] Wolsey and afterward of William III. What park and 3 ½ miles Bushy Park to Windsor. It exceeds what I have ever read. Pictures here, much trash, some good ones, and <u>Raphael's Cartoons</u>. The beauties of Charles II Court by Sir Peter Lely in William III's Bedroom, are so that one cannot trust because eyes and bosom all the same. But the duchess of Portsmouth different from all and not half as good looking. But, I had almost said dear Nell Gwynne is very fine, still quite as aristocratic looking as the others. But Raphael is Raphael. That certain gaze within me of perfection, the, how shall I call it, the Dolce-forte, the Grand-umilde, the elevation and yet bowing down, was felt by me in looking at the cartoons. I liked best the fishing and Paul preaching at Athens. Strange, that cripple in the right corner of Peter and John at the Beautiful Gate, who always appeared so horrid to me, gained now much — he looks intently yet not knowing yet shall he believe or not. See my Catalogue. Walk with Parkes from Station over Vauxhall Bridge to his house along the Thames. See Lambeth over the river. We talk on ballot. Much fear entertained that Queen will one day become deranged; she is melancholy, figidty, no fine character. Parkes read officially many letters of Baroness de Lehzen and says he thinks her a most uncommonly clever woman but intriguing. At Parkes "meat-tea" in lieu of dinner. Says, I dine every evening at seven, and there are always 4 covers for my friends, so come in when you like. They come always over from Parliament and dine with me. —Penny postage stamps have become exchange in lieu of copper, in shops, also little debts of 2, 3 shillings are paid off by sending stamps in a letter (cocoa of the Mexicans). Going home many most stately girls in Regent Crescent (considered the beauties of Great Britain's Vice). Grand Effect of Gas in Piccadilly near Green Park.

22 April, Monday. To Parkes, with me to New Bailey where the sheriff admits us to the passing [of] sentence on Barber, Fletcher, etc., the will forgers. Justice Maule and others. Transported for life. See the *Illustrated Times* of the case. Ask the man at Charing Cross, who marks how long each bus stops at the corner, how many buses there pass daily. 800 alone that spot. Go to Inkton & Roth, Tailors to Prince Albert. Dine in the City at a Table d'Hôte, an old man begins to talk with me and tells me that it is believed 100,000 copies of Channing's *Entire Works* published in England. There is a people's edition. Also that his son was told by his master with whom he studies law, that he must study Story on equity first of all Equity books, and how much Prescott was liked. Saw Everett — frigid in manners as ever. A fine and grand view in front of Buckingham Palace on the left side back toward palace — before you that now charming St. James Park, with Nelson and Duke of York columns, the houses, and vast & green plain of green park up to Piccadilly. It is very fine. —Three horses before stage coaches and one before private chiefly consequence of income tax. I meant to go to the House of Lords, but came too late. How very odd bishops look with their aprons. Anything but priests. No doubt it is the last remnant of cassock. Association of ideas does everything — or at least very much. When I stood at the foot of Canning's Statue I felt that that spot between St. Stephen and Westminster is greater than any spot in Rome or anywhere — between the dead and living rulers of the world. Fine horses of members led by grooms. No letter from Matilda, and it is right, yet that brought me to the city. I cannot sufficiently admire the physique of the horse guards. Enormous fellows, well made, fine faces surely they are the finest looking soldiers in the world. What thighs these rogues have! They ought to be used for breed[ing]. What a race there might be produced, if Socrates' plan were adopted, only for 150 years. Clergymen here go freely to the theatre and now only a few "who are by no means bigots" begin to give up dancing. [word illegible] have no objection to card playing, dancing etc. Parkes is so far my efficient friend; he thinks for me, makes long notes of what he will get for me, to whom he will write, etc. An Irish beggar woman said to me, when I said: "My poor woman I have not a solitary copper" — "God bless you Sir even for that." —No rag and patches in those parts of London at least which I have frequented. London Palace Part, Busy City Part, Genteel but not Palace part, Huddled masses part, Semi Country part, Shipping part, Black manufacturing Part, Park Part.

23 April, Tuesday. Breakfast at home. See with Parkes's Clerk all the courts — all the judges and lawyers one has read of so often; from the wigs and gowns to the bear caps and red coats at the Wellington barracks to the left of Buckingham Palace. The musicians of all the infantry guards together with drummers. To McCollough, the political economist has an office in the Stationary, a tall, raw boned Scotchman, talking with a terrible Scottish accent — speaks against International Copyright and not very philosophical or thorough. Found letters from Lord Morpeth at Home. Go to House of Commons. Mr. Miles lets me in, through permission of the Speaker to the benches reserved for peers, peers' sons and distinguished strangers. Row, laughing, "hear-hear-ing" such as I never heard in Congress. Loud talking. Of course now & then more personality in Congress but far more order. The affair was about a charge Mr. Farrand had made against Mr. Hogg. Peel, Graham, Lord Stanley, L. Russell spoke. Before that Bowditch, Roebuck, Sir Robert Inglis. So far I was fortunate. Go at 7 to Parkes, dine there, long talk, good Port, he shows me the exact spot where Charles I was executed, go to Reformed Club — luxe, splendour, comfort, grandeur. (The Reform Club costs £5000. This large number of clubs is a new feature and element of English life) See there Admiral Napier. I wrote this day to my Matilda and to the boys.

24 April. Breakfast at Sir Robert. Harry Inglis, ladies there, Rogers the poet, Miles MP and others. Very sprightly and fine — anecdotes, discussion, etc., until ½ past one, from ten. Rogers asks me to breakfast with him on Monday. Write to Morpeth, Mrs. Bunsen, Mary Mackintosh. [Here Lieber inserted a copy of a Letter of Credit with the comment that "not more than 5£ allowed in one bill, but an unlimited number may be taken."] Find letters to sundry persons here from Sir John McNeill. Find in the streets a similar cage as formerly on Waterloo Bridge, with rats, cats, guinea pigs, starlings, pigeons, owls and what not all in it, in perfect peace. To the National Museum. Free access to every one. Collection but small, some very fine pictures. More anon of them. —Rogers at breakfast said he liked the prepos[ition] at the end if well used; I supported him with Hooker's "Shall there be a God to swear by and none to pray to." Until then Miles and Inglis had been against it.

[Here Lieber inserted a penny post card with an engraving by John Thompson after W. Mulready with the comments: "This is one of the first post stamps. I am sure it was designed by a German." and pasted down a one-penny postage stamp in the margin with the notation: "This is a penny postage stamp. Twopence ones are blue."]

I wrote a good many letters, received many from Sir John McNeill. Dinner at Kenyon's 40 York Place. Booth, MP and "Ubiquity" Young (he has £2000 for reading over acts of parliament) and a Mr. Harley there. Good wine, good but not excellent talk. Kenyon wants me to dine with his brothers on Monday.

25 April. Breakfast at Roebuck's, radical MP born in India, portrait painter in Canada, Barrister in England — but poor. Queen's birthday. Horseguards in full dress. These men and horses are unequalled. A low, poor, dirty woman asked me in St. James Park "when will her Majesty pass?" Concourse of people. Behave well. Police/white but fellows in green, evidently belonging to the Forest department rude. Splendid but old fashioned coachmen and footmen. At last the Queen and Prince Albert pass; no one could see anything of them, the coach all closed. Previously I had seen Wellington and Albert riding from Horse guards to Buckingham Palace. By three I go to the City. Call on Levin — not in. Old Hambro takes me home and I dine with him. Only Danes with him besides me. Speak freely of their king. Illumination in the Streets; some by gas looked well enough; but the whole no great thing — a ready made affair. Victoria Regina and Victoria Regina again. Many people in the streets, no swearing, no yelling, no cursing and swaggering. The population of London is improved, and to what is all this owing? To many things, and among others to the fact that people are treated more like improvable beings, from the criminal up to the mechanic (National Gallery). I had this [day] a note from Mary Mackintosh. Hambro has a house in Algiers. At least he established it there and has, of course, an interest there.

26 April. Breakfast at Monkton. Miles, MP, 26 Pall Mall. Marquess of Northampton, president of Royal Society, Rogers the poet, Kenyon, etc. there. Miles in red silk morning gown and golden slippers, mandarin girdle. When he went out for a moment, all joked about him. A touching poem of Hook's on a girl, who jumped from one of the bridges was read; I gave Longfellow on War. All except Marquess Northampton found the end too moralizing. Miles read a long poem Lilly by I forgot. Old Rogers spoke of <u>tact</u> and said to me "in short that in which our host is very deficient" when Miles was in the room. At one o'clock go to Pentonville prison, saw Crawford, very friendly. Briefly, I will here remark — though I must go again — that the prison is preparatory for transportation — only for 18 months, if possible first offenders; incorrigible sent back, from 18 years to 35 only; men only (?). Therefore this cannot be considered precisely a model prison in general. The modifications of the American prison, which struck me immediately were these: The School, the Service, Each prisoner can ring a bell and is attended to (no abuse resorts from it); has writing materials; are often taken out, though without communion; more frequently visited by officers; separate officers and trade teachers who are also paid; much improved privies; gas light. Separate recreation yards. The black cell suffices. No self-pollution. See my parliamentary papers. At 5 to Parkes, who takes me to House of Lords, where the recall of Lord Ellenborough by the East India House against Government became known. (In the Lords was read the 2nd time Lord Lyndhurst's Dissenters Chapel Bill, which is what I predicted in my *Hermeneutics*, speaking of Lady Ewley's will) (The Lords looked very ordinary. Duke of Burlough had dark pants, white stockings, yellow vest and brass button coat) Go to dine at Parkes at 7. See Lord Wellington. Return with him to House of Commons. Go home by 12 o'clock. (Find a mass of letters, among others from dear Matilda, Madam Bunsen, Mary Mackintosh).

27 April. Breakfast at Hallams. Macauly, Lord Mahon, author, Lord Willoughby (?), Everett and Mr. Philipps, lawyer not the lawyer, there. Macauly says English drink much ale in India, yet not bilous in consequence; learn that Mr. Philipps is universally condemned for his behavior in Courvoisier's trial, so Lord Brougham for what he said. Take Lord Morpeth's letter to Duchess of Sutherland, had given orders to show me in immediately but I could not. Go with Frank Levin to East India dock by railroad. Into what narrowness and dirt and poverty we looked down from the railway. Saw a new East Indiaman. Staterooms much more commodious than liners, but not as elegant. By steamboat to Westminster Bridge. The Thames swarms with these little sharp built black steamers. Go in the evening to French theatre but a German Taschenspieler spielt [magician performs]. Neat theatre.

28 April, Sunday. Duchess of Sutherland sends to ask whether tomorrow at 12 will be convenient to see Stafford House (an exquisitely dressed servant with top boots). Go to Temple church. Roeback as a bencher had given me permission. Lately fitted up. It is an exquisite church which belonged to the Templars. To me a model of small Gothic church. Fine dark marble pillars, which the Reformation had filled and plastered over. The restauration [*sic*] cost very much. No church ought to be without painted windows. Service again very long, near 3 hours. All the people and only gentle folk, many lawyers, etc. follow the service with great propriety. But all kneeling in the English Church is but symbolical — they cheat the Lord. Preaching very common. To the bank and take a long omnibus — Piccadilly, Hyde Park, Knightsbridge, Kensington Road, Kensington, Hammersmith, Kewbridge (Thames), Furnam Green. Brentford where I eat some cold meat. We pass the parks of Holland House, Duke of Devonshire (Chiswick), Duke of Norfolk. Here 6 miles from Hyde Park the houses a little sparse for a short distance. Immense, immense! In Piccadilly a well dressed man gets on the back and when he approaches Green park exclaims: "How beautiful, why all the leaves are out," and they have been out for near a month. He told me he had not seen a tree for a year: always in the city, and near to no park. Everett had called again. The brass plate of the coachman has the number and the word <u>driver</u>. I also heard people say Fall. Buses run to the distance of 20 miles from Bank.

29 April. Breakfast with Mr. Rogers the poet. Found Marquess of Northampton, President of Royal Society there (invites me to Dinner of that Society at Crown & Anchor) on Thursday. Sir Robert Inglis there, and, somehow people speak of me as "the particular friend of Sir Robert Inglis." Odd. Two or three questions of English history I know better than anyone at table. At 12 o'clock go to Stafford house, built for the late Duke of York, bought by Marquess of Stafford, now Duke of Sutherland, brother-in-law of Lord Morpeth, eldest son of Earl of Carlisle. Generally a dreary thing to go through palaces, but here! Splendour, taste, luxurious repose, courtliness, inventive genius, roominess, art, magnificence, grandeur, chasteness, all combined — and in all this beauty, the beautiful duchess with her liquid smile and beaming good nature, and Thorwaldsen's *Ganymede* and the 2 Murillos, and other good pictures. The house stands as an <u>impression</u> in my mind. I saw the first picture of [name left blank and following word illegible] Boccaccio's women. Some very fine but not Landscape. A copy of [name left blank]'s *Jews in Babylonian Captivity*. I had seen the engraving at shop window and instantly recognized it as <u>German</u> from the spontaneous remembrance of Cornelius' paintings. Is it his mind, or has he received it from still farther back, something common to him Veit, Schnorr? I believe this. Probably a fraction of Italian liquidity and German accuracy and candour. I found a German Candidat der Theologie [theological student] there (!!) and Rev. Mr. Bunsen, son of <u>the</u> Mr. Bunsen who is now in Berlin to aid in drawing up the statutes of the <u>Schwanen</u> [Swan] Order. (I ought to propose to carry it over to America!) To Putnam, who came from Paris in 22 hours by way of Brighton, brings me letter from George Sumner offering kindly. Inspected the building of new parliament house (see 4 pages on). Dined at Mr. Kenyon, who is married to a Vienna woman. (I learn, Oh it pains, that Mackintosh was considered a renegade, at least not to be depended upon, and his virtue flaccid.) [see entry for 1 May for additional comments for this day]

30 April. Breakfast again at Rogers and he invited me a third time, but I decline. He has all sorts of beautiful rarities, in short his apartments are a beau ideal of rooms of a gentleman scholar and poet. Fine pictures, even Titian. Original contract of Milton's with Symmons (so written but afterwards printed Simmons) for Paradise Lost for £4. Fine autographs. —Northampton there again. No person ever says mylord or your lordship. In short, English Aristocracy sits altogether in Institutions, and red breeches. —To the exhibit of flowers in the garden of Botanic Society in Regents Park. 5 shillings. A prize had been given for the best flowers of £300. I had never seen flowers so gorgeously and artfully developed and spread. Azaleas in particular fine, and Cartopodiam or whatever the name was. Very cold; many ladies; no beauty; costly but not tarty dress. Dine at bachelor Kenyon's; Altogether 11 — many ladies. Write to my most beloved Matilda. Mackintosh calls and many others. Have sent the following letters of introduction from Sir John McNeill with my card: T. G. Lockard, 24 Sussex Place, Regents Park; James Swinton, Bulstr Street; Red. J. Murchison, Belgrave Square; P. J. Tyller, Devonshire Place; John Murray, 50 Albemarle Str. — Mr. T. J. Phillips (7 Lincoln's Inn) calls. I met him at Joseph Ingersoll's and now at Hallams. —Some priest was transported for life for rebellious practices and Parkes (?) expressed his sorrow at it to Sir James Mackintosh. The latter said: "He is very bad, he could not be worse." Parkes replied: "He is an Irishman, he might have been a Scotchman; he is a priest, he might have been a lawyer; he is a rebel, he might have been a renegade." Can intercourse continue after such things?

1 May. Shoemaker (who by the way says that all his workmen admired the way lasts were worked). See Mary Mackintosh. Sad indeed. All her characteristic traits remain, and so altered. How shall I feel in going. [Here are inserted additional comments from 29 April] belongs to April 29. Mr. Booth, MP sent me a card of entrance to parliament building. As I said before the Gothic Art is still a living thing in England. They <u>do</u> it, execute it, as their own, not by way of mere imitation. I dislike however, and upon this very ground the old Gothic inscriptions. They are nuisances. Even shopkeepers have begun to˙ use them. They ought to be indicted. I found the below as a print of a letter sheet. Thus the river front will look. An enormous building. And yet I fear it will be one great mass filigree work. Will not all this minute work be puny, or be lost, totally lost for the general impression. [At this point, an engraved view by J. Schury of the "New House of Parliament" was tipped in and the entry of 1 May resumed] (see the last page but one). Zoological Garden in Regents Park. Very fine arrangement. First beaver I saw alive, and gull which I saw near. Many of our birds. Beaver evidently a rat. The large South American rat close by. Also the first otter I saw alive. I rode on the elephant, which had the proper houda. At home I found a note, a sweet one

London

belongs to April 29. Mr Brooth, M. P. sent me a card of entrance to parliament building. As I said before the Gothic Art is still a living thing in Engl. They <u>do</u> it, execute it, as their own, not by way of mere imitation. I dislike however, and upon this way grows the old Gothic inscriptions. They are nuisances. Even shopkeepers have begun to use them. They ought to be indicted. I found the below as a print of a letter sheet. Thus the river fronts will look. An enormous building. And yet I fear it will be one great mass

Francis Lieber's Journal, 29 April 1844, with an engraving of the British Houses of Parliament

from Matilda; I answered a few lines and went to Sir Robert Harry Inglis for dinner, at 7 o'clock. Mary Appleton there, Lordbishop of Salsbury, a Mrs. [name left blank], wife to the Rev. Mr. [name left blank], who was tutor to the present Crown Prince of Hanover and is now principal of the King's College London. His wife a born von Schlippenbach in der Ukermark. Strange how they admire Niebuhr here. She remembered at once my name from the *Lebensnotizen* [biographical notes: the *Reminiscences of Niebuhr*], and Inglis and others, I find, always speak of me as connected with Niebuhr. What is the reason? His historical core it is clear it cannot be. It is because he who was so learned was so heartily against French revolution and modern Liberals, and wrote so longingly of religion (without having himself any of what they would call so). A variety of wines. The head of a large unfinished picture of Wilberforce by Reynolds (?). Invitation from Lockard to breakfast.

2 May. To Pentonville. See April 26 in addition I have to say that there is a bell even for the "refractory cells," visited the recreation yards, the pump with the gangs at work, kitchen (no prisoners at work here as at Sing Sing), the baths (every one has a warm bath every 14 nights). If a man sincerely repents and the governor is convinced of it, he is not allowed to stay the full time in the refractory cell. Punishments are made known at the discretion of Governor who desired it. The Commissioners were a long time against it. I am let into many cells. Most of them appear rational and apparently under good effect of the system. The prisoners learn very quick as in America. Some said to me that they never felt loneliness much. —The aristocratic character of the English appears oddly and strongly I think in the fact that <u>livery</u> is the prototype of all distinctions of dress of civil officers; or wherever a distinction is desired and where on the Continent a <u>military</u> uniform would be given e.g., railway officers, etc. At the Angel Inn, City, read this: "Lane's Cork Stout Draught and Bottle." Real Chinese juxtaposition. The following (near Blackfriars still more: "London City Branch National Joint Stock Linen Ware House." Without <u>of</u> or <u>and</u>. People seem to me peculiarly polite in <u>showing</u> way, etc., walk a long way with me. That one fellow in the Temple only excepted — a real old fashioned rude John Bull. —With old Heine to the West End. Dine at Crown and Anchor, as the guest of Marquis of Northampton, Royal Society Club. Remarkable! Dirty carpet, <u>smeary</u> screen, superannuated servants, common dinner, common conversation, very common wine. The toasts: The Queen; Prince Albert; the Queen Dowager and the rest of the royal family, were drunk are rather merely said by the president, without the least attention to it by anyone or repetition. With the marquis to Royal Society. Some papers on Natural Philosophy read. —Book with all the names of fellows in it. <u>Charles</u> begins as patron. These books you find everywhere in England, e.g, Oxford. Puerile.

3 May, Friday. At 9 to Southgate, on Bus. Old Stamford Hill. Beyond Edmindton, of Gilpin fame (the Inn still existing) begins country. Lovely. Mrs. Bunsen out. Mary receives me kindly. I dine with the children at ½ past one. By two or so Mrs. Bunsen returns from town. Altered, of course — fat woman, strong tor [*sic*] as she always was. Son, who was in the army with me to the Inn. Mrs. Bunsen encourages me to write to Bunsen. By 7 o'clock at the flower pot jump into bus for Charing Cross. Go to Parkes, who takes me to House of Lords, where we found bishop of Exeter speaking against Dissenter Chapel Bill brought in by Lord Lyndhurst, object: that dissenters shall be lawful owners of land and property which their congregations have possessed for the last 20 years — caused by the great hardship in Lady Ewley's Fund's Case, which nevertheless was according to law. I wrote at the time in my *Hermeneutics* that Parliament must correct it and would, and, strange now find them about it. Lord Cottingham answered the Bishop of Exeter (Philpot) severely as he deserved. Lord Kemble followed and then a mouthing lord [spoke] against the bill. But all parties for it, so no division. Duke of Wellington there — walks like a very old man now, but I saw him riding brisk gallop. Ate a steak in the "Kitchen" in parliament house with Parkes and some others. Bishop of Exeter is of low extraction — mother a dissenter.

4 May. With Putnam to Tower. Formerly the Knights harnesses impressed me always as something at least dignified — I found them even handsome. They have now something ridiculous, very ridiculous for me. How different a modern grenadier, who without steel or plate mounts a battery or stands exposed to shell shot for hours in a square. — Axe with which Ann Boleyn was executed. Room where Raleigh wrote his history. Very remarkable to Japanese armours. One of them like coats of mail of knights. Crown jewels. To the [name left blank] Docks, where American Packets lie. Prince Albert — how it impresses at once with the idea of bright neatness and elegance. Give me American vessels. Saw old Hambro. Went to <u>Gaedecher</u> and Sieveking. Did not see Pauls. Gaedecher very glad to see me. Eat steak at Simpson, old steakhouse whither George Oppenheimer took me; but the <u>breeches</u> of the servants are gone.

5 May. Breakfast at Lockharts. His amiable daughter. We are very soon <u>au courant</u>. "You look very much like Webster, it struck me at once." The sculptor Clevenger, in New York, said so too, but I had hoped for a letter from Matilda by the last packet, but none. The public women in Regency Circus and Waterloo Place, very handsome after all. I mean the best dressed, but then they are the handsomest women I understand. It is fearful how they swarm and the best dressed sometimes will ask "at least for a sixpence for a glass of wine" if a person declines going with them. Took tea at Mackintosh's.

6 May. Breakfast with Sir Robert Inglis (7 Bedford Square). Archdeacon Wilberforce, son of Wilberforce, there. Talked a good deal [on] interesting matter. Called on Dr. Ferguson, thence to Hallam. Long, interesting conversation, in which I found and he said so I thought much deeper on Political Philosophy. If I remained here longer I should soon [get on] famously. Thence to Everett. He will manage my presentation to Guizot. (to Paris post office Poland street) To Whitehall (Sir James Graham permission to go to Parkhurst and then to chapel) where there is now a chapel, which is all that remains. Pictures of Rubens on the ceiling on canvas. The *Apotheosis of James I.* He who believes in the resurrection of Ruben's flesh may as well believe in the resurrection of all meat, beef not excluded. And then these eternal Jameses and Charleses and Georges, for one has no particle of respect. Who cares for any one except William III, and you cannot move without meeting the long noses of the Stuarts, or the insignificant faces of William IV or George IV in their tawdry dress of the garter. Thence to Parliament. Heard Peel make his first speech on Bank Charter renewal. He <u>preached</u>, yet very insignificant things, besides he showed that he did <u>not</u> know what measure of value is, although ridiculing so many who indeed had said nonsense enough. The speaking part of the speech and the long winded introduction were no great things and wholly unequal to what I have heard of Clay, Calhoun, Webster, even Choate. Dined with Parkes at the Reform Club — that splendid mansion. I am an Honorary member for a month. Some time or other I will give a description. See the rules of the club. At home I found a letter from dear Matilda. She is dissatisfied with my letters which I own are very hasty, but what can I do?

7 May. Go to Windsor. By railway. At one time we went a mile in ½ a minute. At Slough I inspected the electric telegraph. Slough from London 18 miles; yet answer back in an instant. There was something awful in it, as always when relations (here of space and time) to which we have been accustomed from childhood are suddenly suspended. See description of a new one, in papers. These rest simply on the fact that galvanic battery produces current of electricity — this turns a needle — therefore connection and disconnection of the poles of the battery. From Slough 2 miles to Eaton & Windsor Castle. See the book. I was most interested in the glorious English landscape — that exquisite verdure, elms; part of the foremast of the Victory, the views from the windows, perhaps the Waterloo room — There are Jameses and Georges enough. Round tower. Park tour of many miles. Statue of George III of a poor crazy man! Many deer by herds, but Virginia water where tradition still tells the nefarious doings of George IV with Marchioness of Cunningham <u>and</u> daughters. After all, although the long-walk is beautiful, a drive on the boxseat through a fine part of England is infinitely better; and — less expensive. This expedition cost me, without a dinner, 1£,10s. On arriving home I found a permission to see the apartments of the Queen; and invitation to public dinner etc. from Mary Mackintosh.

There is far more repose in English life. Going home, passing Eton, numbers of boys out on that beautiful green under those lofty elms playing chicken. A beautiful sight — the best here. Well dressed handsome boys in this landscape! Finer than the deer in Windsor Park. Pass <u>through Paddington</u> — Oxford & Cambridge Place. Always with something green, etc., how very different from old towns or on the continent.

8 May. Write to Matilda. Pay calls, go to the City to arrange money matters. Dine at the Reform Club and go to the Covent Garden Anti-Corn Law League Meeting, Parkes having got me a stage ticket. The whole House crowded full — I should think 4000 people, in short crowded to the highest top. Good many women. Warburton, MP in the chair. Spoke nervously, and not much to the point. Villiers, MP spoke better; Gibbs a "Buckinghamshire farmer" was a show; good deal of laugh[ter], but he did not look much like a farmer; Fox, Unitarian minister, who on Sundays preaches or lectures for 1 shilling admission, very fluent and redundant, not unlike some American eloquence. But all tricks bad, so his to set out. Swell on and end by accumulative sentences, e.g., a charity which — a charity which and this 10 times until at length a forcible sentence closes as the two or three heavy strokes of an overture or symphony. This does well once, but he did [it] regularly, about 6 or 7 times. His speech indeed consisted of so many pieces constructed in the same way. But of course that catches. The applause was immense. Upon the whole nothing particular was said; behavior excellent. When I came home found another invitation by Sir Robert Inglis and many people had called.

9 May. At breakfast read *Morning Post* which gives an account of last night's meeting of the Corn Law League and a lie from beginning to end. Positive fiction. Oh ye newspaper liars! Oh ye public liars from Bulletins down to no cure no pay. Finish writing to my dear Matilda and take the letter to the City. Old Hambro has the gout, and I cannot arrange my money affairs, so I must wait till tomorrow and give up my Cambridge trip. At 6 to Merchant's Taylor's Hall, Threadneedle Street, where the "Sons of the Clergy" dine (Lord Morpeth had sent me the invitation). Sir Robert Inglis places me by him at the elevated table. The Lord Mayor takes always precedence in the City, so here before the Duke of Cambridge. At dinner, Duke of Cambridge to his right, Archbishop of Canterbury to his left. The speech of the Duke of Cambridge nothing and never have I heard such embarrassment, catching and recatching of words and actual failure of finding words as the Archbishop's speech. He is however very old. Good singing. The others I did not hear speaking; many bishops, judges (Tindal), etc., there. The faces are not so well marked, the heads not so fine and bedeutend [distinguished] as in America, which I know does not say much of itself, for the lowest Polish Jews have some of the finest heads. There is more constant thinking and Gespanntheit [intensity] in the American face. I went through rows of police men [here Lieber sketched a shield with a cross] to a cab which they had sent for to Holles Street, but Mary Mack[intosh?] had left; followed her as directed to Baron Alderson, of Regent Crescent. Found none but women first. They dress now very low. Some girls there, with ⅓ of breast certainly bare, and deep under the arm — but then they have something to show. One girl of perhaps 14, very low but very beautiful. A fine woman talked long and animatedly with me.

The other day I found at Punch's window, his framed appointment as jester to the Queen, signed and sealed in regular order. I wonder he dares such forgery even in joke. Old Mr. Rogers called on me. The Hon. Cpt. Howard had invited me for the festival in St. Paul but I thought it too tedious to go there at 3. An Alderman on my right who grinned whenever I turned and told me he had had once an introduction to a count in Paris.

10 May, Friday. Write to "Mademoiselle Marie de Bornstedt, Dame d'Honneur de Son Attesse la Duchesse de' Anhalt Bernburg" enclosing Mrs. de Hassels letter, begging her to write one to Paris. Write to "Chevalier Bunsen" now in Berlin. Go to the City; Old Hambro will send letter of credit tomorrow. Forget what else. In the evening to the House of Commons on the Peers' benches for the "Hon. Cpt. Edward Howard," Morpeth's brother has obtained for me a standing "Speaker's Order." On Lord Ashley's Amendment to the Factory Bill, to substitute 10 hours to 12 during 5 days and on Saturday 8. Heard Lord Ashley, Sir Latimer Graham, Lord Howick (Earl Gray's son) who used the most curious arguments, Roebuck (who is all the time pugnacious and bitter to no purpose), Ferrand, etc. Eight, ten or fifteen members starting at the same time. Great interruption, yet I doubt not but that the strong expression of a few strong impulses or ideas is upon the whole very good. They evidently aid in guiding. I mean 1. approval (hear, hear, which of course is expressed in very different ways) 2. denial (no! no!) 3. expression of considering an argument or allusion very unfair (oh! no! oh! oh!) 4. ridicule (laughing or satirical hear! hear!). In the course of debate Lord Howick most sharply reprimanded Roebuck for talking loud with his neighbor. — The <u>machinery</u> of the Commons is very different from the Representatives. For instance <u>chairman</u> here one, who is paid, appointment of committees, etc. Very young members. The best American speakers, Webster, Calhoun, Clay, even Choate and River I think speak better than here but there is not so much eternal blarney and rigmarole. —I find far more stiff joined (even young) people (paralytic) who can hardly get into the coaches or buses, and people with twitchings in the face. What is the reason. In the shops, in the streets altogether in language etc. less <u>extravaganza</u>, but the eternal royal arms are ludicrous, although the V. R. [Victoria Regina] everywhere — in every bus — <u>shows</u> that the Queen and her initials are here far more a civic institution than a personal affair. In other countries the initials, etc. and the word Royal is a <u>noli me tangere</u>, high distinction, the monarch's <u>own</u>; here a hundred inns are called the Royal Inn, etc and how many "Her Majesty's." Sir Robert Inglis catches me and I must now breakfast with him tomorrow. I go to bed at two, but the House does not often sit longer now than one. Enormous cry of "Adjourn, jurn, jurn," this latter repeated like a shake. Others clamour "<u>divide</u>, vide, vide, vide." The two galleries along the House belong to the <u>house</u>; one or two have even spoken down, because so little room at present. Lying on the benches, sleeping, but I saw it in the gallery only.

11 May, Saturday. Lord Brougham had sent me word he wished to see me ½ past 9 to apologize. I go. "What's the matter? What do you want? Eh! What! Be quick, I have no time?" So odd and crazy that I laughed. Come on Monday. I go away on Monday. Then tomorrow at 5 o'clock (but Parkes has told me already that he has said to a friend of his, he had approached Monday = I write this on Sunday).

11 May. Breakfast at Sir R. H. Inglis. Find distinguished people there, one who accompanied the Niger Expedition, one who goes to Arabia to study inscriptions. Lady Inglis insists upon my going to see Mrs. Bick, daughter of Sir James Mackintosh. She wanted much to see me. Odd. But she lives near. I went. Intelligent woman; to John Kenyon, 40 York Terrace, Regents Park; to Mary Mackintosh. Long and last talk. I cannot help thinking, that she must generally have a prevailing longing for home, although she acknowledges the advantages of Europe. We agree very remarkably about America and Europe, or rather not "remarkably" because it is natural. Write hastily to my own Matilda on account of money affairs should be upset in the Channel. Go to the City to see Lord of Credright, and in spite of the greatest hurry I cannot see a gallery. So I read in the luxurious library room of Reform Club. They know what comfort and style is, these Britishers. Dine with Parkes at the Club — for the first time White Bail <u>probatum</u>. Go to see Cerrito in <u>Undine</u>, Opera House, but "un accident arrivait à la lune [an accident happened to the moon]," so she did not dance the dance with her own shadow. There was a great deal of good humored uproar. Cerrito dances well, graceful and unquestionably has the true <u>trampe</u> of the dances, but she seems 1. to move here hands too quick and not sufficiently <u>liquid</u> 2. she has not Fanny Elssler's soul. All are dancers, Fanny is a priestess of dance. And indeed excellence in any time cannot come so often as to have two Fannys in the same age. Grisi dances very well. The gauze trousers are ridiculous for they cover nothing. I saw Grisi repeatedly as high up as the girdle and the <u>linen</u> drawers of the <u>chose</u> is really too bad. In going out of the opera, lines of public girls. Parkes insists upon my staying in his house on my return and he invites me to do it like a man. But he found what I said immediately, that the private rooms of the Queen are not seen on Sunday. Again what I hardly ever deviate from: make your plans and settle them for yourself alone.

12 May, Sunday. Breakfast at Parkes (could not with Kenyon, who had made up one for me, e.g., Mrs. Jamison). There Mr. Basil Montague came — now old but the first lawyer after Sir Samuel Romilly, so Parkes says, and author of *Punishment of Death*. How he quotes Latin. Invites me. In going to Parkes, along the lane between Green Park and the back of the houses of St. James' Place, turning round the corner of the gate, into St. James' Park, I run against the Duke of Wellington, who balanced on his feeble legs for some time. I of course supported him and ask his pardon. No, no matter he said. He was walking at this early hour (7 o'clock) by his carriage. So I had a recontre with England's Duke. But he walks very what is called in low German "spök [shakily]." —Yesterday I saw a cart in Ludgate hill, neatly painted and in large letters on it "American Ice" while two men were busied in getting dirty, brown, broken rubbish of ice out of the cart. Write to James, and Augusta — the last Queen's Heads — and ah, the luxury is at an end. Goodby England, goodby letter-chatting; goodby Water-closets; goodby trim fields and refreshing verdure; goodby exquisite ale; goodby luxurious clubs and paradisiacal reading; goodby sensible newspapers and best servants, goodby excellent yet ever polite police; but also goodby <u>dear</u> pavement and shilling sucking land; goodby green-yellow red breeches and lumberly carriages; goodby ye eternal Charleses Jameses and Georges and the royal arms almost on every bumfodder. Among my acquaintances here is Miss Priestly (Mrs. Parkes' sister) and Mrs. Austin both of whom have lost everything in the U.S. Bank, and Kenyon gets no interest of his Pennsylvania stock. This is very dreadful. And I know this only accidentally, not by conversation on the subject. Probably there were several more. Saw Lord Brougham; very different; asks me to let him know when I am here again. Says cannot understand Niebuhr, that he ought not to have published the work thus. I asked whether he meant the artistical arrangement. "No, the thoughts." He knew Niebuhr well at Edinburgh. To Levi's, Upper Gower Street, to dine there. Not long ago they tell me, people only regretted that by 1850 or whenever it was, the Pennsylvania stock would be paid off.

13 May, Monday. Breakfast at Parkes and with her, a little like Mrs. Otis, and a young lady staying with her, to Windsor to see private apartments of Queen. There are "searchers," who search every car after arrival, and every article kept 12 months, then sold. The oddest collection. Great many boys out at Eton School but one cap. The cap is considered in England servant and laborerlike. —I was disappointed for I expected something unthought of by me in the line of royal English luxury, refinement, elegance and soft luxury here royally excellent as at Stafford house supremely so for nobility; but nothing of the kind. The Windsor apartments like thousand other royal palaces. I have no doubt some of Louis Philippe and Nicholas grander, superior. Some things even great bathos as it seemed to me, e.g., passage out of the dining room. Exquisite views from windows; but some of them again, look on the roof of the lower story. Much pleased with the great simplicity, in some cases, shabbiness of the books in the cases of the Queen's drawing room. Shocking pictures of all the daughters of George III in George IV's dressing room, dressed in the English style of the beginning of this century, with breasts as big as bushels. Immense number of Canaletti in the Corridor. Hayter's original of the Coronation — where all the ladies of the court are. Walter Scott's portrait. Many busts. But the most glorious view is from the window of the "Ruben's Room," "State Apartment." I should have that for private room. Pleasing that the benches in private chapel are for the maids and livery. Access to the Queen's box very narrow. Lunch at Parkes. The ladies had gone with me because permission not easily got. I had mine through Hon. Edward Howard, Cpt. Royal Navy (Morpeth's brother). —At 5 from Nine Elms by railway in 2nd class because I can see more — all the world goes in it. Part of Northamptonshire dreary. At ½ past 8 at Southampton, which again swarms with public girls, but these are pretty, some very pretty. Some dressed well, others, as in London young (15, 16 years) with dirty shawl, bare neck, as in London and Manchester.

Southampton and Isle of Wight

14 May. ½ past 5 morning in steam boat to Cowes, meet the steam packet, Liverpool from Alexandria. They must always be 21 from Alexandria before they get practice whether at sea or here. In 1 ½ hours at Cowes, Isle of White. "Cowes & Market." Saw distant Norris Castle, bought by the Queen. To Parkhurst, about 4 miles from Cowes, near Newport. For girls no establishment yet. All these boys, some 9 years, sentenced to transport. But many would not if this excellent institution did not exist. This, therefore, no house of refuge. Elder ones sleep alone, younger together. All sergeants officers. Service when I came. They get fine letters from some boys in the colony. Those at New South Wales do very well; in New Zealand not — too disturbed. Pass through Carisbrooke where Charles I was confined. Window through which he tried to escape. Good view. Romans, Saxons, Danes, etc. here. Well 300 feet deep through rock. Sand pictures. Returning at the barracks between Newport and Parkhurst inspection of soldiers. Highlanders. Ugly new Infantry caps. Many ladies there, and Highlanders in folding knapsacks, very bare; but it is nothing to them. By 12½ back to Cowes. I paid 10 shillings for gig <u>and</u> driver. In steamboat to Southhampton. At 4½ for Havre in the Monarch, Not like American vessels.

France

15 May. At 5 we arrive at Havre but can go into port, round the pierhead, only at 7 on account of tide. At eight custom house opens. They are very polite and gentlemanly; just now far less exact than English. —One might suspect Louis Philippe giving soldiers the present mean, dirty, tasteless uniform to wean the French from pleasure in military. Passport. At ½ past 9 start in diligence; odd buildings. I sat on the banquette. Small horses, bad harness. 6, 8 horses. Drivers cruel in beating, use often the buttend of the whip; as I know them. But drive very fast. Good road. At [name left blank] touch the Seine and now very fine to Rouen but how different the culture, trimness and full verdure of England, just having seen Isle of Wight, which by the way so far as I saw it is not better than many parts of England and not so fine as Herfordshire. Coachman & Conducteur chatter.

Rouen to Paris

16 May. Bad breakfast. Stroll about. So last night. Curious town, with its most narrow streets closing in over you, gable ends, winding serpentlike and up-hill, almost transporting like Oxford. No street coquetry, which I mean here in no bad sense, i.e., no dress, no trim walk or as in America. No public girls apparently in the streets, no looking at you, this even not late in the evening. French cafés full, in the day time, talk, smoke, clicking of domino, etc. What immense time there must be wasted away constantly in the cafés all over France. Go into the church of St. Ouen. Fine building. But Catholic service seems to <u>strike</u> me no more, though I insist upon, the churches ought always to be open. Cathedral does not please me, filigree work. Other churches, see Guide book. Palais de Justice; important trial of an attorney for false sale. Young judges, and no one can tell me the name. In England the people consider and feel them <u>their own</u>, much like their aristocracy, and every one knows their names. The <u>president</u> was all the time adjusting his robe, feeling his hair, his shirt collar, gesticulated, talked, etc. — so very different from England. Place de la pucelle, where she — the best, purest, bravest, noblest girl was burnt — a saint indeed. Old church close by now livery stable. Rue de la grosse orloge. How unspeakably mean the soldiers look. Fine quays. Corneille's statue on the bridge. Bridges are fine places for statues. Mean dinner, meaner dirtier water closets. The police suffer no girls in the streets to stand, etc. Women in the cafés. At ½ 2 o'clock on railway to Paris through Normandy. See the little book. Officers of the railway like the English dressed, and they like the English police. The [illegible] often road chiefly English. These capitalists light the continent, build railways, etc. At ½ past 6 at Paris. [word illegible] Octroi [toll-house]. Cannot get in at Hôtel d'Hollande. Must go to Hôtel de l'Interieur 51 Rue neuve St. Augustine. Boulevard des Italiens. Place Vendome. Napoleon's Column.

Paris

17 May. (Found letter at Rougemont de Lowenberg from my good, my dear, my true and sacred Matilda) Deliver letters, go to the Chamber but could not get in, for Tocqueville just in the Tribune. Crossing the Place de la Concorde I could not help seeing all the human gore which had flowed here from Louis XVI to the last of the Commune of Paris. It is a most fearful spot.

18 May. Deliver letters.

19 May, Sunday. Breakfast at Tocqueville, where his wife and Beaumont. B. & T. truly glad to see me, warm and hearty. George Sumner tells me that Beaumont mentioned me very honorably indeed in Chamber of Deputies. They, too, feel deeply the bad odour in which the U.S. "for we are deeply attached to them." I write in utmost haste. The making water in the streets, which first struck me in Liverpool, and has increased now at its height here. Little Rambeautot or Vespasiennes on the Boulevards. It is shocking and the worst of it is, one makes use of it. —No reading any longer in the Chamber; if a man reads, the members go out. This is great improvement, very great indeed. It has rained these two days. In England but one morning a little rain. Paris strikes with its high and often fine houses, but the Anglican race will live but one family in a house, and although it makes flatter cities and spreads them more, it is highly important, socially, morally, politically — highly and essentially so. I hate these street-houses. Not half the wealth appears here as in England. Paris is no[w?] very dear. Exhibitions, my first hasty visit disappoints me, but one must see. How beautiful the French sounds in the mouths of the lowest. How plain the women are. All polka here as in England. A rage for a vile dance. Varieties very amusing. Must go to Heckscher [this last sentence is crossed out].

20 May. Rains cats and dogs. Breakfast in café with George Sumner, who gives me *Boston Daily Advertiser* with Texas Correspondence and Mr. Clay's letter, which is very reasonable. To Edward Heckscher and make plan of proceeding. To Chamber of Deputies, passing again that most beautiful and most fearful Place de la Concorde. Look closely at the Statues of the chief cities. Rouen surely ought to have had among other things a spindle. Go to the Tribune du corps diplomatique, the ticket given me by Mr. Ledyard. De Tocqueville has given me his medaille de Deputé. House very much like ours only more elegant in some things. Picture of Louis Philippe swearing the charter. 2 deputies were <u>reading</u> prosy essays; the others spoke free, fluently and but too lively. Perrier shook his hands, and body, etc. They have water as in America. In England they suck oranges. Houses built like ours always bad for hearing. The Deputies have desks and paper. But such a noise. The speaker beats with his paper folder; so do others; ringing bell (which sounds very undignified), calling, etc., etc. I think House of Representatives in Washington the quietest. —Forgot to mention the good news that Pennsylvania has made provision. I feel quite happy. See the plan of the house of Deputies. Dined at de Tocqueville's; a Mr. [name left blank] there. De Tocqueville had not read St. Martin's work on French, American, & English Parliamentary law (Reglements). Tells me that the change of demanding ays and nays was lately lost only by a very few votes and will be carried without doubt ere long. Ça marche toujours, viz. I had mentioned my astonishment at the fact that the secretaries <u>estimate</u> but do not count those who stand or sit, and that 20 votes only can demand a counting. Dividing is what I love. Opera francais. Fair singing no more. Fair dancing no more. None, none equal to Fanny Elssler. O heavens, what a new idea of dancing she gave me, just as Raphael when I first saw the *Madonna de Sisto*. That sacred moment. Café au grand balcon. Bed.

21 May. There are flower shops in Paris (bouquets). How pretty! There are wood shops (bois au poid!) how odd for an American. Vegetable shops; ironing and washing shops! I am very unfortunate with my letters. Most out of town. — It rains still very hard. Breakfast with Sumner in café. Errands. Bossange, who gives me this curious piece of secret police information about the U.S. "There is evidently a great intellectual movement in the U.S. They import only good books. I cannot send trifling ones. Charleston, Philadelphia & Boston import the heavy good books. New York not. There are but two or three people in New York for whom I ever send to Wiley & Post[?] books" With Sumner to Louvre. Could not see all; but the pictures no great things. [name illegible] gallery. Marine models very interesting. Place where Henry IV died. It is very curious. <u>In</u> England one is reminded of <u>one</u> history, but here so many histories, totally different. Place Concorde (blood Louis XVI); Vendôme, Napoleon; Tuilleries, Louis XIV; Henry VI and St. Germain de l'Auxerrois, Bartholomew, Chamber of Deputies (quite different again). St. Germain de l'Auxerrois. From this place then came the signal for the greatest crime in history. St. Eustache, interesting on account of Gothic passing over into Renaissance but mouldy, dirty, and childish altars. Corn Market. Enormous roof. Meant to have gone to the theatre au Palais Royal but all seats taken. Went to Felix, long talk on last revolution, Louis Philippe, Guizot, etc. Home, bed.

In Rouen . . . [rest of sentence crossed out]. How unutterably uncivilized, barbarian. I remember having seen this and even worse in Berlin.

The House of Peers sits in the Luxembourg. They do not know here the joint committee. The two houses ought always to sit in one palace. I venture to say the English History would be a very different one had the House of Lords not been sitting in the same Parliament House. In England and America always messages from one to another. —De Tocqueville tells me that no member of the Deputies would allow himself to be made a peer, as long as he can get elected deputy. He instanced Passy. All the world wondered but it was found he could not have been elected. Bossange tells me of new good German International Copy Law namely that if a German bookseller is interested in a foreign book, no German booksellers can sell it. Also Sardinia [has] a similar law.

22 May. No letter at the general post office from Mittermaier, as Felix told he had written him. To Heckscher, thence by cabriolet to Luxembourg; not bad taste of building, but Italian Modern Gallery — flaringly dead women and flaringly disconsolate men or vice versa, besides out of the way scenes of old Persian, etc. history. Scamander, etc. No one cares a fig for. There is keine Weihe [no inspiration]. All theatrical, opera women, etc. But sculpture better, decidedly. Some very sweet things. —How very difficult composition is in art, in writing, etc. We all can very well produce a single good thing but many of these pictures appear to me like a string of fine conceptions; but there is not one great mind weaving through the whole as in Raphael; and the same is the case with the lives of men. Only in those of the great is one composition, one general coherency pervading the whole. I also found many originals the engravings of which I had known. Poor and middling pictures or statues improve by reduced engravings; only great works of God and men improve by being the more and more magnified. —Thence to les Chambres de Marie de Medici, sa chambre à coucher, with gilt ornaments, etc. The arabesques, painted by Italians, at once striking and warming up. What amount of art there was in Italy then. —Thence to Chamber of peers; like Chamber of Deputies; not fit for debate. Cousin spoke, or read, or preached, or lectured — it sounded most charlatanlike to ears of ours. Adventure avec la petite Belgoise. Thence Pantheon. Perhaps of all modern buildings in Greek style, which I know the best; uncommonly fine. But kahl [plain] and this regularly putting away great men like in the stores of greatness is repulsive to me as the vases in Rome, of aunts and uncles were. Very high; vast and instructive view from the top. St. Genevieve close by — dirty, mouldy, cold, with all the little smeary tapers on the tomb of the saint and wreaths on the crucifix, as I used to know it. It is very repulsive and deeply impresses you with the fact that it can be and is carried on without any connection with morality. Besides such as it appears very pusil-lanimous. They go and pray a certain prayer at the tomb of the saint, pull out a sous piece and the woman puts two tapers on certain points of iron made for it, while the person is gone long ago and forgiveness of sins is obtained. This it is which leaves the heart void of religion as we find in the first Revolution. To Notre Dame — vast, dirty, mouldy. Very old architecture. Close by, Hôtel Dieu. God bless you devoted nuns. A temple and a magnification of charity and kindness. —Daily die 5 in average. Close by again l'Administration des Charite's (?) de Paris. Close by Morgue. No one there. Hôtel de Justice. Flower market on the Isle de Paris. N. 14 rue Arbre-Sec, where Coligny was murdered. Dinner in café, Boule-vard des Italiens. I am so sorry I do not hear from my Matilda.

23 May. With George Sumner in Exhibition. Some fine things; the most remark-able seem to me the two gigantique panes of glass. Soap very fine; embossed orna-ments covered with cloth. But I must rather mark out when I can get a classified catalogue. Buy, if possible *Journal de Débats* with the feuilleton on this Exhibition. — Arc de l'Étoile. a folio of history, and what a folio! It is stupefying. But there must be others with other conquests, science, literature, etc. The arch is very beau-tiful indeed. I think much better than any Roman one. But one sole thing I dis-liked. The arms of the Fames, put in their sides. View from the top. One can easily imprint a topographic picture of Paris on one's mind. Saw Mrs. Austin. She has seen nearly the whole world. (She lost her money through dues) I gave them let-ters to Niebuhr, which made the beginning. I dare say they will do nothing for me. (Saw Kate McLeod, Mrs. Calderon)

24 May. Went at last to Rougemont de Lowenberg & of course he had a letter from Matilda, although I had given them my direction at once. Took 500 francs, rather 20£ sterling. With Edward Heckscher to Jardin des Plantes. Enormous col-lection of animals, fine of minerals, comparative anatomy, etc. but living animals not equal to Zoological Garden in London. We dined together at Very's. Went to Franconi. Very tasteful amphitheatre, and some fine riding. The whole very fine, tasteful, impressive.

25 May. Saw Mr. Lucas, Inspecteur General des Prisons. Very polite, wishes to send me his works, etc. —but against solitary imprisonment. He says that the most admirable effects have been produced upon bad girls by the "sisters" in the Maisons des Jeunes de'Tenues in the provinces and complete reforms. Che lo crede? [Who believes it?] —At 2 to the Institut Public sitting of Académie des Sci-ences Politiques et Morales. Nandit presides. Mignet, secretaire perpetuel reads the eloge of Count Simeon, whose name I heard when a boy, by way of exception as a good Frenchman (organizing the Kingdom of Westphalia). At ½ past 5 to Foelix, who takes me to a Mr. Klintworth, who will take me to Duchatel, Minister of the Interior, and Guizot. Home. Went the whole length of the Boulevards. That the Opera is closed! I feel so anxious to get to Hamburg.

30 May, Thursday. Laffitte's Burial. Boulevards full of people and troops, line and national guards. I like the <u>new</u> uniform very well, except the red pants but they were given, I understand, by Charles X. With Edward Heckscher and Riviere, professor of minerals in Jardin des Plantes, and his wife to Sèvres. Start from Tuilleries in omnibus. See *Galignani*. I had no idea of the beauty especially fruit pieces and table ornament. Large pictures, portraits, etc. and nothing <u>porcelain</u> about it in color. Professor Brognart led us partly about. The guide an Alsatian. The common price of pieces, we asked was from 20 to 30,000 francs. But also small things and cheap though none unornamented here. Collection of porcelain from all countries and of all times. Walked through St. Cloud garden, p. omnibus (for railway would have been too late) to Paris. Dined with Heckscher in Palais Royal.

31 May. With Sumner to Column of July. The golden Fame on the top, though certainly well made reminds of Newspapers. Model of Elephant, very fine indeed. Pére la Chaise. In approaching shops of stonecutters with epitaphs and <u>wreath shops</u>, to be hung on the graves thicken. The wreaths made chiefly of yellow immortelles and of a white shaving, I believe of quills. The cemetery what I always thought a great cemetery ought to be — a city of the dead. You walk in streets of greatness. Names crowd one after the other. Casemir Perrier's monument fine. A woman takes us round. Tomb of Abelard and Heloise. Girls have hung immortelles here too. These wreaths are a sort of votive and no doubt connected with some distinct belief of efficacy. Rods made for them on the tombstones, with tin covers to protect against too quick withering. It has become mechanical. Some very fine and appropriate tombs. Down to Maison des jeunes De'tenus — between House of Refuge and Penitentiary. While Sumner went in to parlabre — for we had no permission I waited on the stone bench and with me sisters and mothers to see young prisoners. They had <u>bouquets</u>, some books. There are about 500. Eremitic plan. Very healthy looking. Since Eremitic they have ½ less recedives or recommittals. The boys do not find it difficult to endure. Good system of reward if 40 good points, they can choose some book or <u>Reisszeug</u> [illustration] or other. Religious instruction given together but different from Pentonville. Encaged. Like to work. Take airing in a yard not attached to cell because the building first for the <u>Arbeit</u> [work] plan. But I think this really better. Some officers in this Institution who have been here imprisoned. —To Montmarte. Good view, instructive.

Place of attack. Dine with Sumner in <u>cave</u>. Go to Mariani, one of Espartero's ministers. Is writing history of last 4 years in Spain. Was to have seen George Sand there, but left for the country. To Howe and the sisters (Wards), 22 Rivoli. Dreadful news of riot in Philadelphia. I have always said that the problem of religious excitement and great individual liberty with large cities not by any means solved in the U.S.

1 June. Early to Mr. Visconti architect of the tomb of Napoleon, with Mr. Vetet's letter through de Beaumont. He receives me well. Shows me the whole plan and makes appointment for 2½ o'clock at the <u>canons</u> [cannons] of the Invalides. To Howe. Breakfast with Sumner. To Mr. Warden, poor old man, with vertigo, having lost his property in America lonely in that bustling Paris. What a mass of people have been rendered miserable! He tells me that the distinguished Mr. Lieber is here, not having been able to read Mr. Preston's letter. St. Sulpice. Prussian Embassy. No letter from Bunsen. Palais d'Orsay, one of the finest Houses I know of — exquisite. To the "canons;" wonder how these Prussian and Austrian guns got there now. They must have been buried. Visconti shows me the tomb so far as done. Parts strike me as very fine but not the altar and will be fine that hole down to the Tomb? Dined with George Sumner.

2 June. Breakfast with de Beaumont, his wife granddaughter of Lafayette. An officer there from Africa, de Tocqueville. With Heckscher to Salle d'armes or "Academy." some fine fencing. With Sumner in the evening to Mabille a <u>grisetees</u> place in Champs Elysees. Cancan and Polka!! Headache. So I did not go to Howe.

3 June. Letter at last from Matilda and good news as to boys. —To N. 52 Rue de la Victoire, whence the 18th Brumair broke forth. Bonaparte's and Josephine's dwelling. Long alley of elms closing over in French style. Bourrienne, if I remember right, gives all details of the day. Louvre to see the gobelins and Sèvres exhibition. Some landscape gobelins; very fine but most so the borders for some panels. Also Mahmud and massacre of the mamlooks [mamelukes] which I had seen. Several other things. An hour and a half with Kate McLeod for Mrs Calderon went out. How against England as to Spanish politics and Espartero! —Engravings exposed at the window are here far more decent than in London. No <u>ballet</u> prints with nudities just so much covered as to make a little more exciting.

4 June. To Messageries Royales. With Heckscher to Versailles by railway. Statue of Hoche — close by the palace. Such [a] palace can never be built again, for oriental despotism with refined European spirit can never unite again. It is enormous. Windsor like the modest palace of a Stadtholder [town leader], and so it ought to be. We got terribly fatigued before we were through and this is but a small part. It is the opposite to a savings bank. It cost at the least *Galignani* says 50,000,000 [*sic*] £ Sterling. The idea of Louis Philippe's of a historical gallery is very grand and this probably the best place, but a pity [it] is here because it is so enormous and so historical that one must study it and for that one ought to be able to <u>drop in</u>. A traveller ought to <u>live</u> 4 days at least here. Immense number of battles. Statue of L'Isle [Aile] d'Adam and the doors of the Hospital at Rhodes interested <u>me</u>, for I admire that siege. Statue of Jane of Arc most lovely and happy. Jane of Arc in marble by a French princess and that placed in Versailles by Louis Philippe King by revolution. There is what I call a historical <u>grape</u>. The long Saloon of Louis XIV. One has not even dreamt of such splendour. His council table with the identical green velvet cloth in his council room! His bed in which he died. Window from which the King and Queen with Lafayette [showed themselves] to the enraged multitude. Fine marble staircase. Here again you find strikingly how certain periods if active have their peculiar faces — revolution, Louis XIV, Reformation, etc. The gravel offends me. I like to see the common <u>paysant</u> women explain to each other the pictures and take the most earnest interest. Dined in café. To Paris, I to Theatre Francais to see Rachel in <u>Catherine II</u>. The piece [is] very silly. Her declamation and pronunciation the finest French, the greatest I have ever heard. But she does not <u>play</u> with the face; she only moves the <u>eyes</u>, but cannot even it seems open them very wide. Framboise in Boulevard, cigar and bed.

5 June. Breakfasted with de Tocqueville and then to Mignet, fine conversation on representative principle. With Wards (Howe) to Hôtel de Cluny to which Visconti had given me a ticket. Sorbonne, hear a lecture on philosophie. St. Germain du Pres with Sumner, the oldest ante-gothic church of Paris. Shocking capitals — monsters. To see Dupuytren musée but could not. Found two students singing loud and cutting away on some dead woman. Ecole de beaux arts. A fine idea indeed to save arches, etc., by transporting them and embodying them with taste as here. Very good idea indeed. It is reviving it. Dined with Sumner. To French Opera. Saw Taglioni in <u>Dieu et la Bajadere</u>. Very light, but not liquid like Fanny Elssler — not the soul. I thought it would be so.

6 June. Occurrence with a sparrow, and Tocqueville's expression. Thomas Crawford, American Sculptor, called on me. Engaged to Louisa Ward.

7 June. See Crawfords. Pay last visits, Madame de Beaumont very kind and <u>herzlich</u> [cordial] to me, yet different way from Madame de Tocqueville who is an Englishwoman. Abbé de L'Epèe's tomb in St. Roch in Latin that, imitating his Savior, he made the dumb speak (rather French) and the manual alphabet engraved — good idea. In the evening at Howe's. Little Anne begs me to send her a flower from the spot where I was wounded. Mignet paid me a long visit in the morning.

8 June. With Howe, Sumner, Crawford in the café; with Crawford on the top of the column place Vendôme; agree as to ancient architecture for modern times. I think like the ancient tragedy — great but naked — void of incident, variety, and extensiveness. We want Shakespeare, and so as Hôtel des Invalides, not St. Magdalene; at least only for very, very peculiar purposes — a pantheon to bury great man in would be well like Magdalen, but a Gerard College! How much finer a palais d'Orsay here or Venetian palace in Rome — But it requires imagination, which the Americans have not yet, because not yet repose. Then went to Brooks, Hôtel Mirabeau. They have been here a week! in the same street! She the same (How free she speaks of Powers' *Greek Slave!*). Home and pack, and write these lines. Crawford and Sumner accompany me to the Messageries Royales (which is a mere name to distinguish it from the messageries generales). At five we start for Lille. The last house sign in Paris I read (near the Messageries) was: "Cabinets d'aisance inodores." I have a place on the banquette. Paved road as far as Lille, and indeed through the Netherlands; very wide. Country level; hardly now and then an undulation; well cultivated — in large, even masses. Through Peronne.

Belgium

9 June, Sunday. At 7 in <u>Cambray</u>, recollections enough. Good breakfast. Douay, Fete Dieu, Great exhibitions; all shops open. By 2 o'clock at Lille. One of the signs: "Café au grand St. Esprit" with a painted dove. Railroad to Ghent, through Courtray battlefield of the Spurs. Belgian custom officers very polite and easy. These railroads will break in upon passports, prohibitive systems and all. I used formerly to say that if people could travel through the air it would have the most decided effect on politics. Railways effect this in part I suppose. How very bad and odd the Flemish talk French. I had a totally different idea. In our car — and I went in the third to see more, not knowing that the second is as good, or rather as bad — was spoken by people of the lower classes: Flemish, Dutch, French and German. Sign boards, ordinances, advertisements, in French and Flemish. Toward five at Ghent. Walk about after dinner.

Ghent and Brussels

10 June. See the Belfry. What silly anecdote in Murray's guidebook. Impudent fellow with me who does not know a single house to point out to me. To the

Marche de Vendredi. History enough here! The iron cannon. Now this clumpsy thing of wrought iron has been used and Stockton's must burst. Beguinage. That is the sort of convent, if indeed they can be called so, which the Protestants ought to have. Small houses, with a little garden, common service and common meals; attending sick, schools and prisoners. No vow but, of course, certain promises; with a Superior at the head. It would be a great blessing. Maison de Force. Of historical interest for us penologists but otherwise not much. The officer who led me about told me that formerly "sous le rois Guillaume" the prisoners were allowed to have birds and flowers. But it was abolished (2 years before the revolution) and it is now more difficult to keep them in order. Prisoners are paid for all they work; yet punished if they will not work. "Cachot" even 3 months. Two men in one cell often, but it will be changed. No women here. Cathedral of St. Bavon. Van Eyck's picture. Uncommon minuteness and accuracy. The faces are exquisite, but otherwise the composition is very poor, or rather there is none at all. No doubt a painter may study them and learn, but we cannot be touched or elevated by such pictures. Buy an engraving. The man in the shop said calmly and unpretendingly, yet it sounded very bitter: "Monsieur, nous otres ici, nous n'avions pas une patrie. Nous avons ite Autrichiens, Espaniols, libre, Hollandais, Francais, Belgois." ["Sir, we others here, we didn't have a native land. We have been Austrian, Spanish, independent, Dutch, French, Belgian."] This sounds odd and melancholy when one comes from France where the glory of France stares you everywhere in the face and where you are everywhere reminded of the totality of France from olden times. At 2 o'clock to Malines & Brussels. Very level country, very cultivated and green but not as in France in large masses. More like England. Also hedges. By 5 at Brussels Hôtel de l'Europe. In the evening carry letters and cards to Mr. Hilliard, American Chargé d'Affaires. Count Arrivabene from Ticknor and Foelix; Mr. Vickers (cousin of Foelix) and Diepetiaux, Inspecteur generale des Prison, from Barclay and Foelix. Stroll. Bed. I found here a letter from dear Matilda. —Tocqueville spoke once to me of "la fureur de l'uniformité des Francais."

11 June. (Written at Antwerp). The people called, some had even the evening before. Offer all services.

12 June. The King at Laaken, otherwise Mr. Hilliard would go with me to him. He describes the king as a very well disposed man of sound sense. Strange Belgian troops look very well; much better than French. Hôtel de Ville; much better than that of Ghent; and it looks indeed historical, but to imitate such a thing, no! The place in front where Egmont & Horn were executed very old and curious looking, more so than any other I know. [here four lines are crossed out] This porcheria [obscenity] is well executed and it cannot be denied more <u>natural</u> than the spouting water out of the mouth or squirting from the breasts. The Museum is absolutely shocking with its nasty daubs; collection of prince d'Aremberg better, a Miers (?) there with all the exquisite execution of that school, also Gerard Dou. But, I have no longer real taste for these pictures. The refuge for old men and women. God bless it. The Hospital large and grand. The botanical garden, with "Resource," music, gentlemen and ladies walking, the first I have seen again. Diepetiaux gives me a mass of his writings. Arrivabene takes me to see Brussels lace making. The finest are sewn altogether, i.e., from the ground, and the flowers on it. Women earn from 2 to 3½ franc a day hard work. Begin early. Very fine, but one of those things which <u>unexplained</u> would not be valued so high, not absolutely beautiful of itself like the French cloth, e.g., at the exhibition of shawls.

Waterloo Battlefields

13 June. Early to Waterloo. Cotton, the Sergeant Major of English Hussars my guide. Mont St. Jean. Hougoumont, etc. The mound and Lion a <u>worthy</u> monument. Good idea. Back by 4. Dined at 5 at Count Arrivabene, where several people, also Quetelet. These dinners at present are really too short and flimsy, the very opposite to what Hamburg dinners are or were. At 10 o'clock by diligence through Waterloo, Mt. St. Jean, Quatre Bras, to Quatre Bras le Docq near Sombreffe, ¾ Lieu from Gembloux.

14 June. I at 4 o'clock. Heard my old <u>Walloon</u>; kettle over the coals, all old things. Such fearfully ugly women. At five I set out with a boy through Sombreffe to Bry. Found an old man who had been guide de Napoleon. Here we drank on the 16th. The man remembered that all wells were exhausted. Found the place where we were so long exposed to the cannon fire. To the windmill where Blücher stood. A foot path leads nearly the same way down the slope which we marched down to attack Ligny. Found the hedge through which we passed to attack French grenadier guards; the house where I first fired and killed a grenadier; the church, the road from Fleurus where I, the first, scrambled up; where Bagensky was wounded; where Neuman was shot — all, all, even (I believe at least, the well where I gave water to two officers and some soldiers, and one said: "Jäger, das soll dir Gott vergelten" [Trooper, God will reward you for that]. The deep hollow way where layers of dead and wounded lay and I shot a drummer — all, all I found. Where we <u>last</u> stood, now two houses built; the old woman whose house it is confirmed that they were not built then. Inn near the church. Strange, as I now drank quietly my glass of beer here. Oh, it was a full day. On the milk sonnet: "Hier hasst ich nicht, selbst nicht die Feinde" [Here I did not hate; not even the enemy]. With my boy across the field to road from Fleurus to Quatre Bras de Docq, and back to Quatre Bras de Docq. I [word illegible] inquire: "Qu'est ce." Boy: "ça fait uff, uff, uff." I: "Mais, pour quel object." Boy: "object." I: "Mai oui, pour quoi est ce." Boy: "C'est pour fair peur." [I: "What is it?" Boy: "It goes huff, huff, huff." I: "Yes, but to what purpose?" Boy: "Purpose?" I: "Yes, what's it for?" Boy: "It's to frighten."] I cannot make out what Bagensky in his History of Regiment Colberg, the battle part of which I had with me, means by windmill of Bussy. No one could tell me. With diligence de Mons to Namur. Entered Namur [along] the road on which I was taken wounded in the car to town. Brussels Gate. Hôtel d'Harscamp. Found a man in the Hôtel who had about on the 20th served the wounded. Spoke of the <u>collets</u> <u>blancs</u> [white collars](us), praised the Prussians that they had not touched a thing after entering arms in hand. Saw the penitentiary for women. Near 800 here. Work together in pretended silence, but talk, even before us. Nuns serve, get 600 francs a year. Sleep separately. No classification except for good behavior inside the walls. I could not see anything peculiar except cleanliness and decent behavior. The nuns say prisoners tractable.

15 June. Horse. Great difficulty in finding my place where wounded for 1. now a new road to Gembloux 2. the little wood cut down. Road [rode?] as far as Suartée. There a woman sent me to her father. He had fled during battle, but his son, who would take nothing, [took me] to another old man. They led me, with children following, to a farm and now I came nearer and nearer and began to <u>orientiren</u> myself. Rode about. Found an intelligent wood cutter. "Bon Wallon," where great fight. Saw the place where I approached Col. Zastrow. At length at <u>the</u> place left of Bellgrave, plucked flowers, mused, prayed. Circle concluded. Road home. Missed for the first time the boat (to Liege), baggage had gone without me. Not my fault, for the captain had told me my watch went right. So I got permission to see the citadel. There I found a man who had served in Chevaux legers de l'Empire. Spoke always of "collets blank" and how they had lain strewn about. "Ah! Ils se battaient bien monsieur." [Ah, they fought well, sir.] I, of course, said nothing to get the story out of him. Fine view down on the Sambre and Meuse Bridge. In the morning had visited the church yard to find if possible Zastrow's grave, intending to have a stone erected, but no trace. The grave digger, old man, had been there only 4 years. Knew nothing. The man on the citadel told me that a feast is celebrated every 20th of June, in honor of Virgin Mary because she protected a little chapel near Porte de Fer, towards Porte de Bruxelles. "Not a ball touched the chapel." I did not know until now that some one besides Col. Zastrow had commanded our Colbergers.

Liege

16 June, Sunday. Embarked at 6 o'clock where the kindly girls dressed my wounds. Now down the Meuse where 29 years ago I with so many wounded [were brought] down to Liege. Port St. Nicholas, uncle Toby. Bouge, where Don Juan of Austria was poisoned? Looking back, beautiful picture of Namur, Citadel and Bridge. Approach to Huy. Well fortified, ranging up and down the river. (Andenne first) Looking back the most charming "cut out" picture: bridge, Huy, cathedral, citadel and river. Fine shores. Beautiful situation of Chaquier castle high on a rock. Serain, where [the] late Cockerill's enormous establishment since 1816, King of Holland his partner. Liege at about 2 o'clock. Found my baggage. Landed near Pont d'Arc (Ici les Liegiois ont vue briler leurs fers [Here the citizens of Liege are seen to polish their iron]). Went to Hôtel de la Pommelette. At dinner, table d'hôte music for the first time, women play violin. Strolled about. Found Rue de la Barbe d'Or, but the stone bench on which I had rested so many a time my wounded head, gone. To Harlez, Portier rue, close by. Not at home. Went up the hill to the old convent de Saint Laurent, Benedictines, then hospital, now barracks and hospital. The large Gothic doorway through which I was carried, the yard where I lay on straw. Here a salle de la galle. In America unknown. Wild boar's head with motto Suavitate et Robare! Still here the painted inscription (though faded somewhat) of Republic Francaise l'Hospice des Liegeois. Went down the way I trailed when a little recovered, passed the church Saint Croix, of Norman origin. Everything came back to my mind, though I went here but once. The bridge over which I passed so often to have my wound dressed, and the chapel where it was done gone — all pulled down and built over. Palais de Justice, Maison de Ville, wells. To Harlez again. Found Simon. He did not know me. Kind. Said they had often spoken of me, but lately again. He remembered Bärwald and Jung — remarkable. Told me that my old hosts lived in another part of the city but could not tell me where. Harlez was emigrant, lived 7 years in Germany, studied in Jena. When Prussians commanded here [they] made him Sous Intendant. King William continued him. But [he] lost his place by the revolution. Even he says that the Dutch government was very unwise in forcing them to do all legal acts in Dutch which was of the greatest difficulty. The cousin of Countess Outremont [was] one of [the] chief promoters of the Revolution in Liege. Went to rue Pot d'or where Julie Lessoine lived, now dead. Entered the gate, I had so often entered in my first love, which I did not know was love, in rue d'Amay. Saw the room in which I found her so often. A wall drawn across the yard now. Lessoines do not live here now. Young Lessoine is deputy in Brussels. Walloon here as Flemish in Flanders in the accent and more and more against French. This is droll. Much written now in Flemish. I became, wandering thus about, very sad. Oh, my Matilda, I pressed you to my heart, that you have never interfered with my remembrance of Julie. Traced back my way home. Bed.

Louvain, Malines, Antwerp

17 June. At 7 by railroad to Louvain, passing over battle ground of Neerwinden, passing Tirlemont. At 10 at Louvain. Cathedral, Hôtel de Ville. Was sitting in Estaminet; Louvain beer and cheese by my side, which I had obtained after much pains for they speak little French here or none at all, but I patched up a jargon of German or English; the Hôtel de Ville before me. More a carved boil than a grand thing. Tasteful puerility. The immense number of those gothic bases with still another number by their side, without figures as now, are nothing as everything in architecture without use is bad and if the figures were on them, the whole would remind one more of those show boxes on hand organs. My Gothic enthusiasm is gone. Fine, by way of history, but not to be copied, though surely use can be made of it. In England except House of Parliament, they know this best. They carried elaborateness in Gothic architecture evidently too far. This Hôtel de Ville is besides too small. Inside the plan and a model of the steeple of Cathedral as it was until 1605 but blown down. In the Cathedral fine Messys and Memling with all their elaborateness. (except the Lord in *Lord's Supper*. Horrid. It cannot be his.) A figure of Virgin Mary who descended in 16 and some years and averted the balls. Now they adore it. It is very disgusting. A private collection of Mr. Vandenschrieck, very fine as to Dutch school. A Ruysdael, *Cascade*, the finest I think I have ever seen. Also Rubens' *Marriage of Constantine*, with the two boys playing pipes near the altar. Also Rubens' *Death of St. Catherine*. Beautiful coloring and no overgrown masses of flesh, but that trunk with the blood spouting! Why not covered? Because Rubens had very little taste. Strolled about. At 3 to Malines by railway. Notre Dame. The *Draught of Fishes* by Rubens very fine. Cathedral. Van Dyck's *Crucifixion*, fine, yet it seems much spoiled. The interior of this noble church most damnably spoiled by ornament of Louis XIV time, but the sacristan told me it would be taken down. I think the tower of the Cathedral in its simplicity the finest Gothic I know. It impresses me grandly, grandly. There is no childishness about it. Here that remarkable woman, Margaret of Austria — diplomatist, regent, promoter of arts, music, poetry, literature and religion resided and Charles V created by her. A statue will be erected. Plan of Flemish periodical. At 8 to Antwerp where we arrive by 9¼ — a full day indeed. I dreamed at Florence that Luther took me on the imperial Eagle over Germany, Rhine, Nuremberg, etc. Well, this day was nearly such an excursion.

18 June. Write a line to Herman Shaeffer, partner of Agie & Co.; he comes and we walk to the cathedral. Then home and wrote this out until 12 o'clock. For the first time with a "commissionaire" Snyder, 62 years old, to the Cathedral. Inside beautiful, treble aisles, etc. Rubens *Descent from the Cross*. This seems to me the finest picture I have seen of him. There is more <u>taste</u> in it than in all others and less <u>outré</u> [excessive], although also <u>flat</u> faces here (see for the others guide). With the little girl on top of the tower. Distant view of Scheldt, country, citadel, place where heroic van Spyke blew himself up, etc. I do <u>not</u> greatly admire the architecture. As Napoleon said it reminds [one] of Brussels lace, besides, what architecture is it for a tower of a cathedral which consists of bits of stone-work strung together by iron bars; a manner more fit for moorish architectural playfulness? I prefer the simple noble tower of Malines. To the <u>Baisons</u>, the great work of Napoleon, made for men of war, but now for commerce. Immense horses and fine, one for wagons of enormous load. 1000 francs. To the museum. Rubens, Rembrandt, Ottoveniusses (teacher of Rubens, from whom I think he forgot too much, for Rubens has not what O. has, repose). See Catalogue. To the commandant, permission to see Citadel. Room where the gallant Chasse lived long and received Gerard's etc, visit. to compliment him on his <u>belle defence</u>. Everywhere large congregations of children going to church, led by some old rich lady or <u>religeuse</u>. Catholicism reviving everywhere and also in strictness. They remove pictures, in which there is too much nudity, even of the finest and first painters, Rubens. Dined at Herman Shaeffer, partner of Agie & Co (flannellier). His wife pretty, at once reminds me of America. I do not know whether any national face is more distinct than American women's faces, and why? This is very surprising indeed.

Belgium to Holland

19 June. Early to church St. Jacques. Exquisite pictures. See Murray. At nine in Diligence to Rotterdam by Breda. A monotonous, waist [waste?] country separates Belgium from Holland. North of Breda, indeed a little South, begins that most peculiar character of Holland — canals, fine brick roads on the dykes, long alleys, good even fine brick houses, vast meadows. Meuse [Maas] at Moerdijk. Romping in the steamboat with little Dutch boys. More and more Dutch character; fine, truly fine women; exquisite complexion and figures. Dort of Calvinistic memory, canals, narrow streets, great cleanliness, driving in constant circuitous route. Ferry to Rotterdam; this side Rotterdam the first stork. Curious gold head ornaments of all sorts begin. (Most so in North Holland.) Steamboat over Meuse. Rotterdam at about 8 o'clock. Walk about. Canals of all sorts.

Rotterdam to den Hague

20 June. In the morning on the top of Church. Dutch view. If any man were to say: It is possible to <u>make</u> a whole artificial country and that this country can be one the very richest, though the making costs enormous sums, and Holland did not exist, he would [be] called a fool. All Holland is perhaps the most striking instance of reality against the greatest improbability. At 12 o'clock, noon, by diligence, at the Hague, passing through Delft, and the finest mansions on the canal, with iron gates and names of the mansions in gilt letters, many ending in <u>burg</u>. Deliver letters to Mr. Hughes from Preston, Wyse and <u>the</u> one from Upshur; and to Gevers van Endegeest, Councillor of State, and member of States General and W. A. Gevers, brother to the Dutch Chargé d'Affaires in U.S. With Hughes to States General. Very quiet and sedate. They speak very fluently, but without passion. Assembly small. The most remarkable, nay most astonishing [thing], is that according to <u>Reglement</u> no amendment can be made by States General; either adopt the whole or reject the whole. They have committees as in France. The government proposes a law (for though the States may initiate, it is very rarely done); it is given to the bureaux or committees. They elect a member each. These form a <u>central bureau</u>, which communicates with the ministers and what is then adopted must be adopted by the States General whole or rejected whole. The States General are <u>not</u> according to nobility, clergy, and county; but the <u>provincial</u> are.

Den Hague, Delft, Leyden, Haarlemer Meer

21 June. See Museum. Potter's *Young Steer*, and other fine pictures. See the catalogue where I have written as usual. John de Witt's portrait interested me much. This great, great citizen. Japanese collection. Dress of Willem I, when murdered. Miniature of Spyke — light blue eyes; round uncharacteristic face, light blond hair, mouth not even peculiar. Full head rather. Yet such a soul! He was 22 years old. Everywhere I see yet the influence of this great act. A great name, a great deed, a great work are inheritances of nations of immense value. Dine at Hughes. The two Gevers call, sorry I have so little time. Gevers van Endegeest introduces me to Librarian and Archivarian Tells me that Catholicism greatly increases, they buy much land and eliminate protestants; so protestant mechanics do no longer succeed in Catholic parts of Holland. One half of the present Netherlands Catholic, not the best educated, because from former exclusion but that is daily vanishing. In going from Rotterdam to Hague saw the first travelling mechanic; today the first smokefilled room at the club where Gevers introduces me. I had not [thought] it would be so utterly repulsive to me. By chance in strolling about through a street of houses of bad fame. For the first time again that brutal exhibition of breasts at the window and tapping and calling to come in. Oh, Germany thou doest not announce thyself pleasantly, especially when I consider Keibel's letter I received in London, which was like being suddenly reminded of old nauseous medicine. —Spot where the De Wits were torn to pieces, and de Wits' prison. John de Wit's house.

22 June. I resolve not to stay until steamboat of 30th from Amsterdam. It drives me too much; having no news. Though I must give up Leyden, etc. but not <u>Haarlemer Meer</u>. Great work. Yesterday I sent the flower which Anne Ward so sweetly asked from my place of wound. Write also to my dear Matilda with flowers. Today I write to Oscar to expect me with the boat of 25th. King's pictures which most liberally can be seen every day. The first I see, a Titian *Venus*, with the man in Spanish dress looking round. Ah, spiro Italia! Spiro Italia! — The best pictures here seem to me — at least my soul fastened most on them: 1. That Titian. 2. Portrait of Penni by Raphael. 3. *Columbine* by Leonardo da Vinci, the finest Vinci I recollect if it be not the Christ with the Pharisees in Dresden. This *Columbine* has nothing of his mannerism of the female beauties. 4. Dirk de Harlem, 1470. Two very fine pictures. Relating the story of emperor Otho and his faithless wife. Better to me than any I know of those times. To me is much finer than van Eyck. 5. N. 88 Perugino. *Holy Family.* Oh <u>very</u> fine. Moreover an Andrea del Sarto *Holy Family;* a Sassaferato, a Virgin contemplating bambino; fine Portraits of Peter Pourbus; Memling, fine execution of faces; Murello *Holy Virgin* fine but the Virgin's face I think no great thing. 35 & 36 two fine Mabuses. Two large pictures by Titian, *Triumph of Religion* & *Science.* Probably to study, but for <u>us</u> not great. Titian was no composer. Venuses and portraits for him. In the room the horse, which the present King rode in battle at Waterloo. —I learn the voluntary loan of Holland which had excited my soul so much was not <u>so</u> voluntary or disinterested as I had thought. Thence to Librarian; thence in Treekschugt to Delft. Oh, how beautiful along the canal. I pay 4 styvers only. In Delft, the tomb of Willem I and the place where he was murdered 10th July 1586 (?) now a barracks. Here William I murdered by the instigation of Philip II, a monarch, there de Wit murdered by a wild democracy, yet siding with Orange. There is history for you. God bless the memory of both. Are you <u>two</u> not walking arm in arm there above. Saw those canal boats in which families live. Fine girls. Dinner at the Canal. Walk to the Hague as far as [word left blank], where jump again on board a schugt. One lovely, smooth park. Birds sing. On board I find market women, singing, rumping [*sic*], kissing men, etc, etc, Very brutal. I had just met two old women dragging, like horses, dogs, and men two separate canal boats. I wonder what Betsy would say to all this? She would look down on them as poor slaves and brutes, she being the lady. Back by 4 o'clock. Through

Jewish streets, though not obliged to live here. The common dress of servant girls here very becoming; tall, flying jacket, fine breast, and walk so stately. Bookseller (Deef); Theatre La Muette de Portici. Ballet naked enough.

23 June, Sunday. Write journal; by about 2 o'clock Mr. Gevers, brother to Dutch Chargé d'Affaires in U.S., fetches me to walk in the Park. Fine beeches and oaks. Dine at Gevers; his wife and several children. Glass screen with ivy growing from boxes at the bottom; beautiful. Children from Java there. In Giver's carriage to Schevelingen [Scheveningen?] village on the sea coast. Fine peasant women. Gold ornament. Tea-garden, rather Tea place close to the sea — odd contrast of fashion and surf, tea and sea. Hughes. Home. Mr. Gevers, talking of the shame of advertising for wet nurses if <u>unmarried</u>, directs my attention to the accompanying [article] which I cut out. [Here, Lieber attaches a Dutch newspaper clipping]. It is literally translated thus: "Gladly one would see placed as speedily as possible within or without this city, a respectable maiden (printed with caps) as wetnurse. She is 22 years old, of protestant religion, very sound and strong of constitution, and has plentiful of suck. One may have the best testimonials, etc. N.3" "Meisie" means and only means an unmarried girl. [In the margin another short Dutch newspaper advertisement is attached.]

24 June. First railway train to Leyden, where at the Station I find Professor Schlegel of Leyden, a Saxon, and Mr. Gevers van Endegeest, who has been speaker several times and is now member of Representatives and chairman of the board appointed by the King for the desechement [draining] of the Haarlemer Meer. In his carriage, through several <u>polders</u>, to a fine Dutch village, where we find a schooner (built in 1713) regular old Dutch built thing; sail through canals and wider water to a place where we could see the dyke which this board was obliged to build before the emptying of the Meer could begin. Thence in schooner to Leeghwater, the steam-engine with building, to empty the lake. Leeghwater is the name of an old engineer who 200 years ago proposed the drying of this vast lake. They properly called this engine and place after him. (Happily Leeghwater means also <u>emptying</u>.) In the vessel further on; then meet carriage and drive to Catwijk, the sluices which separate Rhine and Sea. Thence to Mr. Gevers' house, his wife. Dinner. Hurry to Leyden Station; railway to Haarlem, Amsterdam, at 10 o'clock on board the steamboat to Hamburg.

Mr. Gevers has published the following very interesting work: *Over de droogmaking van het Harleemer Meer door Jonkheer Mr. Gevers van Endegeest*, Haarlem, 1843, with maps and engravings of the machines, etc. One map which shows the gradual encroachments of the Haarlemer Meer. It was once only wide canals; many villages where now only one lake. The danger of the Haarlemer Meer was so great that the annual expense of keeping the dyke in order was 40,000 florins. For the drying 8 millions at 5% were allowed, which will all be wanted when finished and all the land gained will be sold, it will not even cover the cost but then the danger of breaking through was imminent. It is a national affair; but the two provinces of North & South Holland pay in addition 60,000 florins annually for ten years. This great work was commenced in 1839. Perhaps one year yet before pumping begins, which will last two years, with 3 engines of 400 horse power each or 6 of 200 horsepower. An entirely new machine invented, made partly here, partly in England. One piston lifts 9 balance beams. The dried area will be 18,100 <u>hectares</u>, about 21,000 acres (?) of which ⅒ or ⅟₁₂ will be lost in canals. The work of Mr. Gevers will be probably translated into French. Of the highest interest. The circuit or district of the ancient "Rhineland College" is 123,000 hectare, of which 25,000 water and 75,000 polder! The <u>Rhineland foot</u> called after this college. The Rhine sluices under this college, but the Drying Board had to widen the Rhine canal and to add 2 sluices for the water of the Haarlemer Meer to flow off. There are three sets of sluices in case of breaking through. A thin board separates this whole part of Holland from the North Sea! But it struck me, this is more thought than reality, for the board does not separate from <u>the</u> North Sea but rather from North Sea, that is part of its water. We use a name for a whole part of the Ocean, the North Sea; we see it on the map; we imagine it as one thing which, in many respects is correct, but when [we] apply it in this case it is not logical, for we only mean a very small part of the water which operates here — highly important nevertheless. — See Murray. Great almost English comfort, uncommon cleanliness, riches at Gevers — high red curtains and sofas — Hippocras [spiced wine]. <u>Krender wijne</u>. Ice <u>in</u> the wine for the first time. Parks, fine and must be very expensive since <u>land</u> is so very dear. The Board of Drying consists of 11 members besides Gevers, hydraulists, engineers, 2 Rhineland college members, citizens, etc. The late king had a counting house with 15 clerks in the palace for his commercial operations. He had capital in all important commercial enterprises; lent money to the government, etc. Pitt immediately sued an editor for having stated that Pitt had speculated in funds, although he allowed everything else to be said, and Thiers has lost immense part of popularity because people believe that he used knowledge which he had as premier for speculations in funds with his father-in-law. Say and other political economists speak of propriety or impropriety of <u>governments</u> competing with individuals, but here even individuals of government. The constitution of the Netherlands exempts King and family from personal taxes. Holland is enormously taxed, especially after the addition of the 400,000,000 florins (?) by late troubles with Belgium. —Everything in Holland relating to King seems to be bourgeois like; small palaces, etc. In literature the

Dutch in line far more to France than to Germany. Bookseller told me that he sells far more French books. All educated people know French, English; very few German.

25 June. At 3 o'clock we sail; pass by into Sea. Rain. I sleep almost the whole day.

Hamburg

26 June. At 3 afternoon arrive at Hamburg. Oscar, with white handkerchief at Neue Hafen, but we sail to Baum-haus. I in boat to Neue Hafen; thence in Droschke [horse-drawn cab] to Baum Haus. There at last my [boy] in my arms. With him to fetch the boys, viz. Hammy, Normy, Felix, Emil, Carlito from school and drive to 13 Esplanade. Carry, Herriet, Matilda. Little girls.

27 June. Revue, with the boys to see it. Uncle Jacob. In the evening Adele and Senator Haller.

28 June. Aunt Minna; Hesse found only pretty Capedeville.

29 June. Visits. Chateauneuf, who explains somewhat the rebuilding of Hamburg, which is truly grand. I must have more explanation of the whole. Talked over Rome. Many dead. Dräper (?) whom we used to know in Rome, jovial and practical, for he saved a whole fortune for some of his relations shot himself because he could not, as he thought, succeed in copying Raphael in Spain!

30 June, Sunday. With all to Niensteiden, dinner at Jacob Oppenheimer. Walk after dinner through the Danish park. Very fine. Senators Arning and Haller — sons-in-law of Jakob Opppenheimer there, Grabüge. Thorsperre at Altona and Hamburg gates. Together two marks. —What I saw and felt first on landing in Germany. [A peasant woman p— in the street.] A travelling <u>Handwerksbursche</u> [itinerant apprentice], well-dressed, begging alms at Dr. Schleil where I fetched the boys; woeful pavement; ugly types of bills on the corners. Not pleasant this, with such cold weather that I could see breath. The dresses of Vierländerinnen strikes me this time as ugly, unpleasant, barbarous, somewhat Indianlike. —Write this journal always in Carry's pretty garden-room.

1 July. With all — after having missed the railway train by 5 minutes. Went to Ham[burg], wild beasts.

14[?] July. *Reminiscences.* Enormous expropriations on account of improvements after fire. A history would be very interesting. Perhaps never so great before. — All governments, even French, but <u>never</u> English complain here occasionally of newspaper articles and demand the reprimand of censor. The French, when answered that far worse things are said in French papers against Germany. Answers that they have liberty of press, but where censorship there government becomes answerable, etc. Principle of self-election or completion not only in Senate but even partly in Bürgerrath. Not so in Lübeck. Ancient guilds were re-established after French in all exclusiveness, e.g. Waizenbäcker [wheat baker] and Grobbäcker [coarse breadbaker], not allowed to do the one or the other. So Kleinhändler [retail dealer] and Grosshändler [wholesale dealer]. —All baked things excluded from importation, but if the bread cut not, so poor people sometimes cut a piece off to bring bread from Altona. Until of late great fear to publish finances. All debates, etc. of Senate most secret. No amendments can be made. Senator Haller says we are "sehr kindlich" [very childish]. —Much Bavarian beer. Steamboats to Potsdam, Magdeburg, Britzeburg. All on the narrow English plan, not wide American. For the first time in my life I saw on the Elbe the man at the wheel <u>sit</u>, and the wheel, in consequence, inclined, to make it more comfortable. Remarkable! They still like to give people here money to go to America — c'est a dire, mauvais sujets [that is to say — bad subjects]. Mr. de Roenne President des Handelsamtes. Who will go to U.S.?

(Bergedorf near Hamburg belongs both to Hamburg and Lübeck! They hold courts together. An odd exception of the exclusiveness of sovereignty and an instance how nothing is abstract belonging to practical life.)

At Professor Wurm on the Alster. There a professor of the "Gymnasium," an institution between gymnasium and university here, from Switzerland told us of the easiest way of opening letters, because the parties practiced it in Switzerland against one another. Thin lead, on it hard wood, the seal on hard wood; one severe blow. Senator Ferdinand Haller, intelligent, jocose, etc. was first lawyer here. They have not even the decency here to ask a man whether, if elected, he would like it; yet he must give up lucrative practice and go away or give up his nexus as citizen, even if he resigns afterwards as Senator Schlüter here. Temperance societies begin here, but, as Oscar at least says, allowing brandy to working people. One day went to Bergedorf, by railway thence to Eimsbeck. One day to Donner (Conferenzrath Merchant) in Altona, to see in his garden Thorwaldsen's *Graces*, *Shepherd Boy*, bust and vase. What a pity those black veins. I confess the boy did not charm me any longer so much as formerly, though head beautiful. Schumacher, the astronomer, had got me the permission. Carry, Matilda and Augusta Ahrend with me. Dinner at Richard Parish, where Schumacher and Minister von Steine, Russian service, Altona by birth. He told us that a well known fact, acknowledged by every travelling Cossack and observing astronomer — by all, is that nothing keeps so warm as tea, which being so compendious is excellent. —Generally I find here a total ignorance of <u>organization</u> of U.S. A notice about me in *Berlin Vossische Zeitung.* In Hamburg it is prohibited to sell or use common phosphorus matches for fear of fire.

> Carry, Henriette, Matilda. = Edward, commonly
> called Cantoor. Clara. Felix. Emil = Matildita,
> Carlito, Clarita = Oscar, Hamilton, Norman.
> — Frank. Und solch Spectakel!!
> [and such a row!!]

14 July, Sunday [date repeated]. Carolina, the most furiously curious daughter of Eve, sitting and grinning at my side, stuffing me everyday overfull — all her plans gone! Rain — Hail — Thunder and Lightening. Reinbeck, Friedrichshain, Stahlwagen. Eisenbahn — Cold meat and cucumbers as large as my arm and fabricated by Dutch adherents of the Mosaic Religion.

12 July. With my Oscar at 10 o'clock from Grassbrook to Hoopte, Ham[burger] village by steam on the Elbe, passing Vierlande. At 1½ at Hoopte. In a very dirty, clumpsy omnibus, with 2 horses through Winsen — small, reading Königliche Leinen Legge [royal linen law] (where Leinwand [canvas] for the market is examined, measured and stamped) past Bardewyk [Bardowick], on paved road, but how paved! To Lüneburg, where we arrived at 5. See the distances! 2 German miles from Lüneburg to Hoopte [actually 25km]! Chanoiness Charlotte von Lasperg, whose brother married sister of Duchess of Berenburg (both Princesses of Holstein Glückstadt) not yet there. Dinner; good Brathahn [roast chicken]. Lüneburg is the oddest looking town I have ever seen. The gable houses with vaulted stories for the gable, crooked and odd as if made by children, to cover the gable thus: [here, Lieber draws a sketch of a stepped gable] Some houses had grass growing on the top of these pottery looking arches, and, of course before the windows above. We stood before our inn, the Deutsches Haus, and to the left a house built 1548, over the door. Awful pavement; inclined tower, and <u>redness</u> of town which makes the newness of colour contrast with oldness of form. (Extensive Rathskeller under old Rathhouse [city hall] and Hall where formerly judgment was held.) Walk with Oscar to Kalkberg, of geological interest. Met prisoners in chains, and by hasty counting, I found actually one guard with carbine and small sword to two prisoners! Extensive view. Monument in castle remains. Returning Chanoiness von Lasperg looking out of the window. I came only to give her account of Mrs. de Hassel in Columbia. She had received my letter only at 4 o'clock (though sent from Hamburg two days before!) and at once set out. Gebildete Frau [educated woman]. (Frau von Lasperg says she knows I shall remain in Prussia.) Oscar and I take tea with her.

13 July. She up next morning to take coffee with us at 4 o'clock. Start for Artlenburg, above Hoopte, at 5. Arrive at 7. Boat from Boitzenburg. On the right Lauenburg (Danish), left Hanover. At 10 at Hamburg; we saw the steamer for Hoopte start, in which, we afterwards found was Mama, Carry, Harry. At 2 we went all to meet them and missed them again. The day of failures! Read Dahlmann on English Revolution. How can that book make noise! It has rained everyday in Hamburg and of summer pants no one could think.

Edward	18
Clara	13
Oscar	13
Felix	10
Mathilde	9
Emil	9
Hamilton	9
Carlito	8
Clarita	7
Norman	7

[The names of the children evidently are written in their own hands]

Before Mr. Martin Haller became President of the Hamburger Handelsgericht [commerce court], nearly every article of importance such as rice, sugar, corn, etc. was not only sold by different measure but according to different <u>currency</u>. All was made uniform except sugar because the sugar-bakers opposed in mass. It is still sold in [left blank]. To this day there are in common trade some stuffs [that] are sold by <u>lange Elle</u> [long yard], and <u>kurze Elle</u> [short yard]. (English prints are sold, lange Elle. French prints short Elle. Flannels and woolen cloth all lange Elle. Silks all short Elle.) The difference is some inches. Some silks long Elle, some silks by short Elle. This sounds precisely like the beginning of the history of Pommerania which I have. There it is said that in some commercial towns a number of <u>Rechte</u> [rights], Roman, Wismar, Hamburg, German, etc. Recht for different purposes and different people.

14 July, Sunday. The whole day sunshine and gushing showers alternated; so that we could not stir. Grabüge. Theodore writes that his little Isabelita, who learned speaking in Hamburg and has retained the words of endearment in German, has lately begun to call him "Lieber Vatita" [dear little father]. She is 5 years old and has been now in Porto Rico [Puerto Rico] two years. I ought rather to have written "Fatita." What philologer would recognize that word! Geography is now taught very scientifically in German schools. The impulse given by Ritter. Altogether beginning, as it ought to be, with natural geography. Excellent maps.

This is what I have always said ought to be in so called Political economy (Political Social Economy). The case is parallel.

15 July. Rain. Clearing up; with Carol[ine], Mathilda, Oscar and Norman to Ham[burg], where little Mexican, 7 years old, who had come with Capt. Dr. Werner not at home. After dinner to Eimsbüttel, fair, Walzing in barn. There was a very suspicious booth, though open.

To Berlin

16 July. My parting this time lies so heavy upon me. (I spent in Hamburg 3 of my most happy days of my life.) At 4 I received a letter from Bunsen which had been delivered to a Mr. Bieber, our neighbor. Very friendly — see it — but I cannot go to see him in Hamburg, as he wishes — too late. Carry continued her attentive presents to the last. Green pocket book. At 6 in the evening in Magdeburg steamer to go as far as Wittenberge. Among my passengers a lion, hyena, vulture, etc. Their owner a Vienna man: "Ja, mein Herr, in Berlin und Dresden hat aber der Bürger gar keine Rechte, da hat er in Wien viel mehr." ["Yes, sir, in Berlin and Dresden the citizen has no rights; in Vienna he has a lot more"] "Der Kaiser ist halt eben niemand, rein niemand." ["The Emperor is just a nobody, just a complete nobody"] The German twaddles more; people, I mean shopkeepers, etc. can talk the silliest trifles, bring in the stalest witticisms, for hours. Far more it strikes me than English, French, or American. The Germans always speak with a cloud of: Ja nun hören sie einmal; [Yes, now do listen] "ach" [Oh] on all occasions: "ach, geben sie mir mal den Teller." [Oh, hand me the plate.] I say Germans, I ought to say perhaps Mark [Brandenburg?] Prussian people. nu [now], mann [man], Bene [instead of beine, legs], nicht [not]. A man on board of the name of Schrafford, a common farmer of Lewis County, N.Y., who went to Bamberg to receive about $40,000 property, left by a grandfather. A groschen Stolbergisches Geld. About 5 or six German miles from Hamburg begin uneven banks. Steamboats burn English coal which stands in baskets on deck. For berth paid extra pay per night. Meals as one wants them. Here as everywhere in Europe no bells from the pilot to the engineer, but cpt. on the paddle box calling to a boy, the boy to the engineer.

17 July. At 10 o'clock morning at Wittenberge, Prussia, small town. Very polite and fair custom officers. I must wait until 2 o'clock. A man who showed me to a place where I could get a bottle of beer, a mechanic, leads me into the room with these words "Bruderkin, disser Herr will ne jute Flasche Bier haben. Gieb em eine solche! Aber erscht gieb mir en Kuss Bruderkin" ["Little brother, this gentleman wants a nice bottle of beer. Give him one. But first kindly give me a kiss, little brother."] and he actually kissed the unshaven, pipe-smoking, dirty, old innkeeper. My very stomach revolted. (I wrote here to my Matilda.) So I saw an hour later two old [word crossed out] Custom officers in uniform, with large mustachioes, one snow-white, walking hand in hand in the street. The town all the flatness, jejuneness, insipidity, with low 2 story houses, want of character, which the Mark [Brandenburg] has throughout. I know no towns in the world so destitute of character as those of the Mark. This place 18 German miles from Berlin. To Perleberg, excellent and straight highroad through fearful sand, pines, this [word illegible] to Perleberg, this as Kyritz, Wusterhausen, Spandau and Berlin have all the same character of utter want of character so the rooms. Sand. Insipid furniture, etc. Except the roads I cannot see much change.

Berlin

18 July. At 6 through the Brandenburg Gate in my $3 extra post at Berlin. Hôtel de Rome, after all night through. Try to sleep, cannot. Write to the King, to Geheim Cabinettsrath Uhden. To Hitzig. See Clara! Mother of 3 children. Fearful smell of stagnant gutters. Low houses; horrid pavement; silly looking droschke men, Friedenssäule. At 4 I could get nothing in Restaurations. At length to Gustavus. Ernst.

19 July. Look for lodging. See Matilda Benicke, Keibels, dine; with Ernst & Gustav to Hofjäger. Very good music. Thiergarten improved. A very fine statue of Venus of [name left blank], in zink, painted white. If found to answer more shall be placed. —In a shop I saw porcelain buttons for all orders, and infinite variety, not only all classes of red eagle, medals, etc., but for having served 15, 20, 25 years, for having saved the life of person, for God knows what. The soldiers who were present at the revue of Kalish have actually a distinguishing mark across the Achselklappe [shoulder board]! Everything is marked as on animals as it were. Young Knoblauch tells me that lately on Neander's birthday, the students ornamented his lecture room with flowers. Touching. Students here very quiet. Doctors often receive 1 or 2 Louis d'or for giving certificate of want of health to free [them] from serving. It is said to be very common. (G. confirms this. Money has been often offered to him.)

20 July. Pay visits; deliver letters. Many call immediately again but see nobody because out. Museum. The Amazon by [name left blank] seems to me out of place because not calm enough not dignified there. In the midst of a busy place it would be more becoming. The idea certainly good; yet there are disturbing details, e.g. the pending tail of the lion. — Caesar and Napoleon, a great poem. The praying boy of bronze is beautiful — I remembered him from Potsdam. Polymnia's drapery probably the most remarkable I ever saw, perhaps, ever made. I took but a glance of the picture gallery. Wheaton tells me that Kamptz always speaks in the highest terms of me. In the evening at Geheimcabinettsrath Uhden; the King wants to see me. Tuesday at ¼ before 8 o'clock, before the Vortrag [speech]. — Von Kamptz, Major Paalzow's Frau are in Eastern Tirol. —Everything here is so very <u>mince</u>. Pot, basin, bed. My bed — and I have rooms which have been occupied by high titled people — is 2½ or 2¾ feet wide! The Hôtel de Rome, first hotel here, was dirty, things out of order, etc. Yet there were princes and princesses lodging in the house. I now live [at] 56 Mohrenstrasse, Widow Preuss. Price of droschke any distance in town I believe only 5 silbergroschen. But dinners are not <u>very</u> cheap it seems. They smoke in dining rooms in most "Restaurationen."

21 July, Sunday. Dr. Julius — who speaks in the highest terms of Matilda and tells anecdotes of King. Dine at Gustav. Keibel fetches us in his carriage; visit Charlotte Stiegliz' Grab [grave] of which this ivy; to Treptow, where it was fearfully cold. (In the evening with Felix to Professor David of Copenhagen in Hôtel de Brandenburg.)

22 July. Matilda's, dear Matilda's birthday. Museum. Saw the Raphael's — no great masterpiece of him in those locked rooms.

23 July. Early to the Schloss [castle]. In the waiting room pictures with their painters; neat boxes with pearl shells from the Isthmus of Panama; a cane chair with broken seat. (Everyone in common boots except myself.) At about 10 minutes the King came in in common undress, no star or order, (blue pants, spurs) his cap and kerchief in hand. (Everyone spoke to him with great ease and the Majestät was but sparsely <u>parsime</u> [sprinkled].) He looked at the picture acutely, praised it much and kindly; passed me with a very friendly bow to go to the shells, looked at some prints and then came to me and said: "Are you Mr. Lieber? Do come in." He opened the door, which I ought to have done but forgot and went into his cabinet, the corner room I think of the bell floor to the Long Bridge. The large table of plain oak-wood. The room was full. No luxe whatever, no grandeur, no soldiers (except quite outside on the corridor, one sentinel). He began by saying: " I am very sorry that you want to leave again. I thought you had wanted to settle among us again. It is a great pity, etc., etc." I replied: "Your Majesty, I have a wife and children, no fortune and my salary is there." King: "How many

Replica of Franz Krüger's *Friedrich Wilhelm IV in his Study* (Courtesy of SSG Potsdam–Schloss Sanssouci)

children do you have?" I: "3 boys." King: "Where are you from?" I: "From Berlin." King: "From Berlin? Indeed." I: "From this very Breite Strasse." King: "Ah, I didn't know that." —All these questions were made in the common tone of politeness and kindness, no brusquerie. He has small blue eyes and uses frequently [word crossed out] a glass to look at pictures, etc. He has a considerable beginning of a pot belly, low down, so that the waist coat — a black silk one, buttoned to the neck, makes the folds it always does with potbellied people. His sandy hair is a good deal gone. —He asked about my residence; about South Carolina.

I told him of the Proprietary Government, (Slavery, etc.), and Charles II. King: "Do say. Karl II donated knights from Nova Scotia. I have to confess to you, I do not know where that is. Where is it?" I explained. King: "Ah, so it is still called that, etc." At length, I wedged in my thanks for his pardon. First, he really did not seem to understand me, and at length said: "Oh, in that I have done nothing more than my duty. You've been done an injustice. I am only happy that I have learned about these matters properly. I could not have acted differently. One has done you a great injustice. By the way, you had a testimonial that after the Evangelio [the Gospels] is the highest for me — from the late Niebuhr. That was a noble man, etc. I remembered how lovingly he talked about you in his book." My affairs led to Jahn, whom I called "one of the most erudite persons." King: "He was a mean man. Imagine, on one of the 18ths of October he had a fire especially for the King of Saxony, etc." (I did not precisely understand it, but it was some gross vulgarity regarding the King of Saxony, who was then a prisoner. Jahn was always an eminently vulgar man.) I: "I have often been surprised at the high pension which is left him." King: "Ah, he had a considerably higher salary, and one has never transferred anything to him. He surely never intended any harm." I introduced the subject of commerce, the new treaty, and told him that I feared it would be thrown overboard, and why. King: "Ah, do you think so?" This led me to say how the Americans were the chief people worth courting in a commercial point of view; I told him how they are the most consuming people on earth, and how this increases, of emigration, etc. [and] gave him data on Congress. He was astonished and listened attentively. At length came Penitentiary [reform]. He declared himself for [the] Pennsylvania [system]. "but," said he, "the people here are against it. You would not believe the difficulties they make for me, and all that sometimes from people who do not want it because of philanthropy. It is strange. They do not wish to put the people in solitary confinement, for humanitarian reasons, but they want to whip them like dogs. The system probably requires modifications for the German, who, as one says, is more easily affected in his feelings, etc." I: "I don't much believe that the German is of a heavier, despairing nature. He is easily saddened but I have never noticed that he is more easily affected in a bad way by the Pennsylvania System. The German is a finder of difficulties." King: "Yes, and we in the North are worse than those in the South. And it is only getting worse." I: "Why is that?" King: "I don't know." (But I did know it, I believe perfectly well. It is the natural consequence of the two causes, German character and the absence of all public, oral life and liberty of practical discussion.) We continued. I said: "One says that so mechanical a means as 4 walls will not achieve such a spiritual result as the improvement of a human being, whereas a piece of bread is also mechanical but it has the spiritual effect of furthering my thinking, or if I do not have it, it might produce the thought of stealing. Everything is determined by mechanisms, for as long as we live. The first big question in this instance is: Does the State, in whatever situation it is, have the right to make a human being worse than he already is? Surely not." King: "No, truly not. That is very clearly presented." I: "But now the State makes itself directly guilty of this offense when it puts human beings into a situation in which they have to turn worse according to the eternal laws of ethics. Because it is a steadfast law that people driven by the same thought, impulse, or passion, or endeavor will strengthen each other and advance when they are brought into contact. The pious will be more pious, the daring more daring, the evil more evil and if you bring together criminals who are bad to 6 degrees, they will leave prison 12 degrees worse, etc., etc." King: "That is very good, very honest, very true." I told him yet much of instances especially of the German I lately saw, etc. He then said: "Do you know Humboldt? Do go and see him. He will be happy to make your acquaintance. Talk to him about this. And go see General Thile. An extremely solid, pure human being, but he is against it. You have to convert him. There was a Mr. Tellkampf here, now also an American. He appeared to me to be in favor of the Pennsylvania System, but the gentlemen said, he was not particularly in favor. So you see, they are themselves against it. They may be wrong. Do you know Dr. Julius? What do you think about him?" I gave him my sincere opinion. —We talked of German books, and I said, "The greatest misfortune in Germany seems to me to be that the learned aristocracy think science is degraded when one attaches a purpose to it, etc." King: "That is completely true; that is the way it is. It has never appeared so clear to me but I have always felt that it was so. The English thicken everything too much but here one writes as if it [science] concerns ephemeral beings, etc." —Toward the end, he said: "I am very sorry that I have to leave you. The ministers are waiting for me. I wish I could see you again, but it is entirely impossible. I have promised the Emperor of Austria that I will come to Vienna when I take the Queen to Tichel and then I have to go to Prussia, etc. Should our paths cross somewhere, make sure to have your presence be announced to me. I sincerely thank you for the very, very dear moments you have given me." Before he said: "I have to see whether you could not be employed in the penal system. I really will have to think about that, etc." I also said: "Your Majesty, let me touch upon a point that is very important and one of which I have studied a lot. Now that you are reforming the law, you should do away with the scandalous public executions." King: "Think about this. At the last execution there were 40,000 people, boisterous, etc. A fellow erected bleachers. One forbade him to do so and the 'infamous rascal' still goes there at 4 in the morning with a cart and some boards and erects some bleachers. I have now, at least, given the order to move them to Spandau. A while ago someone said an execution would take place in Spandau, which was not true, but an enormous crowd of people were there."

31 July, Tuesday. Hitzig, Julius. Dinner at Geheimrath [privy councillor] Heydemann, Professor Juris and right hand of Savigny in the Law reform. From 3 to 9 o'clock. I felt sure and instructive. Heydemann tells me what Excellency de Savigny told me the day before that my ideas as to extramural executions have been adopted and will be proposed in the Staatsrath [state council]. Here I have had real, positive influence. In the evening to Knoblauch, who has arrived, but I did not find him. —The day before I dined at Gustavus'; went to Matilda Benicke, to Savigny — ¾ of an hour with him, very polite and kind, to Marcus Niebuhr, to Jay where I found 7 or 8 Americans, studying here. Savigny spoke peculiarly well of the Americans who have studied here. The most remarkable thing here appears to me the working of ministers and cabinet with the King. It is thus: Each ministerium has a minister. These ministers do not habitually work with the King but their reports, etc. go to him. Upon these, one of the two <u>cabinet</u> ministers (Thile & Bodelschwingh) or some Geheime Cabinetsrath [privy councillor] (as Uhden, etc.) makes reports and the King decides. There is indeed such a thing as a conseil des ministres called Staatsministerium, presided over by the Prince of Prussia (so that even here the King is only occasionally) but this acts only on certain subjects, i.e., those which interest two ministers. Frequently it has happened that the King has acted without any ministers knowing it. Friedrich II corresponded even with his foreign ministers without the minister of foreign affairs knowing it.

1 August. To Knoblauch, who follows me and on the steps of Gustavus' house we meet at last. With him to Ratzinsky's but no time to look at pictures; with Theodore Fay to Bülow, leaving cards; to Massmann, where Vetters and Wackernagel. Hafergruzsuppe [oat gruel soup] and Mrs. Massmann waits upon us, which made me feel horrid. Massmann & Wackernagel maintain against me that the German language is at least as melodious as Italian and Spanish. All four in rain to the new Turnplatz [exercise field] ; went over the old one, now a shooting place for Neufchatel-Schuetzen [a marksmen's club]. With Knoblauch to the Theatre. Zampier. Tiresome. I knew Crelinger's quondam Mad. Stich's voice — the best sounding German I have ever heard.

1 August [date repeated]. Professor Heydemann fetches me at ¾ seven for his lecture on Naturrecht [natural law]. What superficial stuff; what phrases without substance. A parcel of letters from Matilda. To Gustavus, not at home; to Knoblauch, not at home; to Count Ratzinsky's Collection [on] Unter den Linden.

Kaulbach's *Hunnenschlacht* [*Battle of the Huns*]. Truly great, except two reminiscences of Michel Angelo's *Last Judgement* — the group to the right (in M. Angelo's to the left) and the two grappling men (in M. Angelo the devil who pulls by testicles). They might have been avoided. Cornelius' *Christ Visiting Hell* is a failure it seems, but how did he come to commit it? At Matilda Benicke's; dine at Keibel with the Knoblauchs and Ernst, etc. Jay fetches me at ½ past 5 to go to Bülow's, son-in-law of Humboldt's at Tegel. (Bülow is minister of foreign affairs.) Fine casts, of antiques, of villa Luisine[?], which I did not know, of Thorwaldsen's *Spes*, of Rauch's child of Humboldt — Rauch himself there; Alexander Humboldt (of course very polite because King had been so), many ladies, countess Haak, dame d'honneur of Princess Karl, lively, etc. Servants with Axelbänder [shoulder boards], Tomb of the Humboldts', etc.

2 August. Write to my Matilda. Massmann brings me galvanoplastic reliefs. With Knoblauch to Institute for Deaf and Dumb. They teach speaking. See books. Dine at Mr. Ward, an Englishman lawyer (on account of Pondichery claims ? here) where Ehrenberg, Wheaton, Marcus Niebuhr and his wife and Julius. Ward shows me my name in the lately published letters of Dr. Arnold (the historian of Bussby). I was much pleased because I honour him much. Went in rain to Marcus Niebuhr. I like his wife, a von Wollzogen, much. And I see that they like me — Sent letter to my sweet Matilda.

3 August, Saturday. Letters to Bunsen, through Ministerium of foreign affairs; to Geheim Cabinetsrath Uhden through his wife. Celebration of late King's birthday (as founder) of the University. I found Jay and Ward there. Imposing "Nun danket alle Gott" ["All praise to God"] which Jay felt deeply. Pay visits to Bülow & Humboldt. Dinner at Knoblauch, where Jonas, August, etc. (Jonas of Jewish parents, a pastor here, married to daughter of Count Schwerin and much beloved by the father-in-law.) Neander, who says I must come here to the University. Go back to Knoblauch who presents me with Cornelius' engraving of *Niebelungen;* books on instruction of Deaf and Dumb. Keibel gave me at dinner a letter from Matilda in which the following from Julia Ward, the first I ever received, nor had I written to her. v.z. I had sent a flower of my Namur spot to Annie at her request.

Julia's Letter, Züllichau. August. 1844.

"Flowers you send to Annie, dear Lieber, and to me you wanted to send thorns — quite correctly for am I not a little wasp and have // I continue copying in Karnow's garden, Saturday 10th August // continued to plague you on and on but I still love you with all my heart and nobody shall say anything false about you in my presence because your picture is, I don't know how, connected to the remembrance of my old days. Back then, when I first knew you, I lived in Heaven and with the dear beautiful angel who has now flown back to his own paradise. Oh God, how close it brings me to you that you loved Heinrich, that you cried over his death. Heinrich, was he not an angelic soul of a beautiful nature, what strength of intellect, what tenderness of feeling. And all that had to die — what now? I still don't understand it. God has given me much but this he took away and never gave it back and could not replace it. I assure you, my dear, I have changed from my heart— whatever I may seem to be, I am not the old Julia anymore and will never be again. At one time I was proud in my happiness; I did not walk on the earth. I had wings and floated into the golden light of morning and was carried to the highest heaven and I wanted to hang my head and hide my tears. Back then I said to everyone, 'Do not get close to me. I don't need you. I live alone with my woeful thoughts, even the ghosts of the invisible world bring to my soul godly sustenance.' And now my heart says, 'Do not go too far from me. Don't leave me. Do not mock me — give me a tear, an understanding word, compassion, and sympathy because I have lived and suffered.' — But why all this? I really don't know. Does this happen to everyone. I almost think so, because what am I missing? Do I not have everything? My husband sleeps, my good Howe, because there is no one better than he. My child also sleeps and how beautiful the small hands are [word illegible] held out, the roselike mouth lies partially open as if it would receive an angel's kiss — upon the beautiful forehead reigns the deepest tranquility in every small feature. I see that this is still and unspoiled, a happy creature. Thanks be to God, my child will love and be happy and enjoy everything beautiful. This thought is dear to me. But we, do we have to die? Goodbye, my dear Lieber. Could you buy for me a complete Herder and in addition engravings of Luther and Goethe? I desire also one or two children's books which I want to translate into English — but they have to be nice. But don't bother yourself with my wishes if its not convenient for you. Greet your wife from me and write to me from your heart. God be with you. Farewell. Julia Howe.

3 August, Saturday [continued]. With Theodore Fay in university celebration of late King's birthday. Lachmann spoke. Fay was deeply touched by the universal. Nun danket alle Gott [All praise to God]. Dinner at Knoblauch's where Jonas, etc. at Neander's. Back to Knoblauch, who gives me the beautiful engraving of Cornelius of *Niebelungen*.

4 August, Sunday. Ernst packs with me. My hostess asks: "Wo gehen Sie hin?" ["Where are you going"] I: "Wozu das?" ["Why do you want to know?"] Sie: "Um dem Commissarins zu sagen." [To tell the police."] I: "Sagen Sie ich geh zum Teufel." [Tell them I am going to the devil." Sie: "Gleich?" ["Right away?"] To Gustavus; walking in the street on Sunday I heard at the same time Weavers, bowling and piano and at Mrs. Keibel. Knoblauch comes late because he had been in committee. Mrs. Franz exceedingly warm. Zelle (Schwabbeljochen [jabberer]) there. At 6 o'clock with Knoblauch and Kautian to Frankfurt [an der Oder]. At 11 left Frankfurt, in Crossen about 4 where we found Hermann and Jenny.

Züllichau

5 August, Monday. Monday at ½ past 1 at Züllichau, Karsten with dangling arms met us; he knew me. Edward and [?] at the post office, they do not know me. Family dinner general.

6 August, Tuesday. To Edward. Vineyard of Mr. Kingknick, altogether. Visit neighbors.

7 August, Wednesday. Dinner at Edwards. Fürchterliches Anstossen [Furious toasting].

8 August, Thursday. Visit to parent's grave. Kerrier [words illegible] Auction of all periodicals. Wait with brothers.

9 August, Friday. Walk to Edward, who was in the snuff. Hungarian wine; wine pins, snuff dissipates gradually; tea at Julius. Garden, All dictate journal.

10 August, Saturday. Supper at Edward's. Poor Adolphus' book, in which the golden marriage of our parents described.

11 August, Sunday. At ½ past 2 o'clock with Karsten and the brothers to the post-house. With Gustavus and Louisa to Crossen. At about 10 o'clock there. We meet here again Baurath [building surveyor] Kautian and his spritely daughter. In the coupe with two school damsels to Frankfurt on the Oder, where we arrive at ½ past 5 or so. In the "Bahnenhof" [train station] Miss Kautian gives me the little eau de Cologne bottle (of porcelain in imitation of stag antlers). To [word illegible] also Bellstab und Grill. Miss Kautian bespeaks ticket of Singing academy. At 10 o'clock in Berlin. Go to Gustavus'.

Berlin

12 August, Monday. Visit with Gustavus, Boscha and Amalia Lieber. Poor, poor oppressed girls. We see our "Vaterhaus" [parental home], Breitestrasse No. 19, belonging now to Schlottmann umbrella maker. Find a letter from dear Caroline and <u>the</u> one from Geheim Rath Uhden, dated Erdmannsdorf. The King sends most friendly message, and that he wishes to retain me. Many sundry things.

13 August, Tuesday. By particular permission I see Gewerbe Ausstellung [trade show], which will be <u>very</u> fine. Except that all that relates to ships. They reminded [me] of Nürnberg Bilderbogen [illustrated broadsheets], on which all shipping is curiously odd and clumpsy. Previously I had been with Louisa in the singing academy. Excellent singing. Fine institution. (To Marcus Niebuhr. Found only his wife who is most sincerely kind to me. It did my heart so good, so truly good.)

14 August, Wednesday. In the morning I was at Matilda Benecke's, Heydemann. A ride on young Keibel's horse over Köpenicker field, where many people are digging the new canal, to Kreuzberg (I do not like the monument after all, in spite of many beauties. These Gothic <u>tops</u> as monuments will not do.) To Bahnenhof for Leipzig; Massmann, Charlottenburg, home. After dinner I hasten yet to the theatre to see <u>Summernights dream</u>. Beautifully got up, as I should never thought it possible. In the evening, Knoblauchs, Keibel, Carl Lieberin, some Liebers (Breslau), Emil, Ernst at Gustavus'.

Journey through Germany

15 August, Thursday. Fetch Ernst, to Bahnenhof. Start at ½ seven for Leipzig in the 3 class; open as far as Cöthen. 2 Thaler 15 Silbergroschen as far as Leipzig. Through and by Jüterbog, Wittenberg Anhalt, Cöthen, Halle. In America I had never felt the quick travelling as here for there I had been accustomed to it from [the] beginning; but here I had travelled on foot, by carriage, and when I flew through these places and passed the Brocken and the soil changed, and after the sand came the rollers, to break the clods, it appeared like flying indeed. At about ½ past 3 o'clock at Leipzig. Vastly increased, lively. Many additions and buildings. Leipzig's population has rapidly increased. So Dresden. <u>Peace works everywhere</u>. At seven from Leipzig (through Markranstädt). Near Lützen we pass Gustavus Adolphus Monument, over the old stone which I had seen many years ago. The idea started with the students. And now through Weissenfels, Naumburg. I recognized even in the dark night many spots of my former travels. For I went all the time outside.

16 August, Friday. Breakfast at Weimar. At Erfurth [Erfurt] we enter Turn und Taxis past Gotha dinner, Eisenach (world of damsels at the window), Vacha (Wersa), Fulda.

Frankfurt am Main

17 August, Saturday. Gelnhausen breakfast. I travel outside of by-chaise. Hanau, where the miller, so they told me, has a pension yet from the King of Bavaria because he either stowed or let loose the water to aid the Bavarian cavalry. People could not tell me which, on my flight. At 11 o'clock at Frankfurt. Lodge at the Sevau. It was heated. Shave, Bath, dinner, Varrentrapp, George Knoblauch, who is exceedingly friendly, says Frankfurt goes rapidly down. Monument of Friedrich Wilhelm II in honour of Hessians, Dannecker's *Ariadne*. It is a wondrous, enchanting work of art, very original, yet lovely, graceful, liquidly so, true flesh and voluptuous breathing. Three views attracted me most, back, along the right arm upwards, and a underview seeing between thighs. It is truly great and lovely. Has Thorwaldsen ever produced greater work? And no mean thing, the face is <u>beautiful</u> which is so often not the case in female statues of antiquity or modern times. I must see it again. It is decidedly one of the greatest, loveliest, warmest, most ravishing works of art I ever beheld. Effect of rose-colored curtain. The owner, young von Bethmann does not come here for whole years. "Schöne Aussicht" [beautiful view or belvedere]. Goethe's Statue in the Library. Saalhof Goethe's "Vaterhaus," F.N.74 Hirschgraben. An old but not antique house. The old door, over it in old iron ornament J. C. G. the second I forget. Goethe is not yet popular here, because people still remember his shameful selfish egotism. Take place for Monday to Heidelberg; go to Bahnenhof to take beer, to the theatre. So far all with Knoblauch. Find the representation of Cortes tiresome, very fatigued go home, and to bed at last.

18 August, Sunday. At 10 o'clock again to Dannecker's *Ariadne*. It is a glorious work! The most remarkable view seems to me when you stand behind the hind-part of the panther a little towards the right and look upwards. The originality and boldness of the conception appears thus perhaps most. Such a motion and crossing of limbs (not quite unlike in this quality to the *Laocoön*) and yet leaving the impression of calmness and repose as all true grace and elevated beauty must. This contrast (somewhat as in Fanny Elssler's dance) still dissolving in the sweeter harmony has a powerful effect. The back view with the voluptuous flesh; the front-side view with the heaving breast; the view from the head down, with this bold yet serene head upwards — all are beautiful. Is not the right hand resting

Terracotta model of Johann Dannecker's *Ariadne on the Panther* (Courtesy of the Staatsgalerie, Stuttgart)

on the panther a little ungraceful, failing in the opposite to Canova's too taper-ing hands? Is not the ridge of the upper nose between the eyes a little too high; and the right thigh resting on the left foot a little too <u>tight</u> (straff)? In the latter I may be mistaken but it appears to me so. Further study might show me that I am mistaken. —The first effect of the pink curtain is very curious and fine; but the roseate colour changes soon into bluish, when it ought to be removed. I could sit for hours and hours dwelling on this heavenly production which unites grace, boldness, voluptuousness and purity in a most remarkable degree. Thence home where I found already Mr. George Knoblauch, who did not understand why I had insisted on seeing *Ariadne* alone. (However many visitors, men, women and girls came in.) Then to Dr. George Varrentrapp, the penologist, who lives in his mother-in-law's palace. To the Städelen Museum. The finest picture seems to me the Domenichino, *Sebastian* with the two women. The portrait of Guicciardini by [name left blank] was interesting to me, so the Giorgione, a condottiere, fine. Overbeck's *Influence of Religion on the Fine Arts*, pale and tame as I find all his things, also a reminiscence of Raphael's *School of Athens* (the boy bent down to see the mathematical figure). *Huss* by Lessing seems to me not great; Schadow's *Virgins with the Lamps and Christ* is beautiful I think in the group of the neg-lectful sleepy virgins. <u>Job</u> by Hübner attracted me most in one of the center fig-ures. To George Knoblauch dinner. To the model of air-railway and the over-head way (centrifugal power). In the Hôtel d'Hollande. Both very interesting. Passed evening with Varrentrapp, most interesting and instructive. He is a peculiarly well informed penologist and seems a man of sound judgment. He can give a mass of important and recondite information on penology.

Heidelberg

19 August, Monday. At seven o'clock to Heidelberg. It is so cold that in winter I could not dress warmer, yet I feel cold. An Englishman in the coupée who learns the whole time something by heart from a written book — no doubt German sentences for he went to Baden-Baden, and thus passes the Bergstrasse! The Bergstrasse <u>is</u> fine. God's blessing. Emigration from here to America all the time going on. I saw the women's caps I had seen so often in America. At ½ past two in Heidelberg. Heavy, cold, dark ruin. —To Mittermaier. Do not see him. His son goes with me to the castle which for a moment was beautifully illumined by setting sun. I saw it with Miss and Mrs. Mittermaier from his study, which looks right up to the castle.

20 August, Tuesday. Between 8 & 9 to Mittermaier in the university building. He is very cordial. At 11 again to him. He instructs at present the hereditary prince of Baden and his brother in Criminal Law. Mittermaier is absolute for orality and publicity and says "to jury it must come." To the Church yard where the parents and little Woodhouse lie. Professor Posselt, who insists upon my staying with him. I go to his house. To Mittermaier again in the evening. All day rainy.

21 August, Wednesday. Make visits for sisters, to Kayser, Winter, Munke's. All and everyone speaks of papa with enthusiastic affection. They call him remarkable, bedeutend [important], ausgezeichnet [excellent] and love him and the sisters. His death, they say was a real loss to Heidelberg. Dine at Mittermaier's. Excellent trout. Enquires much after Hamilton, his god-child. With Posselt and the two Hesses, [name left blank] and Caesar from Bonn to the Kaiserstuhl. Hard rain. Oh, glorious view! See my panorama. Beer (and Heidelberg beer is exquisite. 2 creuzer a glass), etc. in the Kneipe [pub] near "Schloss", fine view. Ladies there, old Winter. Adolphus Follen is here. At Posselts his father, deputy from Heidelberg to Carsten and Winter's son. Eat.

22 August, Thursday. To Weinheim, Hörner's to see Mathilda and George. No rain for the first time after many days. On the charming, comforting Bergstrasse, Neunheim to Handschuhheim and some beyond it; then off to Ladenburg (Lugdinum) thence back to Bergstrasse, Gross Sachsen to Weinheim. It is beyond description beautiful — mountains, vineyards, castles, fields, meadows, heavy large walnut trees, pelty, tri-cornered hats and stiff peasants, plenty of towns, villages, etc. with steeples, fine wine and Swiss cheese in taverns, sheep, extensive plains, — Ah, I love the Pfalz. To be professor of History here, with this modicum of civil liberty and perfect freedom of teaching and this lovely nature — Oh, yes I could stand that. Mittermaier says he wants me here. George in an excellent school of Professor [name left blank] here. Mrs. Hörner tells me without my asking that, although the children are daily, wholly bathed, their bedroom smells very strong and peculiar. The description of the scent is precisely that beetle smell of negroes. I took them with me as far as Gross-Sachsen, an hour from Weinheim. I felt a deep interest in George. He enquired much after his "guardian." Poor Matilda cried in her room because I had not inquired after her. Wine, punch and tea at home. In Heidelberg it had rained again. Smoking and tobacco culture much increased in the whole Palatinate. Foster is a fine "Überrheinish" [upper Rhineland] wine; I like it much. I wrote yesterday to Matilda. Had a letter from George Sumner, Paris.

23 August, Friday. With Professor Posselt, my host, and Ferdinand and Cesar Hesse, in carriage to Neckargemünde, where we dined; on foot to Necker-Steinach (belongs to Hesse-Cassel) coffee — on the way cretins, good many here;

in a "Nächele" [one short night] back to Neckargemünde; rain; home. Beautiful scenery.

24 August, Saturday. I visit old Schlosser; lively old man, near 69 years old (but old Paulus already 84 quite lively yet). Baierns Kirchen [Bavaria's churches?] — und Volks Zustände im 16 Jahrhundert, nach handschriftlichen und getränke Quellen [and the people's condition in the 16th century from handwritten and beverage sources] von S. Sugenheim. Geissen 1842. Twice at Mittermaiers. In the evening supper in the Museum. Professors Vangero and Zöpfe there. Truly fidel [merry].

25 August, Sunday. With Mittermaier, his wife, daughters (Frau von Kraft) two sons, Laura [name left blank], and Secretair Mutts, on foot to Schönau. It took us slow and up the mountain 3 hours. On the left bank of the Neckar to Schlierbach, across the Neckar to Ziegelhausen, up the mountain along to Neckar, and then off to Schönau; dirty little place but excellent dinner, trouts, good wine, fideles singen, Mittermaier the loudest. Walk back. It rains the whole time but the women take it well. Leave of Mittermaier very cordial. Evening at Posselt's father, where several people, and in the next room students and girls of the family, loud and happy. Frau von Kraft uses the word: "Es heimelt mich an" ["It makes me feel at home"] which is oberländisch [upper Rheinlander?]; she has it from her husband. A fine expression und "Es heimt mich an" ["It comforts me"] would also be dignified. She gave me a forget-me-not. We laughed and were happy.

26 August, Monday. I write to Caroline. (Clara Mittermaier now von Kraft said when 9 years old and she smelled roast veal one evening: "Ach Mutter ein Stück Kälberbraten diesen Abend und dann morgen früh tod im Bett sein" ["Oh mother, a piece of roast veal this evening and then dead in bed in the morning"]). I might have gone this morning at once to Mannheim, and on, but I had yet to write too much. I also wrote to Gustavus and Geschwister [siblings]. Dine as always if in family at ½ past 12 o'clock. Pastor Hörner told me that working people at Weinheim always dine at ½ past 11 on Sundays immediately after church; in the small English towns also at 1 o'clock. In the afternoon, Mrs. and Professor Posselt (Wilhelm Posselt, Professor of Medicine, Heidelberg) visit the castle and I for the first time the big tun [barrel]. The larger the barrel, I am told, the better the wine keeps. Still, it seems to me one of the extravagances of grosser minds. The wooden image of [name left blank] the jester of [name left blank] there who drank 20 (!) mass [liters] Wine a day. The Grandduke and town do much for preserving the ruins and clearing them up. (As I walked up the steep hill to the castle with Posselt, someone called behind me: "Franz Lieber." I turn around and it is Senator Büsch from Hamburg, who thus knew me even from behind and Edward not when I was standing before him. This seems easy of explanation. The stranger takes in the most marked outlines and most characteristic features only. These do not easily change, but the brother has an image of all the details as last they were.) At 8 o'clock by railway to Mannheim. All the world and not a few ladies go 3rd class cars. I pay 18 creuzer from Posselt to station; 21 creuzer from Heidelberg Station to Mannheim Station (16 English miles) and 18 creuzer from Mannheim Station to the Hôtel. Good illustration in Political Economy of cheapness produced by combination (and division) of labour. Mannheim reminds me all over of Berlin, straight streets, insipid houses, stinking gutters, in short going from Heidelberg to Mannheim is going from poetry into jejune prose indeed.

Down the Rhine

27 August, Tuesday. At 6 o'clock from Mannheim to Bonn the same boat goes to Düsseldorf the same day. I pay on board the Düsseldorf. Steam company (and the prices of all 3 companies the same — no competition) from Mannheim to Bonn, second place where all go, 9 florins 34 — about 40 Stunden [hours]. Very dear compared to America. They smoke everywhere on deck. Down the Rhine from Mannheim to Cologne about 45 or 50 Stunden in 14 hours. Here on the Rhine I read in Murray's guide, my description of the Rhine copied from the *Americana*. Odd mixture of circumstances. We Pass Worms. Niebelungen host; fight of Chriemhild and Brunhild; Luther, etc. At 11 o'clock at Mayence [Mainz]. I hasten in fiacre to Guttemberg's statue by Thorwaldsen, in bronze. It is very fine, with a Latin inscription, one saying that the money has been collected all over Europe, the other in hexameters & pentameters that the world may read now what was closed to them. Nothing great this. In the left, the statue has a bible, in the right a "form" with types; a fur cap and fur dress. I did not like the trowsers about the abdominal region and that the left foot stepped partly over the pedestal which deprives a little of repose which otherwise the whole statue as everything else of Thorwaldsen has. People ought to pay attention to pedestals. So Blücher's in Berlin too narrow, that the Berlin people say: "Er sagt, 'Komm keener mich ruffer'" ["He says, 'No one can reach me'"]. Hasten back to the boat. An elegantly dressed lady with diplomatic looking young companion comes smoking a cigar on board. She smoked after dinner again. Found out afterwards that she is born in England, educated in France — perhaps an actress. It is so cold that my hands are blue. I could not be dressed warmer than I am in winter. They burn coal <u>dust</u> here in the steamboats, and, says the engineer, the company saved last year 18,000 Prussian dollars in so doing. Pass Bieberich, summer palace of Duke of Nassau, who is so dissolute that he would openly drive to a brothel in Mayence until he married the Russian princess: He owns almost his whole country. How wrong therefore the Berliner boy's song in times of Napoleon: "Der Herr von Nassau Bieberich hat keinen Dreier <u>ieberich</u>" ["The Lord of Nassau Bieberich doesn't have three cents left to his name"]. At Bingen begins the gorge. Vineyards not fine looking on account of the many <u>walls</u> between. Castles. That of prince Friedrich of Prussia, of King, and of Professor Bethmann-Holweg (Benecke's) Rheineck I believe. At 6 o'clock at Bonn Railway, where I leave my luggage and visit Niebuhr's grave. I do not like the arrangement; it wants taste I think. Below the grave and over it against the wall above about 5 feet from the ground two angels, horizontal, looking on the grave and serving as buttresses for two gray Corinthian columns, between which one of those Christ's heads with crown of thorns which look so unpleasant. This in white marble, around it circular: "I am the life," etc. with other similar passages. Above the head is the [here Lieber draws the alpha and omega letters], (which is also over the gate of the churchyard) and under the Head is the haut-relief of a sarcophagus and on this a white marble bas relief, representing Niebuhr and his wife with hand in hand, as far as the girdle in Roman costume (as this position, etc. is found sometimes on Roman graves). Under this whole thing is written against the wall the birth year and year of death of Niebuhr, his wife and child, Francis Philip, and on both sides of those upper columns the following passages in full: on the left side: Wisdom 3:6; Proverbs 4:18; Wisdom 8:8; on the right Wisdom 8:3; Sirach 4,16:17 and "Quis desiderio sit pudor aut modus tam cari capitis. Horace." ["Why blush to let our tears unmeasured fall for one so dear."] I took flower next to it for Marcus' wife. At 8 we start on railway for Cologne. Daily about 1300 persons from Bonn to Cologne. At 9 at Cologne. Go to Hôtel de Dome. Moon shine. It is a most gigantic fabric, or at least intended to be so; but <u>we</u> must finish it, and probably shall <u>not</u>. I walk round it long time. Changing light from clouds passing the moon. At the Rhine end the idea strikes me that a circular Gothic church with high steeple, and probably better not with a high steeple, but a world of turrets shaping gracefully upwards can be imagined. Going home, 19 journeymen met me, singing extremely well.

To Brussels and Paris

28 August, Wednesday. At 6 start for Aix la chapelle. I pay for <u>person</u> to Brussels, 3rd place about 1 Thaler ½, almost the same for luggage. Extremely cold. At 11 at Aix la Chapelle. (Not far from Aix la Chapelle, a well-dressed woman of about 30 stepped out of the car and right in front of all about 15 steps from the car, <u>pissed</u>. So did Mittermaier when we walked to Schönau fall back and then came between the main party and myself who walked with his daughter and there he pissed so that I and his daughter had to pass him. When I afterwards fell far back and went into the bushes so that no one could see me do my morning business, I found when joining the party again that the whole stood waiting for me. I cannot understand the people in this. Surely I am <u>not</u> prim, but this surpasses my comprehension.) On to Verviers, where Douane [customs officers] searching of Belgium, Liege (passing my old Convent). Yesterday old castles on the rock; today the many new tunnels through the rocks. Tirlemont, Louvain, Malines, Brussels, where we arrive at 4 o'clock and a half. Others went on to Ostend, and tomorrow morning in England. Take place for Paris but car starts tomorrow at 12 only. Strolling in the evening, saw Count Arrivabene, but did not speak to him. I am staying this time at Hôtel du grand Café — very clean and good. Strange all the standard of comfort increases as you go forth from Northern Germany (of which Hamburg may make an exception).

29 August. Write, among other things one of the aphorisms on Penology, which I may send to the King of Prussia. At 12½ by railway to Quievrain, the first French place west of Mons, or between Mons and Valenciennes, passing through Jemappes. Heavens what battles here, from Waterloo, Fleury, Jemappes to Compiegne and Malplaquet. Valmy neither far, nor Nierwinden, Justemont and all that group. At Quiverain, we for Paris take the diligence. I paid for a place in the Cabriolet, which I always prefer, from Brussels to Paris Railway included 39 francs, and only 2 francs overfreight (by management, i.e., keeping carpet bag). At Quiverain custom searching, very polite. I find when I say that I <u>have</u> dutiable article, having 20 cigars, they always are peculiarly polite and hardly look at the thing. In Brussels old fashioned teasing by <u>commissionaires</u>, etc. At Cambray we join the route from Lille, Peronne, etc., etc.

Paris

30 August, Friday. By 12 in the Messagerie generale in Paris. One flat, fertile, woodless, gentleman's seatless, meadowless country from the frontier to Paris. Montmartre from afar. How it must have beckoned our soldiers! When we changed horses the last time before Paris, 2 hours from it, the first thing which greeted us was actually one of those advertisements painted on the wall: "Maladies secretes [private diseases]," etc, etc. There it was staring all the ladies in the face. I go to 16 Rue de la Paix, Hôtel de Hollande. A clock in my room of course. Paris is studded all over with clocks. Go to Bossange after most thorough laving [washing]. (Met immediately Edward Heckscher in the street). Dinner at the old place Vaudeville. The last les Marocquains. The French seize upon everything to flatter their military disposition and show handsome women's legs. Walk yet under column place Vendome. Thought again of German forbearance having left this monument of Austrian victory. Going in the afternoon through the Tuilleries garden, all was filled with groups of ladies working and their children playing; or the former, or gentlemen reading papers near the reading cabinets, or bonnes [maids] having clubbed together around one reading. I dare say some novel, and many others, dandies not omitted. It was a joyful sight, something so humane. If one sees France thus, it is impossible to imagine the brutality of the revolution.

31 August, Saturday. Search [for] Mr. King; at last find him, Rue de Grenelle, 71. No one can be presented to the royal family except on presentation days, and none until Autumn. I saw at Mr. King's a medal given by Princess Adelaide to her brother, Louis Philippe. There is a coat-of-arms in the middle of which is a ripe apple, a little open; with the device: "Ma valeur n'est pas ma couronne" ["My valor is not my crown"]. It is certain that the King has not received my book. King showed me also a medal with this device: "Presenté a Mr. Heache, etc." On the other side the portrait of King and Queen, for some books, I think, sent them. —King tells me that Gruet is appointed again consul to Antwerp. To Bossange. Thiers, he tells me, received 500,000 francs for his *History of the Consulate & Empire*. To the Louvre. If I had not returned to Paris! These miles of works of art! Ah, and that end of the grand gallery, where Raphaels & Titians and Guercinos & Guidos, and Leonardos crowd and most of them you have known long by engravings. Near Raphael's *Holy Family* (seems leaping out of the cradle) and *Sleep of Jesus* (the mother lifting the veil), I found 5 and 6 painters, male and female, crowded to copy. Did you see it Raphael! I hope you did. This is great and rejoicing and noble; a picture how great minds work. Jesus and John on *La belle Jardiniere* I do not like as I never did like them in print. They are scrofulous. —But those long saloons. I should like to know how many Frenchmen have been in Paris. Evening in the Gymnase. Je m'ennayais [I am bored].

1 September, Sunday. Café, newspapers. Wrote my penology fragments for King of Prussia. Saw Edward Heckscher. Went [by] railway to St. Germain en Laye, 5 leagues from Paris, passing Mont Calvert, where [there are] fortifications. Henry IV lived much here. Louis XIV born here 1638. Fêtes de Loges. Omnibus to Les Loges in the Park of the Château. All sorts of things and people here; a fair; bad gymnastic exercises; a fat woman to be seen. "Approachez moi, messieurs, vous me pouvez touchez par tout que vous voyez qu'el n'y a pas de deception" ["Approach me sirs and you can touch anything that you can see and that's no lie"], lifting a little her gown. But no one approached. A fellow who ate for a few sous chalk, bricks, sand and sandstone. Weights hanging by a pulley on a cord to hit something; music; shooting; and cafés in number where all sorts of people dined but no such brutality as in that shameful tent in Einsbeck near Hamburg, no dashing dress, no coquettish still less lewd look, no indecency, no public girls, no swearing, brandy or impoliteness. Remarkable. At least nothing of the sort until seven in the evening. Many well dressed paysannes. The train with which I returned had 30 wagons, each containing 40 persons inside and on them many people more. They were to go until 12 o'clock at night. I find many people pockmarked in France. —I have met people in the street who were reading. All shop girls on Sunday were reading. So many women read newspapers in the cafés. The hatmaker found my head very round and said, we work much for the English people whose heads are very oval, far more so than French or German; so it is difficult to find one for you. The Germans are broadest from ear to ear.

2 September, Monday. Louvre not open. Bossange. Hat 16 francs. Bossange says that annually 2 million francs of French books exported and 200,000 francs foreign books perhaps imported. The latter must be too low. Visits but every one in the country. Dine at our table d'hôte; sit next to hostess, who tells me she thought I was a Frenchman. These French people have with their vanity an impudence in making compliments which shows that they do not even think of a semblance of truth.

3 September, Tuesday. To Mr. King & Martin for visa of passport. Martin like thousand others at present longing for religion yet bewildered, incapable of choosing or believing. Wish to see the blind, near the city wine deposit but found that they were at present near the Invalides. Prefecture de police (where Henri IV's bust! odd). Louvre. I only walk slowly through the whole. It is a world of itself — these antiques and candelabras and precious vessels, stones and vases, Etruscan, Greek and modern, mummies, Egyptian furniture, even bread & corn, casts, drawings, crayons, pictures of Spanish, French, Italian Schools. The long room 1580 feet long and all this in munificently built rooms with tasteful corridors, etc. I walked, slowly indeed, yet always walking for more than 2 hours! Much vaster than the Vatican. I cannot help finding something black, hard, unelevated in Spanish school; except Murillo. He is <u>round</u>, and can be mellow, but no elevation. Again it struck me how the French almost always have some long stretched figures — dead ones, or flying with outstretched arms somewhere for protection in their large pictures. Why are almost all women one finds painting in the galleries ugly? Why do we like statuary the better and better the older we grow? Do we become again more heathenish, less romantic? Why are most of the persons waiting and watching in the French museums, here, in Sèvres, etc., Alsacians? (Perhaps some old Swiss Guards would be noble.) Dined in the <u>cave</u>. Opera comique. Some good singing. Fine house. First row of boxes, with a retreat in which sofa, long looking glass to the ground, globular lamp, carpet, and curtains which can be drawn.

4 September, Wednesday. I wrote this morning to my Matilda. Read in the papers that much guano is also found on African coast. An amount and chemical analysis in *Journal des Débats* of today. —There are shooting galleries in London where people practice dueling, i.e., firing at a target in form of a man. To be sure I have seen the same in America, only a common target, but the breadth of a man was chalked out and firing went by command as in a duel. I saw in *Galignani* the extraordinary grants only caused by Canadian revolution amount to more than 2 million of pounds. Louvre again. Spend the whole day there.

5 September, Thursday. Louvre. Write letters, penology. In the evening with young Leopold Bossange to La Chartreuse & Chaumiere. Cancagne, Polka. I was very much surprised indeed that the women, all seamstresses and shopgirls, and in the first works, had no coquetry whatever, no <u>show</u>, no peculiar neatness of dress, no fashion, no enticing dress. One should have supposed this in Paris and in this class. Everything very decent, but then police enough. No lower scenes, no sitting on the lap, and the men no brutal drinking. In the Chartreuse some calling and daring with the pipe. At 11 o'clock all is closed. On the pont de la Concorde, the grand sight of all the lamps along the Tuilleries and the other bridges.

6 September, Friday. Louvre. St. Denis, in a regular French one horse concern for 8 sous to St. Denis. Enormously wide road; ugly <u>white</u> Parisian dust. See St. Denis in Guide. Fine Gothic building. Painted, in the style as it was, with gilt capitals. As it is a little rude and <u>kinkerlitzig</u> [silly], but St. Denis and Church of the Temple, London, have proved to me that a very beautiful painted Gothic building might be built. Ugly idea of Francis I & Queen, Henry II & queen, and Louis XIII & Queen, <u>naked</u> on their tombs. The old queen with long flabby breasts. Chair of Dagobert which Napoleon used when [giving] first Legion of Honor. All the kings below. Very curious effect of the <u>lists</u> of the various races in one vault. To see a <u>list</u> of Kings long from top to bottom, as one otherwise sees lists of students, soldiers, deputies, etc. And then some one has long forgotten. I felt <u>very</u> tired and went to bed at 9.

7 September, Saturday. Louvre — see farther below. Write letters and other things, and pack. Dine at Mr. King's, American Minister's, Martin his secretary there and young widow Mrs. Ellis of Alabama. In King's carriage to Théâtre Francais — "Phedre," "Rachel," and Marival's "Maris et Amiants." "Phedre" was solemn. No crying of "entre-act," no letting down the curtain, no music, no change. Close attention. Many read the piece and very full. Neither the English nor Germans have anything like it. Rachel terribly plain & thin but plays grandly. The whole was very novel and great. In the other piece a very strikingly beautiful actress, who played admirably. With Martin [for] ice, cigars, talk on the boulevards about ah! bitter things.

Through France to Germany

8 September, Sunday. At 8 o'clock morning from Rue des Victoires, Messageries Royales. Adieu Paris, adieu! Je t'aime! Through Cressy. Though Sunday, people work in the field, in all places shops open, even blacksmiths work.

9 September, Monday. At Ligny, Lorraine, about 12 miles west of Nancy German house signs with the French. ¼ to one at noon at Nancy. All the lower people in the yard speak German. Very odd the change from graceful French to this broad German accent. In a large café, where two billiards and a girl, as always, behind the elevated counter, is written over one of the doors in large letters: "Pissoir." Plaque of Commissionairs, Statue of Stanislaus Lesciensky: "A Stanislas le Bienfaisant la Laurraine reconnaissante 1831. La Meuse, Meurthe, Vosges." (Luneville) At the corner placard of sentences; one who has stolen some shirts, 5 years imprisonment & pillory; another who has committed highway robbery, 10 years without pillory. National guard sentinel without uniform. Find that in Paris only obliged to wear uniform. We wait here until ½ past five.

10 September, Tuesday. In Alsacia at once long roofs, gavels, projects of houses, and this difference of North & Southern houses, Teutonic & Lateen houses. At ½ past 9 at Strassburg. Münster [cathedral] appeared not so great as formerly. Clever's statue in the market. Guttemberg by David in another. He carries a sheet of paper in his hand on which is written "Let there be light!" The bassirelievi below all indicating by <u>crowded</u> groups the propagation of light. Very different from Thorwaldsen's quiet statue at Mayence. I do not like, at the Münster, the figures on the architrave in the portal. Marchal de Saxe's tomb in Protestant Church. See printed description. Cheap and good at Hôtel de la Fleur. French ladies go to Baden-Baden, their bonne dines with them. I saw in Alsace & in Baden women plough. The same had often made me sad in Carolina when I saw negro women do it as a thing belonging to slavery and now here. The faces of some women and especially, it seemed to me, in Württemberg shocking, so worn, weatherbeaten and almost black. From Strassburg at 12 in omnibus to Kehl, Baden. Light searching, no passport question. Railway to Carlsruhe, Rastatt, Bruchsal, passing Baden-Baden.

The houses on the road of the signal men in mountaineer style with many coloured roofs. Beautiful Swabian Alps. By retour coach immediately on to Stuttgart, where we arrive at ½ past 4 o'clock.

Stuttgart

11 September, Wednesday. King of England Hôtel. Schiller's Monument by Thorwaldsen close by. Again the foot a little over the pedestal. A stile in his right, a book in his left. I think it does not sufficiently denote the poet. Dannecker's *Christ* in the church where he was baptized [and] married — long, ghastly, like a bade-gast [spa guest]. It is fearful from behind; perhaps only the face not repulsive. Heavens! It is evidently a struggle to show form entirely and hide nudity. Perhaps it becomes a little less shocking by longer look but no work of art must first repel. (Between Rastatt & Strassburg we found much hail on the ground). Fine view from Spital-Kirche [hospital church] (where Dannecker). The people get for living there 26 florins annually. Stuttgart lies in a complete funnel of vineyards, open only toward northeast where the road from Bruchsal. Universal love of the King. To the Museum of the Fine Arts. Casts of antiques & Thorwaldsen's *Christ of Thorns*. Great Erhaben [sublimity], Apostles fine. Sculpture in Christianity must probably seize upon the Erhabene in the religion. Charles Müller's *Romeo & Juliet* very fine. *Apollo among the Shepherds* by Schick. Ruyter (a modern painter) very fine house, etc. Metsy's, a *portrait of a woman*, exquisite. *Sebastian* by Guido Reni. A Del Sarto. Hamilton bear chase. Guido Reni *Christ Head!* In the evening at 8 in crammed omnibus for 2 florins, 30 creuzers to Ulm. I suffer dreadfully from heat.

12 September, Thursday. At noon at Ulm. Sophie Moldenhauer who goes alone from Büren near Paderborn to Trieste. I help her on. On in Eilwagen [express train].

Munich

13 September. Evening at 8 at Augsburg. By railway to Munich, arrive through flat land and most awfully stuffed peasant women at 9 and ½ at Munich Bayerischer Hof. Deliver letters but all the world out of town, except Förster & Professor Auerbach. Post office, fresco of horses, painted theatre, statue of Maximilian. Accustomed as one is to see but daubs painted outside of houses, one must accustom one's self first, nor do I believe shall I ever love the painting of every particle of ornament. It is not quite pleasant to see a sitting statue in an open place like Maximilian.

One expects equestrian or standing. At the end of a forum it would be different. A letter from dear Matilda. Pictures of Gluck's *Iphigenia*. Great music. That still elevates me, greatly. (Of the Arcades and royal cor-de-roy distiches. "Hatchiers" with "cannon" and spurs but they have not horses.)

14 September, Saturday. Förster, Kaulbach. *Destruction of Jerusalem.* Is not Kaulbach the greatest painter living? He like Schnorr, like Thorwaldsen protestant. Portrait of King Lewis I, many other things, portraits, caricature of Massmann. Basilica of St. Bonifacius. Fine frescos by Hess but as to church too much imitation of naive period and overloaded at the same time. Munich has become a museum of fabrics. I know we must work with what is there, nor can we go through ages of barbarity as they did before they arrived at this original architecture. There is an essential difference in architecture, language, etc. whether we live before or after age of consciousness. Besides when we take up the ancient architecture we are original as most of them individually were, for they too changed but gradually. It is the will of God that the farther mankind advances the more it shall receive all the past into its bosom. Schwanthaler's atelier. There large statues of Huss, Ziska & Ottakar for a Bohemian of the name of Veit who is building a Bohemian Walhalla at Prague. It will cost ½ million florins. About 15 or 20 statues there will be. Such a statue costs about 8000 florins when cast in bronze. Several nymphs representing rivers for private persons; models of Jean Paul at Bayreuth; of the Bavarian Jurist, etc. Friezes for the building opposite to Glyptothek. At 3 o'clock to the Residence. See the Guide. Portrait rooms with all sorts of beauties from princess to citizen girl, dancer and countess. Schnorr's *Charlemagne* pictures very fine, in fresco. Throne room. Gilt statues of ancestors of King down to Charles XII of Sweden. Dined with about 30 English and none other. Theatre in the Au-[Weide] Rosa. When in bed, Assessor Lenhard came in.

15 September, Sunday. To Förster. All the lithographers away. Pinakothek. I hasten through merely to gain a view of locality & extent but am irresistibly arrested by that most beautiful of all Francia's *Mary adoring Bambino*. Such holiness; she is in the act of sinking on her knees. It is a heavenly picture. Schnorr not at home. To Ott'winehouse where I give letter of Massmann to Professor Auerbach, very much like old Schweigger. Funeral of a general, who had been minister of war, Härtlein? Good looking soldiers, clean limbs. Nearly all soldiers brown or black eyes but officers blue, yet no different class. Perhaps the officers come more from Franconia. Altogether most brown eyes here it seems. Spent the evening with Schnorr. Handsome wife, Vienna woman, fine children. Mittermaier's Italy. Schnorr has never been in Paris, not seen the Rhine, nor Tyrol, nor Switzerland. Write to Matilda, Mittermaier.

16 September, Monday. Terrible rain. Förster. We hasten through Glyptothek to have a view of locality. But many things strike me forcibly already. With Bessel, President of Landgericht [regional court], Cleve, whose acquaintance I make at dinner, to Kaulbach again. I find more and more to admire in his *Destruction of Jerusalem.* Kaulbach may be the first living painter. He, Schnorr, Thorwaldsen — all Protestants, and decided. Before Kaulbach to "Residenz," different part from the other day, namely King's and Queen's private apartments. See description. I find that <u>arabesque</u> prevails too much. Odd for us to see a king with furniture white painted & gold, for which the King has altogether a preference. *Niebelungen* by Schnorr. The girdle scene pleased me most; but generally I thought him deficient as colorist. Many of his men look painted as on the stage. Long conversation with President Bessel on jury and public trials.

17 September, Tuesday. Förster. Allerheiligen Kirche [All Saints Church] Description. Pictures by Hess. Now, this is too much. There is not a nook or corner where a picture, large or small, could be placed where there is none, so that it takes away all repose, all quiet enjoyment, all simple comprehensive view and, at length, makes the impression of a <u>Bilderbogen</u>, in spite of all the grand beauty. Three or four of the best of these pictures and none other would make a far greater impression. It seems to me like the composition of an essay of a youth; he will say all and everything; like some German books, into which more and more is packed. To the great Foundry. There I find Grandduke of Baden, Wrede, Tilsch, Bolivar, Goethe, King of Naples, and the model of Colossal Bavaria. Enormous. I mean the statue for the attraction, Bavaria, is very thin. Goethe in coat but without cravat, which gives the negligé look. But what can be done? I don't know. Goethe, I think, might have been represented antique with marble, e.g., as one of his own characters, or something of the sort. To the <u>Au</u>[-Weide] Mariahilf. Steeple as I dislike so much. Roof painted tiles, like velvet. I am not sure that it *is* the best. On Cologne dome it would be abominable. But inside! Oh! Fine architecture; beauteous glass painting. Exquisite. Silly pulpit. Those pictures in the windows, gray in gray peculiarly fine and then the window over door opposite to altar, like so many jewels. Oh, it is truly solemn & brilliant at once. Into the theatre at ½ past 4 in afternoon and find it again crammed full, but especially women. Coffee in Hofgarten. Read once more <u>die holprigen Plattituden des Königs</u> [the rough platitudes of the king]. At Ott's Weinhouse Förster, Neumann the Chinese, etc., etc.

17[18] September, Wednesday. Glyptothek. Alone, quiet, and peculiarly fit this morning for observation and reception of the beautiful. See the Catalogue, but quite in general I mention here. The whole roomy, temple like. No. 42 a cow, a real one like Napoleon's old lanzars. I like the equinetic [*sic*] statues. I don't know they please like children; active; *Apollon*, or *Muse* (82), Pallas (84). Entering the Bacchus-room, the sun breaking through just on head and breast of sleeping faun. Unspeakably beautiful. It was overwhelming; the breast hove; *Ceres* (114), resting *Niobide* (125) wonderful, and dying *Niobide* (124), *Medusa* (132), *Venus of Cnidos* (135); fine Arabesques by Cornelius and many things in large pictures; *Demosthenes* (148) again not wide across temple; *Alexander* (152); Hannibal (153), *Pericles* (156), *Socrates* (165), *Cicero* (224) much like Webster over the eyes but Webster has higher forehead; Augustus the Napoleon character. I speak of things which were not imitated by Napoleon's adorers. Thence to Pinacothek (Ah, Sie meinen halt die Gemäldegallerie eigentlich [Ah, you actually mean the painting gallery]); again lost in my Francia; liked Raphael's *Holy Family*, n. 538 much more, and again the flesh of the breast of Bacchante in Titian's 528 and <u>sweet</u> Raphael 603. See description. Then into the Loggie, one of far the completest, most perfect things in Munich. An epos! An old gouty, stiff-necked Englishman looked bewildered about and at length exclaimed: "Good God, did you ever see the like." When I was alone I looked about and thinking of Matilda[?] and our situation and G_____ of all all I was obliged to wipe away. These loggie are all they must be, tasteful, delicate, full of sense, poetry & nobleness. Cornelius, this and Nibel[ungen] your masterpiece. To Ott, dinner. Cornelius *Last Judgement* in Ludwigkirche. Great, but too red and full for me; the angel below Christ is an unpleasant repetition, but fine are the scene below where angel protects a soul, the whole left side, souls drawing upwards. I <u>do not</u> like the painted clouds. Michelangelo's is clearer, grander, higher, calmer. I do <u>not</u> like God the Father (almost a good Jove) over birth of Christ looking out of cloud like a window, nor the creation, Sun and moon look like electron magnetic effluxions. But the single figures in side-halls very fine. St. Lewis in side wing is high shouldered and lame; how could Cornelius draw such a thing. —See at the window of glass shop a most tasteful glass, ruby colored with silver vine leaves. Very tasty. Arcades again, and all the Greek battles — alas, too soon maybe. Beer at the Franziskaner, where all the time at least 8–12 girls at the beer window to fetch beer. Schnorr, long conversation on subjects of art. Three very handsome women there; among others Mrs. [name left blank], daughter of Mrs. Blochmann, Schnorr's sister. This Mrs. [name left blank], I had on my lap at Dresden some 20 years ago, at dinner (Follen dined also there) where she bep_____[bepissed] me in a manner that I did not know how to rise. I had white pantaloons on. Suppose I had told her so. I remember I was very disconcerted, I mean at Dresden.

18[19] September, Thursday. Passport. Post Office. Gallery of Duke of Leuchtenberg. See Catalogue. The picture which seized me most was a Sassoferrato (89 in 2nd room). It is exquisite. So unconsciously graceful, holy & maternal. How different from the famous Murillo (99) close by. The most elevated Morillo I have seen N. 96. Canova's *Graces* modern, very modern. Arms like snakes entwined. (Much more so than Thorwaldsen's at Donner's Altona.) Posterior of the one most to the right standing before, I do not understand — Titians, Raphaels, etc. Again Cornelius' large picture, *Judgement.* My opinion of yesterday confirmed. —The King Lewis seems to have high aesthetic perceptibility or irritability but not much taste, or especially not chaste taste. And vain. The L everywhere. Glyptotheck. Packing; take my luggage to the post and go to the theatre, *Vesta* by Spontini. Thence to the Franciscan, opposite to the post. Fiddling music; beer; smoke. At 10 start in Eilwagen for Salzburg.

[Here a newspaper clipping is attached which briefly reports that, on 14 September 1844, the Royal District Court of Dachau reported donations to the churches of Pellheim and Eisenhofen by Leonard Riedermaier of Pellheim and Johann Berchthold.]

Through Austria

19[20] September, Friday. At 2 o'clock or so at Salzburg. Beautiful mountains before arriving there. Kapuziner-Bühl. A great, beautiful view from 3 distinct spots — but I can no longer enjoy alone. Had I Matilda beside me and something distinct before me! Hectic, poor, modest student from Gallicia, who with maiden-like voice and look says: "Man muss hoffen dass eine Zeit kommen wird wenn es nicht mehr ungesetzlich sein wird die Vereinigung Polens zu wünschen" ["One must hope that a time will come when it will no longer be against the law to wish for the unification of Poland"]. The hectic flush, the tremulous voice, the resignation and desire to think nothing wrong, the mildness of the victim were heartrending. —Excellent trout here. Birthplace of Diezel. At Salzburg, trunks searched. Austrian soldiers have yet the distinct look, expression and character of seven years war; you see the barbarian in his face. This is very remarkable. At the same time ill clad, patched pants. Everywhere triumphal arches are building for the reception of the emperor and as I soon found everywhere in the streets through which he is passing houses are white washing, even the smallest. Cathedral, in the tasteless taste of last century, overloaded with clouds, angels, broken frontispieces, etc. The house where Mozart was born opposite to university church. Amphitheatre used as riding school now. Cells in the rocks where St. Maximus has lived, etc. There was a time when it was cheap indeed to become a saint, to be killed for one's faith or to have lived in solitude; but to live for one's faith is far more difficult. I feel so sultry. At 10 o'clock in Eilwagen to Linz. We ought to have started at 7 o'clock but Rhine too high. The <u>Schein</u> & <u>Münze</u> plagues one and gives opportunity to cheating. One must have a police permit to be able to take a seat in the Eilwagen.

20[21] September, Saturday. At ½ past 2 at Linz. Grossherzog [Archduke] von Baden. Danube. Fine situation and houses without roofs which I like. I feel so sultry. Again passport & permit to go on. I eat <u>snails</u>. Very good, green fat (which appears also in turtle & lobster). Coffee in glasses and brass under cups. Asiatic has travelled along like Tringha[?] in the valley of the Mississippi. Theatre. The silliest representation of Englishmen and attacks on liberty of dress. Many soldiers. Old looking cannoneers. On the heights "Wallfahrtskirchen" [pilgrimage churches]. The man who carried my luggage from the post to the inn said twice: "Ich küss die Hand" ["I kiss your hand"]. I telling him that the waiter would pay him I not having any change. Curious high golden caps keeping a middle between a helmet and funnel and tunnel.

21[22] September, Sunday. A policeman at the entry of steamboat to whom permit must be given. Down the Danube. Some parts very beautiful and quite equal to Rhine. Rhine or Danube, again Meuse, Neckar. Palaces — splendid palaces of Benedictines, e.g., at Mecker. Agrippine de Pisaren with daughter, coach with <u>jardin ambulant</u> [traveling garden]. We get so talkative that people thought they were <u>my</u> party, whom I had met again. She is the wife of Lt. general, governor of Warsaw. The same complaints of serfs as we of negroes. She tells me that she finds herself better served in Germany by servant girls in hotels than at home by her own serfs. The same evil of too many house or personal serfs, who are never sent into the field, as with us. No serf to work longer than 60 years old. Late law that no family must be separated. Young men or women having already their own family of course no longer considered members. The serfs are more boors who cultivate for themselves and pay so much — I believe 20 rubles a year per head. I am very anxious to know those laws thoroughly. By 3 o'clock at Nussdorf near Vienna (Battle of Nussdorf). Thence to the "Line" and here <u>all</u> the visitation of trunk, etc. again and far worse than at frontier. I had much difficulty with my letters of introduction. In Leopoldstadt, Golden Lamb. Make quarter for Pisaren, who to avoid again being searched, had sent their coach with the garden volant [portable] round the town. "Mais dites mois donc comment se tient ça (les États Unis) s'il n'y a pas une tête couronné; je ne conçois pas ça; je voudrais bien savoir comment; se la se fait, etc" ["But now tell me how they stay together there (the United States) if they do not have a crowned head; I cannot conceive that; I would like to know how that is done"]. To the an der Wien theatre, Figuration translated from the French, again the English character in the most grotesque manner as in Linz.

22[23] September, Monday. To bookseller Becker, who is very polite. Deliver letters to Dr. von Würth, who has just published a work for discipline for solitary confinement. American Consul Schwarz, who shows me the first German publication of the discovery of America and a number of the rarest American coins, e.g., dollar with Washington's head and "Washington, President I," a cent with only 13 lines across the whole coin, a cent coined by private persons, before settled that coining belongs to Congress — though even now there could be no difficulty. I'll go there again. Send my letters to Jennifer, who is not here now, to Secretary of Legation Clay, who calls the same day. To Archduke Charles' collection of engravings and handzeichnungen [drawings]. They are of the very highest interest, to me those of Raphael especially. You see e.g., how an idea struck him, perhaps the first impulse from accident in real life; he seizes it but tries twenty times, with the slightest variation, e.g., of the head of the infant Jesus. He tries arms, legs, heads ever so often. The *Transfiguration* appears first as arrangement not as transfiguration but one recognizes the ultimate picture at once. Some very finished, some merely sketched in an instant. So it is with actions, books, great idea. Their first starting point often from without. It would be fine indeed to trace some of Napoleon's or Columbus's great thoughts as here some pictures of the great Raphael. The whole *Transfiguration* naked. Indeed he seems to have drawn all his figures first naked. Raphael shows, according to these hand-drawings, more accurate and detailed study than others, but also more genius, and more variety of one subject. Also drawings of Pinturicchio, Ghirlandajo, Perugino. Some of these very Raphaelic. His *Sponsalizio* has the figure of Raphael's breaking the staff, only on the left side, but precisely the same (or is Raphael's figure also to the left but not in print? I forget). Leonardo da Vinci many studies of the extravagant, caricature. Portrait of Savonarola; it is perfect. Wide space from the ear to the eye ridge but not high head. He looks good but not capacious. The whole of highest interest. One ought to study here once a week for years. Dine at the Kugel "im Hof." The most curious names of dishes. See Speisezettel [menu]. Altogether the Austrians seem to be unsettled in their German by the many surrounding and intermingling nations, nor has a well-rooted literature settled the meaning of many words as in other parts of Germany. Das Eck, das Aussicht, die Maass. A house sign: "Stärke und Kraftmehl Erzeuger" [starch and wholeflour producer], another: "Mehl von eignem Erzeuger" [flour from own production]. Evening theatre, I think Josephvorstadt. Fairies came from the clouds sitting on boards, legs hanging down and one stark naked except tricot because by her posture all the dresses had been pulled up. It looked most ludicrously indecent to see this naked girl slowly descend from the upper part. To Professor Endlicher, in Botanic Garden. I was also in the imperial arsenal. Skillful arrangement. One

English Flag. I asked how? A French grenadier had it in knapsack when made prisoner and now here displayed! Good remarks of some English women & girls who were here laughing and yet irritated. Joseph von Würth introduces me into "Juristischen und Politischen Lese Verein" [Juristical and Political Reading Society] where all journals are kept.

23[24] September, Tuesday. Polytechnic school, Philosophical Cabinet (largest electrical machine), collection of models, and collection of tools of all trades and manufactures. No collection of raw and polished wood. Excellent. St. Stephan steeple: 410 feet high. Wagram, Asperne, Lobau, Esslingingen, Kahlenberg, Leopoldsburg, road to Wiener Neustadt, Hungarian Carpathian Mountains, Styrian Mountains, Road to Baden. Visit Mr. Clay. Würth gives me his book on imprisonment. Evening theatre.

24[25] September, Wednesday. To the prison of Lower Austria with von Würth. 520 prisoners and 75 officers of whom 60 armed prison soldiers! Wretched, some rooms stinky. Sleep close together. But all acknowledge it. Yesterday, I was with Würth at Count Stark von Harkenberg, who is the government officer over the prisons. Collection of Esterhazy. Some fine, and interesting pictures. The finest head of Napoleon by Canova. See the Catalogue. Dine with Würth at Hitzing close to Schönbrunn. Here Napoleon. Here Congress [of Vienna]. All the world, wagons, etc. pass through palace. This patriarchalic way since Theresa. Very different from London, nor should I like it. (Gloriette — fine view) Back to town. Theatre.

25 [26] September, Thursday. Forget what in the morning. In the afternoon to Kehlenberg & Leopoldsburg. Fine day but more instructive and vast than beautiful view. Hungary, Styria, Markfeld, Donaudurchbruch, Klosterneuburg, etc., etc. Theatre, Bellini's <u>Montechi & Capaletti</u>. His music resembles each other too much without perhaps repetition, fine, insinuating. Sit near a Berlin stubnose. How all their enthusiasm, remarks, approval and jokes are pasted one assumed arrogant, patronizing, heartless. All Germany, and Prussia not excepted dislikes Berlin and Berlinese, and complains of dearness and dirt there.

26 [27] September, Friday. Würth with Baron Sommaruga, Referent im Staatsrath [Intern at the Council of State] call on me. I see Ambraser collection. Thence dinner outside the line at Railway Station. Belvedere in the palace which Prince Eugene had himself built for Turkish ransom. Enormous collection, which would require much time. Immense mass of Palmas, Bordones, Renis, etc. A naked woman by Lampi, not bad this but he painted so many as if for sheer nakedness. Many Titians varied and naked. No. 36 *Danae goldrain* by Titian, 61 fine Titian. Room III <u>my</u> Sassoferrato of Leuchtenberg, larger not so fine. Raphael 52 (?) fine, excellent, except left corner of Mary's mouth, 53 Raphael badly retouched, so 50, 47 fine; Perugino 24, room 4 not pleasant Leonardo. No. V 18 excellent Francia. Enormous roundabout walk home. Theatre. In the morning I was also in the Antikencabinet. The glorious onyx with Augustus' Apotheosis. Quite Napoleon's head. Another large Eagle. Costly things. Many vases in Etruscan style. Bronze things, Roman & Greek helmets, found in Styria, with <u>blows</u> & <u>intr</u>. Roman like pickel-hauben [spiked helmets], Greek, with eye-cuts and stripe over the nose as on gems, etc.; rings of legionary soldiers. Perfect steel yards with double-weight. Indeed ours I believe imitation. Bronze cat-o-nine-tails with balls or a sort of medals at the ends of the chains, for slaves or soldiers, may be! Coins likewise.

27 [28] September, Saturday. With von Würth to Staatsrath, Baron von Pilgram, der das schlaffste Zeug über Gefängnisse schwatzt [who chatters the most boring stuff about prisons], and wholly consents to my views. He gave an instance of an Italian who became insane in a fortnight because alone — and alone because he tormented all others so dreadfully. When I said that this impossible, he said of course cannot be an instance; insisted upon my seeing Metternich and Colowrath. But he told me the most horrid things of Hungarian patrimonial jurisdiction and explains administration among others thus: In the prison of Marienroch committed for prisoners in 5 rooms, so crowded that half must stand, the other sleep; sent out if they pay on furlough, those who cannot pay remain and die. Processes last 8 years [or] 10 years and longer. —This is official communication! —Defensor abolished in 1803 by Baron Hahn. At present the accused is notified 3 days beforehand that he may give to protocol in his defense what he likes! Lügen and Leugnen [lies and denials] confounded and both as well as want of respect to inquiring judge punished with stripes!! —Gallery of Prince of Lichtenstein. Immense number but I had but very little time. A Correggio, *Venus with Cupid*. Guido Reni's *Venus*, beautiful but now too green. Raphael, *Madonna del poma* seems not fine to me. Caravaggio's *Lautenspielerin* [luteplayer] very fine. Again <u>my</u> Sassoferrato (Leuchtenberg): this shows how much it must have been liked; Romano's *St. John*. Sketches of Raphael's school very fine. —To Nussdorf, reception of emperor Ferdinand I from his expedition. I dine at the Rose (?) near the Danube, and church, and under our window girls of the village with parsons of the village, music, an <u>Ehrenpforte</u> [triumphal arch], shooting, etc. The emperor came in pique-gray uniform, in covered coach with empress, very heavy face; girls with bouquet approached [and] were lifted up to the window, which was half open and the empress, who was not sitting next to our side grasped across the emperor to push down the window, then he with somewhat shaking hand took the bouquet & napkin, returned the napkin & passed on. NB the Servant behind the coach gave the signal to stop as well as to go on.

—Theatre, ballet in Kärntnerthortheatre. Nakedness enough. The chief dancer repeatedly up to the girdle; indeed she put ultimately one more gauze petticoat on. Yet it is not considered strange, so I hear, if priests visit even the ballet. The young male dancer, extraordinary.

On Tuesday evening I found Agrippine de Pisaren's, nee Dourassoff, card with embossed coat-of-arms on my table and these words written: Avrait bien desire voir encore une fois l'aimible Monsieur Lieber sans ce pendant le deranger dans ces projects de plaisir [I would like to see once more the amiable Mr. Lieber without disturbing his pleasurable projects].

The queerest German, unsettled by the many intermingling neighbors, nor have many words received that distinct meaning which literature has given them in other parts of Germany and some words have obtained different meaning merely because Austria separated from other parts: Das Eck, Die Maass, das Aussicht (on a sign); Realitäten for real property. "Stärke und Kraftmehl Erzeuger," "Mehl von eigenem Erzeuger." "Im Verhinein" what with us is "im voraus." Schweinernei, Gänsernes, Eingemachtes signifies Ragout. A dish is called a Kaisergugelhupf. But see die Speisekarte. Fine bread, called Semmel. Streets just wide enough but no trottoir [sidewalk]. In ballet when I saw how a sort of language has formed itself, e.g., pointing at the digit for marrying because, there is the ring, or striking one's face for beauty, because indicating smoothness, and this with pointing at the and pressing the heart, for love, I thought 1. how Chinese this is, for to make of beauty and heart, love is both Chinese & natural; 2. how in the spoken language the same transitions as here happen. From smoothness they pass to beauty or to express beauty they get hold of what [is] easiest understood and presents itself foremost, viz. smoothness, softness; so is the word schön from scheinen, glänzen, English sheen. As we still say "eine glänzende That, ja glänzende, strahlende Schönheit" [a shining deed, yes shining, radiant beauty] or "Glanz und Herrlichkeit" [glitter and grandeur]. This is to be remembered when people wish to settle aesthetics. Where does pulcher, bellas, and other language come from. Ermose from foremost fine fashioned.

—Everywhere lottery staring in the face. Güter-lotterie [property lottery] and Staats-lotterie. The latter draws from the people 10 millions and gives in revenue 3 millions only! Besides the crime. For it leads to all possible thieving. (Naivete) In the Kugel a young man tells me the secret police necessary to learn the wishes of the people! The Vienna women handsome, luscious, but that only; many fine eyes yet no higher expression. Not coarsely sensual but neither elevated, refined. They look goodnatured, loving senses, capable of strong attachment.

28(29) September, Sunday. Sommaruga & Würth with me. I alone on railway to Mödling; by Stellwagen to Brühl, bad dinner, back to Mödling thence to Baden, thence to Grasnerhütten for 3 florins, C. M. passing Archduke Charles' palace. Back by railway to Vienna.

Somewhere a mistake as to <u>one</u> day.

1 October. Tuesday evening von Sommaruga gives me a fine supper, Würth, Professor Neumann, Dr. Bach, etc. there. ½ past one <u>home</u>, fire in the suburb. They give a most fearful description of the universal depravity in highest circles, men and women. Princesses Esterhazy, Lichtenstein, etc. at the head. The Hungarian nobility outdoing [word unclear] if possible. These ladies even promiscuous interc.[intercourse?] in the street. Yesterday I found written by authority on a board near a bridge: "Die drüber gehenden haben am drübernen Hause, auch K. K. Militär ausser Diensten, zu bezahlen" [those crossing, including off-duty imperial soldiers, have to pay at the house on the other side.] Story of Sommaruga's manuscript of a work on Criminal Statistics, written by encouragement of minister of justice, not passing censorship. The president of the council of war declared he would allow nothing to be said about the army, Consul Schwarz friendly. — <u>Vormerkung</u> [memorandum] for praenumeration used here. I make at Schwarze's a memorandum of some of his rare coins of United States.

I have made somewhere a mistake as to date

Through Bohemia to Dresden

2 October, Wednesday. Evening I start by railway from Vienna to Brünn at ½ 7 o'clock. Sommaruga accompanies me to railway. Joseph von Würth comes yet late to me. He pleases me very much. Modest, pure and loves the country. — It [luggage?] goes stow. By four or five we arrive at Brünn or Brno in Moravia. I go [to] the finely situated hotel on the hill near the station. From one window fine view and the railway. I could not help exclaiming as I saw this railroad <u>here</u>. Oh, Father speed them, speed them, for they do not know what they are doing. —At midnight we were at Lundenburg (?) and waited an hour.

3 October, Thursday. I first went to bed. Pretty Bohemian girl comes in, cannot a word German. Spielberg cannot be seen now because building. I pass an "Apotheke zum Aug' Gottes" ["God's Eye apothecary"]. A sign: "Wollenzeugung." "Der 2te Stock zu vermiethen," "Der Gefertigte zeigt an, etc." "Vornhinein" für "Im Voraus." "Haben Ihr Gnaden Wasser angeschafft" [Have your honors brought water] for "befohlen." In general, many of those compound words in German, which now mean one thing, but might as well mean something different, e.g., <u>unterstehen</u>, <u>anschaffen</u>, <u>verschreiben</u> (ordering) mean in Austrian something different but not incompatible with the word itself and that this is the case only in Austria and not all over Southern Germany shows how effectually Austria must have been shut off from Germany for centuries. Sometimes the Austrians have yet excellent German words, where the others have foreign, but suddenly again the contrary. — Fur jerkins here, as everywhere where Slavonic race; the Asiatic fur with other stuffs. The lottery stares everywhere into one's face and tickets by authority and handbills offered to 5, 10 and 20 creuzers. The lottery draws annually about 10 millions (not 20 as I wrote before, I believe) from the people. One million at the highest goes back in prizes to the people, about 3 million to government as revenue and the rest for administration, not to speak about the engendering of crime — domestic theft. For it heats imagination, etc, etc. and people steal because they will repay, etc., etc., etc. For Austria meat, candles & bread have prices fixed by government; in Vienna the pound of meat 2 creuzers higher. In Brünn, the names of streets in German and Bohemian. In the afternoon at 4 o'clock in Eilwagen to Prague. With us Comte d'Ault-Dumesnil & Marquis de Bouguilbert.

4 October, Friday. Evening at 8 or 9 at Prague. Inns full because [of] races. At last I find a place in a very low one. Bohemia seems fertile but already very cold.

5 October, Saturday. Go to the races; Archduke at the head, only princes and counts. No citizens allowed to join, or at least excluded. An enormous mass of grenadiers, every 20 paces one. The whole tame and therefore uninteresting. No animation as in England or America. Heavens what a mass of police, mounted and on foot; cavalrists, infantrists! To keep a few people in order, who yet are so tame! The members of the club smoked around the archduke when they spoke to him. With valet de place to the Burg church, crammed full without the least regard to service or people. Bridge over the Moldau; View from Ratchin (?) (Gastnahrung over tavern-doors which is Sechl. fleischhandlung.)

Dresden

6 October, Sunday. 3 hours drive to steamboat. Then on Austrian steamboat with Austrian & Bohemian coat-of-arms to Dresden on the beautiful Elbe. Frau von Erenburg, cousin to Countess Hohenstein. What conversation! Rain! At 6 in Dresden. Stadt Rom. Theatre. "Heinrich der Löwe." Poor jumbled thing with Shakespearian reminiscences.

7 October, Monday. Rain. Letter from my dear Matilda. Gallery. Wept before *Madonna de Sisto;* find my old acquaintances; but everything transposed. To Excellency von Littichau, not here. To Baroness von der Decken. Very kind; invites me to see Betzsch, who had shown them my letter on Chess player (the German von Maltiz, the French by Count Cercourt, the English by Tichnor). Table d'Hôte. Theatre, <u>Lustspiel</u> [comedy], well played.

8 October, Tuesday. From 9 to 1 in Gallery. I revel. Dine at 3; <u>Coffee</u> at von der Decken. There Librarian Falkenberg, to whom Tichnor had given me a letter, and several who were invited but Betzsch not. <u>Oberon</u> which I find detestable — like a puppet theatre, and music like so much fiddling, though the orchestre fine. Yesterday, I wrote to Matilda and to Ernst.

Raphael

I saw it again, that masterpiece, *Madonna del Sisto* which, more than 20 years ago, introduced me in the temple of the arts. I wept then; I wept again. It is now more beautiful, more holy, more exalted than ever. That which I call Raphaelism, viz. elevation, <u>Weihe</u> [consecration], simplicity, beauty in its highest degree, perfect harmony of every part and a oneness and entirety, with the warmest glow <u>und Entzücken</u> [enchantment], is here in its highest perfection, so much so that this work stands far above every other work of the same master. Still higher it stands above all other pictures. Look around you. You have in the same room, the best Correggios, the noblest Dolcis, in the same gallery the finest Titians, yet this picture is wholly of its own kind. I know of no work or performance, in whatever sphere, which stands so preeminently above all the rest in the same sphere as this picture in the art of painting or the sphere of the beautiful. It is wonderful! The exquisite grace and simplicity, the slight touch of pain around the mouth of Mary, and yet the holiness and generality, I will say, of the expression, the calmness of her and repose of the whole picture, the mild colours, the airiness of her step, the breath of heavenliness of her as if she came down to appear with her message on her arm, the naiveté of the two angels; the earnestness of the pope, all, all is — one cannot say beautiful, for we have used that word and justly on other occasions; this would require a word for itself. Like everything truly great — it grows mightily upon you. Angels must have their joy of it. It touches so deeply. The eyes of the bambino, were that child's face cut out, would almost border with their intensity, on the look of madness, yet they are beautiful indeed. Only the saint looking down, will not yet please me quite. She looks a little too self-satisfied. Pope Sixtus looks very different. God bless you, Raphael. It overwhelms one and yet leaves my mind clear. I could write hours about it. It has now a glass, from Paris (cost 1000 Thaler) which interferes, but it was turned round for us. The Correggio next to it, to my mind the finest. The Dolcis in the room, *Judith,*

Dresden. Raphael

Yesterday I went to Wackella and to Sinai
Raphael

I saw it again, that masterpiece, Madonna del Sisto, which, more than 20 years ago, interested me in the temple of the arts. I wept then, I wept again. It is now more beautiful, more holy, more exalted than ever. That which I call Raphael-ism, viz, elevation, Weihe, simplicity, stately, in its highest degree, perfect harmony of every flash and a crowd and entirety, with that unsmooth glow and Eubychien, is here in its highest perfection, so much so that this work stands far above every other work of the same master. Still higher it stands below all other pictures. Look around you. You have in the same room, the best Correggios, the noblest Holbein, in the same gallery the finest Titians, yet this picture is worthy of its own kind. I know of no work or performance, in whatever sphere, which stands so pre-eminently above all the rest in the same sphere in that sphere of the beautiful art. It is wonderful! The exquisite grace and simplicity, the slight touch of pain

around the mouth of Mary, and yet the tenderness and gentleness, nay say, if the expression, the calmness of her and grace of the whole picture, the mild colours.

The divinity of her Tyfe, the breath of heavenliness of hue as if she came down to express with her message on her arm, just with her message on her arm, the naïveté of the two angels, the restful mastery of the page, all, all is one cannot say beautiful, for in vain and that work and purely by other occasions, this would require a work for itself. Like everything truly great—it grows mightily upon you. Angels must have their joy of it. It tends to display. The eyes of the bambino were that childic face cut out, would almost tender with their intensity, or the look of madness, yet they are beautiful indeed. Only the mind looking dreamy will not yet please me quite. The looks a little too self-satisfied. Pope Sixtus looks very different. God bless you, Raphael! If overwhelmed me and yet leaves my mind clear. I would write book upon it.

Christ Breaking the Bread, and *Caecilia* the finest Dolcis I know, especially the latter. It is Raphaelic. Remarkable in the room where Titian's *Venus*, <u>the Three Naked Women</u>. This, one by Palma Vecchio and one of Venetian School. Palma's fine, but like a fine naked woman, beautiful. The last, a fine sleeping woman dreaming softly but pleasantly perhaps slightly sensually. (Her abdomen I do not like) But when you come to Titian's! — this transparent yet substantial flesh, this gracefulness, and unenjoyed youth! It is a glorious picture! Few things show thus strongly the different way of <u>Auffassung</u> [conception] as nudity. Some painters, especially moderns painted naked nudity (remember the naked woman at Lichtenstein in Vienna or those of [name left blank] at the Belvedere) but Titian's, I mean this you can look at with the purest joy. (And how does Rubens conceive the naked!) I consider this Venus much finer than anything of Titian I have seen at the Louvre. His *Zinsgroschen* [*Widow's Mite*] also beautiful. See the Catalogue. It was a great joy to me that I find here that all the pictures which made a deep impression upon me when I lived here are really the best pictures by far, or seem so to me now that I have lived in Rome and seen so many galleries, so that I was not then taken by adventitious unessentials. I remembered hundreds of pictures, some of which I had forgotten, but one look brought them back although they are now placed entirely different.

9 October, Wednesday. Cabinet of Antikes. See Catalogue. No great thing but collection of China highly interesting. Mr. Klemme took me round [the] large collection of Chinese & Japanese porcelain. Library. [Saw] Hofrath Falkenstein, to whom Tichnor had given me a letter. He insists upon an autograph. I shall not be able to go tomorrow.

10 October, Thursday. Gallery at 9 o'clock. At ten Meng's cast of *Menelaus Carrying Patrocles* of Florence, exceedingly fine, with so many acquaintances of Louvre. Gallery where I run upon Miss Seidel. Find old Thiersch. Take leave of beloved gallery. With Miss Seidel to the King's saloon, frescos by Bendemann very fine, above all Lycurgus with the naked boy. I should like to enjoy once the joy which the artist must feel after such a work stands there. Dine at one o'clock. Collection of Dr. Klemme of the highest interest (author of *Kulturgeschichte*) — from the stones which nature offers ready made as instruments, to the shaped ones, then the ground ones and bored ones, shaped just like ours, then metal, then arms and tools separate, etc., etc. of ancients and moderns and all parts of the world — precisely for my essays on labour and property. Here occurs this remark in connection with my principle that God lays as instinct in us what must be the beginning of that which is absolutely necessary for civilization: viz. not only furnishes the rolling sea or splitting stones (flint and obsidian in Mexico) but the

The Sistine Madonna of Raphael, 1513–14 (Courtesy of the Gemäldegalerie, Dresden)

savage has the same instinct to <u>collect</u>, <u>gather</u> which we find still in children, who cannot pass pebbles, shells, etc. without cramming their pockets. So the Batucudoes Indians in Brazil, always return home laden with all sorts of stones, etc. which they can, but often cannot, use. Remarkable how clumsy, bad everything of the negroes, whom Klemme jocularly called "das Afrikanische Vieh" [African cattle] though he has derived his notion simply from this his study. Many cases, etc. of pieces of savages. To Miss Seidel, with her to the study of Hähnel, excellent sculptor. Model of Beethoven's statue for Bonn. Fine figure of sacred music (Caecilia) for parliament. Home. Mrs. Förster, who has heard of me, sends requesting me to spend the evening there. Go to Frau von der Decken. Count Dohna there. The other evening, Dr. and Hofrath [name left blank], homeopath told me that hearing [is the] last sense which leaves dying persons and that putting out their tongue, if demanded, one of the last acts. And when we spoke of Laura Bridgman's speaking with one hand in the other, and that after all it was no more curious than our speaking with lips when asleep and not consciously willing it; he told me that he knew of a case of a dying <u>cantor</u> in Saxony who was wholly gone but during his last moments the Currende Knaben [choir boys] happened to sing in front of the house and the old Cantor died beating time with his foot against the foot board of the bed. (Baroness de Decken and Hofrath Falkenstein insist upon having autographs of me.) To Mrs. Förster where I had been 20 years ago with Follen. Three daughters, the eldest, correspondent of Anna Tichnor, translates Bryant for the press; I now believe it was the second of these who once bep[issed?] me so dreadfully when at table.

11 October, Friday. At 5 men come to take trunks. At 6 start for Leipzig. At 9 ½ at Leipzig. Fair. Tremendous rain. At Eckenstein's (?) famous cellar [for] wild boar with [word left blank] sauce and three fried tarts with Nierensteiner. Write penology.

See the letters added to this page. I have not written while in Berlin on purpose.

Letter 1. Addressed: To Madam Lieber
       In care of Mad. E. Lomnitz
       13 Esplanade
       Hamburg
   Stamped Sent: Berlin, 21 October
   Stamped Received: Hamburg, 23 October

         Knoblauch's Counting House
          October 21, 1844

I have your last line, my dear wife, which Dr. Julius brought me and a letter which I found the day before at this place, where I had hoped to find one just now —

or, rather not hoped, but it would have made me happy as every letter of yours does, when it speaks of love and the kindness of your soul. But let me give you a description of my last visit to the King on Saturday, Oct. 19. Minister Uhden had brought me word from Potsdam that on Saturday the King would come by the first train, so that I ought to be at the palace at ½ past seven in the morning but that the King would go first, perhaps to the Exhibition, in which case I must excuse the waiting and return at about 11 o'clock. I went and after some waiting it was announced the King had gone at once to the two Exhibitions with the queen. I took my coffee, therefore with Ernst, and returned at the proper time. Waiting a good while I had a long conversation with the Kämmerer and was surprised to find in how narrow a space his Royal Majesty moves. There is not one of the wealthier English noblemen or Commoners who has so little room. His audience room is his "work room," dressing room and all. Close by is a half lighted little chamber in which he sleeps, has his washing stand, etc. At last he arrived and bowed again to us (generals, Räthe, counts who merely show themselves and a republican) with that smiling eye which is, so far as my knowledge goes wholly peculiar to him. A lieutenant was first admitted. He remained about two minutes, after which the Wing Adjutant came and said: "Mr. Lieber from America." I entered, when I found the King throwing himself into an armchair, quite exhausted, saying" "Excuse me but I am so tired, I can hardly stand." I am extremely happy to see you again. How are you? Are you well? You look well." I: "I am very well, your Majesty, but first off, let me convey to your Majesty my late but most heartfelt best wishes on your miraculous escape." King: "Oh, ah, I thank you heartily. Were you still here when Tschech shot at me? You were then going to Neumark, weren't you?" I: "I was still here and was a witness to that most general abhorrence, etc. I have been since I had the honor of seeing your Majesty in Paris, Munich, Vienna, and Dresden." King: "That is wonderful." I: "The conversation that your Majesty granted me has, of course, often stimulated my intellect and so initiated my 'Fragments' which I now present to you." King: "I appreciate that very much. I was going to ask you for it. I will read it attentively." I: "I also have for your Majesty a copy of my treatise against public executions." King: "So? Have you had it printed? I like that. (and now he started to read, holding the book close to his face and read on and on including the notations and continued like that for about 5 whole minutes when he started again.) "Now you insist on the expression 'Extramural?' I: "I am only concerned that these executions are not to be public because then they will say right away that we who do not want public executions favor secret ones." King: "That point is very important also because of the fact that we have here the 'infamous law' that no clergyman may accompany the offender." I: "My God, how is that possible?" King: "It is; it is printed, I can look it up for you. You know that earlier when one abducted people from all over and forced them into the harshest military service, there were so many people who were tired of living that they wished nothing more than death. On the other hand, careless clergymen depicted the consequences of repentance in such a way that the people truly thought the soul of the offender could be shot almost like a bomb into Heaven by these clergymen. So there were so many aberrants who murdered a child because they thought they sent an angel into Heaven and they themselves, so they thought, would be provided for by the clergyman. It was therefore ordered not to have a clergyman accompany the offender onto the scaffold. Due to your suggestion, both will be taken care of." I: "That is terrible." King: "Yes, but to make the infamy more infamous, the law states that the Catholics may have a clergyman but not the Protestants." I: "But what could be the reason for that now?" King: "The Catholics said that not everyone could be allowed, that your soul will be damaged eternally while the Protestants throw together state and church because that is the meaning of the territorial theory. The happy, self-satisfied state which is all and all. One says that the state which is also the church stays with the wrongdoer. Oh, it is shameful. Now, I have a lot to do today, fare-the-well, I hope that we will still be able to get you. It should not be <u>my</u> fault; I concern myself a lot with you. —Servant <u>exit</u>. Before that he had asked: "Have you seen Thile yet?" I: "I was there twice but have not seen him yet." King: "I'll tell you what! Write to Thile; I told you that he told me that he very much wishes to see you; because he really does wish to see you and ask him at what hour you can call on him." I have seen General Thile, to whom I have given a copy of those *Fragments*. He received me and dismissed me very kindly and told me that he would study my Ms. with the pencil in hand and then send for me and that I also should openly tell him what I wished.

—Yesterday, I dined at Minister de Savigny, who pressed me to see him in the evening as often as my time would allow. You may show my letter to whom you like, but do not let it go out of your hand. The conversation is literally correct but for that very reason I do not want it to leak out in a circuitous way perhaps in a paper. One cannot be too cautious with things of this sort. And what now? That I would still sink down in fervent prayer of thanks did I receive the news of a place, or the place in Cambridge. The home of my soul is I believe there if it be any where besides in your and my boys' heart. Love to all. I may leave Berlin the end of this week but you see that this depends not wholly upon myself. Kiss Carry and [illegible name]. Frank. Pray keep this letter for your Frank. I shall put it in my journal, not having an account there.

Letter 2. Addressed: To Madam F. Lieber
                        In care of Madam E. Lomnitz
                        13 Esplanade
                        Hamburg
             Stamped Sent: Berlin, 26 October
             Stamped Received: Hamburg, 28 October

I mean to write soon and therefore will put here an addition or two to my last description of my visit to the King, to make it quite complete. When he threw himself into his chair he wiped his face with a white kerchief. I say white because it was not coloured and I say it was not coloured because not dyed; otherwise it was all over "brown in brown," chiaro-scuro; repulsively saturated with the effects of a liberal snuff-taking. On his large writing table, made of simple oak, were lying two bladders with Scottish snuff. On two chairs were uniforms, with epaulets, spread out over the back. Keep this, sweet wife of mine, to be added to the last, for the description may as well be complete as not.

Friday Morning. Yesterday I had your lines written after my first from Berlin. I do not [know] whether the term "my soul" be too extravagant, as Carry calls it, of itself but I do know that the strongest term of love used by you to me is not too strong for I know your very soul clings to mine. I merely speak of the fact; whether you are right in doing so, whether you have any even merely plausible reason for doing so, is quite a different question. How easily we accustom ourselves to some things. Whenever I receive a letter from Hamburg without a line or two from your sisters, I — dislike it, at least something is missing. Do you not exclaim: "How greedy you are of love!" And what is the disagreeable disappointment you and Carry confessed to one another and which you say you would tell me but do not? —It is near one o'clock. At two I dine with my brother Julius, at Keibels, and I just returned after having made seven, aye seven, calls. You may imagine that I feel fatigued. Still I make use of this interval to write to my love because, as I mean to leave Berlin at the beginning of next week and many things may crowd upon me, I think it best to write now. Only my wife must put up with a hasty and, perhaps, erratic letter. I saw last night Minister Eichhorn, who received me cordially: "It would have been truly sad for him not to have seen me, etc." NB he had sent me an invitation before which I have never received. I spoke of my new science of penology and the necessity of a professor for it who should be inspector general of prisons at the same time. He entered <u>vividly</u> and said: "But to set such a thing in motion and to carve it out, <u>the</u> man must be on the spot. Have <u>you</u> then no desire to return to your country? Has Prussia so deeply offended you that you cannot forgive? However, I understand your wife is an American lady, etc." I explained. He said he should do everything to draw me thither. I then spoke of Julius, who is here to make his theological examination. I told him that four brothers of us had bled for the country and never yet had our family asked or received any favour of government. He should show it to Julius, etc., etc. He promised to go to the very last limit of possibility, etc. If Julius will now but act in some slight degree cleverly, I am convinced that this conversation will do him good. I shall sort the cards for him and tell him how to play out and lead. General Thile has not yet sent for me. It is not from negligence. I shall probably see him tomorrow night. Eichhorn said of himself: "I wish we could get you in our service abroad in the U.S." —You know me, and I need hardly remind you that I do not build upon these things but I do not undervalue them either. That I know if I would remain here and poke and stir, I might have something to a certainty — but I will not. I know that Dr. Julius has said to Minister Uhden that Prussia would never have another opportunity like the present one to get the right man for the highest spheres in prison matters, etc. He said yesterday to me that he thought my *Fragments* for the King exquisite, etc. I shall see yet Humboldt, Tieck. I have delivered hardly any letters here. Ernst will come and fetch me from Keibels to shop for the children. In the evening at American minister's to see Mesmerism, after that at Matilda B. to meet Eiselen. I was sad to find the other day when I supped at President Bornemann's that his son, 13 years old, had just got into upper tertia and was not high in his class. Oh, Oscar could not think of such a thing. —The young man here who thinks of going with us pleases me. Tomorrow I go to Bötch[?] to inquire about him. —It is absolutely impossible for me to say to a day when I shall press you all to my heart. NB one after the other — but if dear Carry will be reasonable there is no harm. Nothing is wanting but to place my bed in a certain place. That is wanting. —Mrs. Keibel (odd transition from bed to her!) schneidet mir gewaltige Complimente [pays me enormous compliments], and old grandmama Keibel is in love with me — or rather with you and you being absent, I get the shower bath. I want to know whether Clara has thought one solitary time of me and whether the other black and blue eyed rabble yet knows how to spell their uncle's name. I wish you had written more distinctly about Normy's eyes, for it almost seemed according to your last, that he squints with both eyes. Is it so! Gustavus thinks it has its seat in a nervous excitement of the brain. I don't. Kiss the sweet squinter, and the stubborn square-back and the lagging Oscar: Tell him that it pleased me to find his testimonial so much better. Still much remains to be done. I saw this morning Matilda Eichens, now Mrs. Smith. I suppose you do not know her. Have you not heard from the W. Carry dear you do not forget the inkstand? Why I ask? Because all the things I have of you and Harry give me daily so much pleasure. Ever your Frank.

Clara is not allowed under pain of excommunication to have a cold when I arrive. I have just got through with one. Clara here is a kiss for you. Cantoor, behave yourself.

Letter 3 Addressed: To Madam Lieber
                     In care of Madame E. Lomnitz
                     Esplanade 13
                     Hamburg
           Stamped Sent: Berlin, 29 October
           Stamped Received: Hamburg, 31 October

                                     Berlin, October 29 1844

Yet a letter, my heart, instead of myself but I do not linger here because I like it. Still this will be the last letter you shall have. I have had no letter from you; no doubt you fear that it would no longer find me. I will briefly tell you what has happened and if I mention details which may be flattering to me it is because I want to fix these events and also because the letter is for my wife. On Sunday last I saw Thile, who, I have no doubt, is an honest, excellent man but so confused, so unfit to comprehend the present times! The decalogue is the true criminal code, only sin has so complicated human life at present, etc. —The saddest thing I have seen here is that <u>he</u> could rise so high and keep himself there. He, however, wishes me here, has taken my direction, asked how long after I should receive an appointment, I might leave there, etc. He was very friendly to me. Humboldt had written me to see him on Sunday. I could not but told him I would go to Potsdam on Monday. So I went yesterday — first to Tieck, who received me very cordially [and] said: "You are very well known here; it didn't need a letter. You have been at the King's, etc., etc." Countess Finkenstein, with whom he has been living so long or who has been living with him so long, was sitting on the sofa, an old decrepit woman. I told the old man one fib — the only one I think I have told here in Berlin. I said: "I saw a dear old friend the other day in whom you take an interest." He: "Who? who?" I: "The Puss-in-the-Boots." Now the fact was that I found it very tiresome and insipid. But he will not write anymore, so my opinion could not possibly injure his productions. I trust the fib will be pardoned. I then went to Humboldt, who received [me] friendly and flatteringly, spoke to me in a manner that if I were to print but a small part of that conversation it would be seized upon with greediness by the English papers and fall like a bomb here. Whence this confidence? Whatever opinion they may have of me nothing in a man's life is a guarantee for his perfectly gentlemanlike honour but a trial of itself and they never tried me. Let me give you some of his sayings as they occur to me, torn, of course, out of connection: "You are, in a strange way, very conversant in the

German language as your letter, which you threw at me casually at the station, shows. The King talked kindly and at length about you last evening. You have certainly made an excellent impression upon him. One argued about what your role is there. The King said, in his attractive way, that you are a true lawyer there; whether you had studied law or not makes no difference. Do come back here; we need people like you for the true and nobel impression you made on the King and you will always have him. I beseech you, before you sail, to send a heartfelt letter to the King and tell him openly your opinion about public jurisdiction and jurors. Your opinion will carry much weight with him. The King spoke of how especially badly you have been treated. Do go to Mr. von Bülow (Minister of Foreign Affairs) and if the servants prove difficult, tell them I sent you. Yes, I have already lived through [17]89 and the world has come no further than you find it today. There will come a time when humanity will be free but this may take a long time indeed. The only ministers who are liberal are the war minister and von Bülow. They despise censorship, etc. Mr. von Bülow loves the English freedom without the English aristocracy. Yes, you might benefit by solitary confinement because you have the spark. In your soul burns the nobler flame. Minister Eichhorn — whose works I will not undertake to defend. I leave the King every night at 11 o'clock and write then until 2:30 A.M. You will probably call me very daring because even though I am *a man of seventy-five* I have still recently undertaken my great work — the *Cosmos*. A part is already finished. Here is a letter to Mr. Prenot. I have said much good about you. His Ferdinand and Isabella is much better than Cortes. (You know what I have always said.) Prenot is the most tasteful historian now alive." I must conclude, lest I lose the time. All in confidence. This evening Savignys have invited me and in the afternoon I must sip coffee at old Mrs. Herz's. Kiss all the children, kiss the sisters, kiss me when I come. I long so much and ardently for you. This morning Dieffenbach sent to Gustavus to know my house, to pay his respects to me. What the deuce can Dieffenbach want? Ever your true and faithful Frank. I see you pretty soon. Oh, a cup of tea! It is so wretched here. Carry give me a nice one will you? Keep this for my Journal.

Added in Hamburg. Humboldt also called provincial estates without Reichstände ein Unding; dass man die letzten haben muss [without resources an impossibility; that one has to have the last one]; Told me he said to Uhden that for once he was a young minister that he should do something to distinguish himself and should introduce public administration of justice but he found Uhden against it. Humboldt gave me a picture of the King. He spoke also of the incongruity of the present cabinet which cannot pull together. He also said that he had often said that we must have diamonds in the U.S., as he had predicted them for Russia, which he added is nothing for if I find Monday, Tuesday, and Wednesday with a people, it is no great thing to conclude that they have Thursday also. He complained that he could not get any information from the U.S. He had long, long desired to know whether near our gold districts we have not found platinum and several other metals which he mentioned but I have forgot.

Hamburg

11 December, Hamburg. I arrived here again on [date left blank] Fall in this time. Senator Hudtwalcker's request with the whole Committee of Criminal Law reform to lecture on Penology. I will but my journey to Copenhagen is delayed on account of long correspondence with young men who offer, etc. as private teacher. At length we decide for Schultze but it was very hard to decline young Ahrens in Braunschweig. See Correspondence. I wrote a letter to the latter which I hope will show him how I felt.

Visit to the Rauhe Haus with Syndicus Sieveking. Excellent except <u>dirty</u>. Two important principles: 1. Living by <u>families</u>, 2. <u>Forming</u> a brotherhood or Seminary of teachers to establish the same or become superintendents of prisons.

Visit with Mr. Söhle to the prison. They receive about 10 times <u>a year</u> meat and hardly ever make use of permission to take air on the roof because "they lose too much work," viz. the earning is their own. They invariably buy coffee for it. Look very well.

The day before yesterday a cordial letter from Humboldt, who has sent my letter to the King with words of his own to Charlottenburg. See the letter.

The same day down to the Elbe, which has been frozen these 10 days. I crossed it at the Baum. The milkmen went home across with red sleighs. A frozen harbour is a strange sight. Where one has seen and here I arrived from Holland. Loud busy action and weaving motion, there is now silence and solitude interrupted by a school of sparrows making themselves as thick and rough as they can, drawing in their little heads and sitting on the bare yards. Thick air, vast plain, a plain field of ice up and down the Elbe; standing up pieces of ice with frozen foam and sleet or particles. —Pillory in the harbour on the water for thefts in the port. Enormous height of water in August (?) 1825 marked in sluice house.

Yesterday letter from Mr. Joseph Adshead, Manchester, sending me his lectures on "Penology." That word of mine as well as "Extramural" & "Intramural" will get into use.

I write to Dr. Palm enquiring about Count Bernstorff. —I find Ulrich here whom I used to know at Berlin, not <u>furioso</u>. He is Professor here at the Gymnasium. Friendly letter from Madame de Tocqueville and him. Anxiety about the manner of going.

11 December, Tuesday. Fine skating on the Alster. The noblest <u>Bahn</u> [rink] I ever saw. Besser. Books. Fire in the evening. I went with Felix. By mistake my *Fragments* will be printed with German types. Conversation with chimney sweep here — 11 years old; two years already in apprenticeship — 8 years apprenticeship in all. They have every day meat here & good bed. Still what a life in this cold! They wash themselves every day not only face.

12 December. First proofsheet of *Bruchstücke* [*Fragments*] from the Rauhe Haus. Long conversation with woman near Dr. Schleiden's. Her husband Quartier's Mann. 4 form a "Quartier" common gain. A place costs from 2 to 4 mark. They hire the workmen. No doubt the number of Quartiere is limited.

[Here Lieber inserted two German newspaper clippings, one being a short entry from the *Breslauer Zeitung* with a report from Warsaw concerning the censorship of foreign journals in Poland, dated 2 December. Next to this article, Lieber wrote the word <u>Censorship</u>. The other clipping is a longer description of the Rauhes Haus at Christmas time by J.D. Wichern, the director of the Rauhes Haus, dated 8 December 1844. In this latter article, the author explains that, due to financial constraints, Christmas presents cannot be distributed to those at and coming to the facility. He pleads for donations and reports that a book concerning the Rauhes Haus will be available for purchase at local booksellers.]

Christmas of the Rauhe Haus. The Winter is fearful not the cold alone but the fearful whole. What dreadful curtain those thickly frozen windows are! The late morning! Candlelight until ½ past 8 o'clock. The Rauhe Haus will take a sign at my proposal for the titlepages.

[Here is inserted a note from Norman Lieber written in pencil reading as follows:]

Norman

Lieber

Wünsche

ein Buch mit löschblätter, ein Bleistift + ein Bunten griffel + ein Gewehr, ein kleinen Pult + ein ein Bilderbogen + ein Stall + einen Guten Guten papa und eine Gute Gute Mama. 1844

Norman

Schöne

Wünsche

1844

Christmas 1844 "wish list" of Norman Lieber

[Norman
Lieber
Wishes
a book with blotting pages, a pencil + a colored slate pencil + a rifle, a small desk + a picture sheet + a stable + a good, good papa and a good, good Mama.
Norman
Beautiful
Wishes
1844]

15 December, Sunday. With Oscar & Dr. Werner into the Sewer (Siehle) built by English people here. Afterwards on the Elbe in a Hay Sleigh & horse to Grassbrook and back. In the evening with the children to Dom [Cathedral]. The immense variety, ingenuity and minutiousness [*sic*] of German toys (Sonnerberg) is too much. It is as though the nation, neglecting so many serious things, directed her energy all this way. Yet French toys are more tasteful.

16 December. Write to Anna Niebuhr.

17 December. Tschech ist doch hingerichtet [Tschech was executed after all]. Scribe an Ernest [write to Ernest]. Last proof sheet of *Fragments*.

18 December. Great Dinner Party of Carry's. Dish full of trout looked as if taken out of some Netherlandish picture. Pheasants, partridges, venison, etc. Mary H. so low as no one could go in hinerich [unclear].

19 December. Sunshine. Friendly letter from Schultze and his Father. I write to Wiechern not to mention any name about the playthings which the children have made up for the Rauhe Haus.

—A morning here is sui generis. Description.

Candlelight breakfast. Matildita & Clarita at a little table; Hamilton, Carlito, Emil, Normy at the low table; Clara, Felix, Eduard with us at the round table with us. The moment the breakfast is down you hear Clara practicing "Fingerübungen" [scales] at the piano; one of the boys singing a hymn to Harriet; another reciting Geography to Matilda; Felix, perhaps, looking for a book or his luncheon box and calling out "Tante Jette, wo ist denn, etc., etc." ["Aunt Jette, where is, etc., etc."]. Carlito with the skipping rope; the two little girls romping; some grown one calling: "Norman bist du draussen gewesen" [Norman, have you been outside]. At length comes the fitting out period; then follows the launching period; at last they are gone. But first I ought to have mentioned the noise of the boys when at the bathing room dressing room, singing, etc. Yesterday Matilda heard noise there [and] went in, found Emil & Carlito beating each other (good-humoredly, as they always are — and this they have from their excellent aunts who never loose their temper) and asked: "Wer ist unartig hier?" [Who's been naughty here?"] Emil promptly answered: "Beide" ["both of us"]. At length comes Hart and sweeps crumbs away while the little girls are shipped off. Each child kisses aunts & me before they go. And now silence ensues, one wonders how all gets on & along so well and at last Hannchen enters, that rump to which Nature forgot to stick a pair of legs when making it, and perceiving it when too late threw a pair of odd baby legs after her, which had remained unused of some former day. She speaks or rather breathes in whispers — P.S. Nature showed her wisdom in making Hannchen, for destining her for a seamstress, she gave her no legs but only a pair of paddles just sufficient for a little locomotion.

The personnel of the dinner on the 18th besides the guests were first of all Marshal Kellermann, a Lohnbediente [hired servant], Henry of Hesse (Caroline's work), Frau Stoebern the cook, Hermann stuck into white gloves, Hannchen, Bohner Catherine, the two housegirls. All went off exceedingly well — nothing broken. But good & excellent as the dinner was, nothing was so fine as the entrance of the children when the dessert came. It was a picture and [a] <u>living</u> one indeed! When the servants brought the <u>Trinkgeld</u> ([the tip] that Hamburg abomination) to be divided among them a ducat, 3 Prussian dollars were found among the

⅔ pieces. Of course so much was given only because it was a dinner to the bride, on whose and the bridegroom's places bouquets were lying.

20 December. I called with Matilda on Gossler's & Lappenberg's. Sunshine again. Möschen is the Hamburger or perhaps the Low German for milk with bread in it, as children get it. Is this not the same word with the Pennsylvania word mush? I think it is. Siel I understand is of Dutch origin. Very good for sewer. Oscar came yesterday and brought a letter for Mr. Schultze. A letter, yesterday, from poor Theodore. He goes to a warm spring in the woods 12 miles from Ponce taking a cook & carpenter with him because he must build first a hut, etc. The poor, yet so noble fellow! There is a contrast for you who go in travelling coaches to some sumptuous watering place. Ah, George & Parish!

21 December. I sent my *Bruchstücke* on Penology to the following persons: Senator Haller, Assessor Niebuhr, Minister Eichhorn, Savigny, Bornemann, Gustav Knoblauch (Keibel, Stadtrath Schultze, Zelle), Karsten, Hitzig, Prof. Heydemann, Dr. Julius, Dr. Varrentrapp, Würth, Gh. M. Mittermaier, Senator Hesse, Minister Uhden, King of Prussia, Professor Schultze (Liegnitz), Oberlehrer Koch (Wolfenbuttel). Those to Gustavus, Hitzig, Keibel, Heydemann, Uhden were accompanied by letters.

From a bill of the poulterers for Caroline's late dinner:

1 Kuhrücken [beef back], 11 Mark courant
2 Phasanen [pheasants], 10 Mark Courant
4 Rebhühner [partridges], 5 Mark Courant
Speck [bacon], 6 Schilling

[Written in the margin at this point is the notation "Letter from Tocqueville," evidently alluding to Lieber's receipt of a letter.]

[Here is inserted a letter, dated 20 December 1844, written on blue notepaper with a wood engraving of the Rauhes Haus printed at the top of the page. Lieber wrote on the left margin of this letter the following comments: "Chief peculiar features of the Rauhe Haus. 1. Living in families, 2. formation of teachers, 3. connection with parents, etc., 4. capacity of material expansion within itself. The letter reads:]

Geehrter Herr Professor,

Ich komme diesen Abend in ihre Nähe zu Dr. Lappenberg. Finde ich sie vielleicht um 7½ Uhr zu Hause dann wurde ich bei Ihnen vorkommen um einige

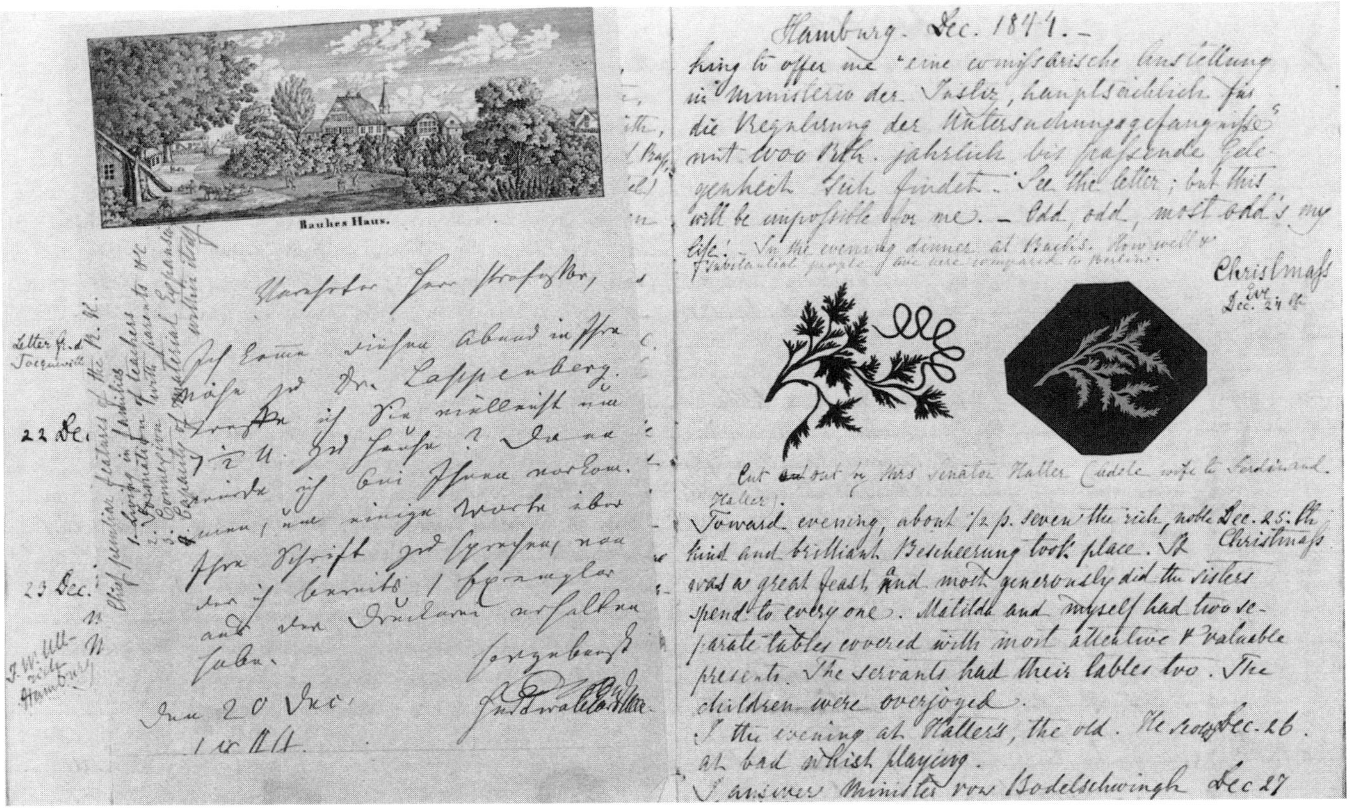
Rauhes Haus.

Hamburg. Dec. 1844.–

king to offer me "eine commissärische Anstellung im Ministerio der Justiz, hauptsächlich für die Regulirung der Untersuchungsgefängnisse mit 2000 Rth. jährlich bis passende Gelegenheit sich findet." See the letter; but this will be impossible for me. – Odd, odd, most odd's my life! In the evening dinner at Bachs. How well & substantial people of the compared to Berlin.

Christmass Eve Dec. 24 th

Cut out by Mrs Senator Haller (Adele wife to Ferdinand Haller).

Toward evening, about 1/2 p. seven the rich, noble, kind and brilliant Bescheerung took place. It was a great feast, and most generously did the sisters spend to every one. Matilda and myself had two separate tables covered with most attentive & valuable presents. The servants had their tables too. The children were overjoyed.

Dec. 25 th Christmass

I the evening at Hallers, the old. The rooms at bad whist playing. Dec. 26.

I answer Minister von Bodelschwingh Dec 27

Francis Lieber Journal, December 1844

Worte über Ihre Schrift zu sprechen von der ich bereits 1 Examplar aus den [name illegible] erhalten habe, Ergebends [signature indecipherable]

[Dear Professor,

I will be in your area this evening, at Dr. Lappenberg's. Should I find you at home at 7:30, I would like to present myself to you to say a few words about your treatise of which I have already received a copy from [name illegible]. Respectfully, [signature indecipherable]

22 December, Sunday. Fine skating. Normy has learnt to slide famously since about 4 days. In the evening good Carry & Harry send off large boxes to Wilhelmsburg and to Hanover with Christmas presents to all sorts of people. Also money. We make a <u>Wunderknäul</u> [surprise ball] for Matildita.

23 December. Send my pamphlet farther to Humboldt, Beaumont, Tocqueville, Foelix 2, Geheimrath Munke, Lord Morpeth, Prof. Wurm, R. D. Ulrich, (J. W. Ullrich, Hamburg). —I write to Humboldt in Paris[?]. Received a letter from Minister Bodelschwingh, charged by the King to offer me "eine comissarische Anstellung im Ministerium der Justiz, hauptsächlich für die Regulierung der Untersuchungsgefängnisse mit 1000 Reichstaler jährlich bis passende Gelegenheit sich finde" ["A commissioned appointment in the Ministry of Justice, mainly for the regulation of the detention prisons with a salary 1000 imperial dollars annually until a suitable opportunity can be found"]. See the letter; but this will be impossible for me. Odd, odd, most odd's my life! In the evening dinner at Buck's. How well and substantial people live here compared to Berlin.

24 December, Christmas Eve.
[Pasted down on the page at this point are two floral cut outs with inscription "Cut out by Mrs Senator Haller (Adele wife to Ferdinand Haller)"]

25 December, Christmas. Toward evening, about ½ past seven the rich, noble, kind and brilliant <u>Bescherung</u> [opening of presents] took place. It was a great feast and most generously did the sisters spend to every one. Matilda and myself had two separate tables covered with most attentive & valuable presents. The servants had their tables too. The children were overjoyed.

26 December. In the evening at Haller's, the old. He scolded at bad whist playing.

27 December. I answer Minister von Bodelschwingh. See copy.

28 December. Send a copy of the letter to Bodelschwingh to Uhden, Minister of Justiz [Justice] and ask him to see that the King sees the letter and not merely the naked result. Salomon Heyne [Heine] died Monday 23rd at one o'clock P.M.

30 December. Presents from Züllichau; written to them. So to Fr. Schultze, Prof. Liegnitz. We made a little punch in the evening. Children have all coughs and make sometimes terrible noise. Poor Normy the most.

[Here are inserted two short newspaper clippings offering rewards for job placements, with the notation: "*Hamburger Nachrichten,* 6 Dec. 1844" and a newspaper death notice for Gerthrude Juedel, born Mayer, with the notation "*Hamburger Nachrichten,* Dec. 31. 1844."

1 January 1845. Went to Catharinen Church. I think a German Protestant Church in wet winter a most melancholy thing: vast, not calculated for the sermon, dark, gloomy, cold, damp. When Oscar and myself entered women offered "Küken" [chicks] (<u>mariti</u> in Italian) with hot coals ranged on a board.

MDCCCXLV

One woman went with us to give us a place in a pew. Before us some Senators in the official dress — like van Dyke's portraits — before each of them and other citizen-officers were lying printed papers with the names of the ministers & time when they were to preach, the songs to be sung, number of burials, copulations, births, legitimate and illegitimate, Communicants, etc., all of which formed a better sermon than the one we heard, which was slip-slop. Besides the organ playing there were trumpets, trombones, kettledrums (and cymbals belonging to the organ). It was very cold, foggy, damp in the church. The prayer after [the] sermon very long. The minister, after sermon, asked pressingly two favours of the people, 1. to give to the poor at the Church door, 2. not to leave Church before the whole service was over, and to wait quietly for song, altar prayer and song. —Caroline tells me that the ministers often make this request. After this I went to old Haller. Uncle Jacob is not well, since the burial of old Heyne. How many living have thus been sacrificed to the dead.

2 January. Write to Julius and several others. I go about to propose for starting. In one shop long woolen stockings to pull over others, etc. in winter, knitted in Iceland, sold in Copenhagen. Carlito is the most amusing, funny, nimble, engaging fellow, seizing upon every ridiculous point, and yet seizing upon it with grace. Felix is a boy of much substance; much can be made of him. Normy will develop himself a fine character. Botteck's *Staatslexicon* (now out for 100 mark) was for years prohibited in Prussia, now permitted; yet by the same minister.

[Here is attached a blank letter of credit from the bank of Johann Heinrich Gossler & Co. with the notation by Lieber that "This must be delivered personally by one of the partners or one who has the power of attorney for one year."]

5 January, Sunday. Pay visits with Matilda to take leave viz. to Hudtwalcker, Arning, Maurice Oppenheimer & Gabe's [name unclear], Jacob Oppenheimer, Old Haller. Having breakfasted at Aunt Minna's (how very clever Augusta is, translating for publication from German into English), called before at Labat's. Lappenberg yesterday here. In the evening Senator Haller and Adele here. He teaches me game with saying first 100. Adele is very clever indeed. Last night there. She cut out that green vine which [I] pasted in my travelling writing box. Write an additional letter to Senator Hudtwalcker which may be printed.

[Here is attached a newspaper clipping itemizing the estate of Salomon Heine, much of which went to Jewish and Christian charities. Also inserted at this point was another clipping giving financial details in the life of Salomon Heine (born in Hanover in 1767)]

6 January. Run about to ascertain whether the Elbe will hold yet; the Alster ice is under water. A melancholy day. I saw yet the plans for Nicolai Church. Those of Scott & Atkinson — Englishmen — the best. But the former had the stiff triangular tower of the Strassburg minster which I consider a graceless finishing. Otherwise fine, Gothic, yet nothing but pure imitation. Söhle comes yet in the evening.

Through Northern Germany and Belgium

7 January, Tuesday. The leave this time was the saddest thing. First the boys, the two little girls, then myself. Go to Haller & Söhle and at eleven I start with the mail; sledge and horse; between the islands. Two stoppages on the ice; mulled beer in huts. Cracking near the shore; rents through which water comes, and round holes, bubbling up. Water on the ice. The whole peculiar. At one in the White Swan at Harburg. Lament visitation. Saw for the first time an Auerhahn [mountaincock]; they weigh from 4 to 6 pounds; like a partridge or a Waldhuhn [woodcock]. This was shot near Winsen. Start in Omnibus for Bremen at 5 o'clock; pay 2 Thaler.

8 January, Wednesday. Not before ½ past 8 in the Morning at Bremen. See Gloystein, Spitta, Shipbroker Heinke on account of Matilda. Sad news as to vessel. Take a Frankfort sausage & wine in Rathskeller and see the Apostles, etc. No great thing. Roland. Wooden shoes begin with the Weser and through North Germany, Holland, Belgium, France. In Holstein again I believe North German girls have so peculiar a head — the same in Berlin — that they cannot part hair like others in a sweeping line at once but must first take back some hair before they can part down. The reason is that their forehead flat and hair low down; no oval shape. This is not slavonic? Write to Matilda but cannot finish for Omnibus starts at 1 o'clock P.M. for Osnabrück. I pay 2 Thaler, 6 Groschen and no over freight. Great numbers emigrate from Osnabrueck to America and always write that they immediately marry and that it goes well. They earn here from 8 to 12 Grote, a man thrashing in winter from 3 in the morning for 8 Grote per diem. One Grote about one cent. They would all go had they the means.

9 January, Thursday. At 8 in the morning at Osnabrück. I run to see Justus Möser's statue, fine and simple; by whom? Enter Cathedral and pray for wife and child. Start immediately in omnibus and make: "Oh, lasst Sie ladend offen, der stillen Kirche Thor; es trägt sich inniges Flehen, zur Stunde inniges vor. Das gute Werk wird besser, die rechte Stunde thut und das Gebet thut doppelt zur guten Stunde gut. Die Kirche ist zum Beten, so lasst den Beter ein; wenn er am besten betet wird es am besten sein" ["Oh, leave invitingly open, the quiet church's door; for our prayers will be rewarded, as we approach the holy hour. The good deed is made better, when performed at the proper time, and our prayers will help doubly when the holy hour chimes. The church is meant for praying, so let the prayers in; for all will be best, when the prayers can begin"]. At 5 o'clock at Münster. Immediately on by Schnellwagen to Düsseldorf.

10 January, Friday. Arrive at Düsseldorf at 7½ morning. Go to bed but cannot sleep. Read Schlemiehl, which dear Carry had yet sent for Tuesday morning, I merely having mentioned it. I do not think much of the book. It is too pathetic and elevated in some parts (speaking of love) when immediately after passages about mending the shadow follow, which require the mind not to be reminded of reality, etc. and the seven league boots come in quite unconnectedly. Thorough toilette. Write to Matilda. At 12 o'clock to the Academy. Picture of Tasso & Two Eleonores (one very handsome) by Professor Sohn and Landscape by Schirmer. In Professor Hildebrandt's atelier, *Desdemona & Othello.* A long conversation with him about the character. Poor collection. St. Andreas Church. Hügler's *Christ tied to a column.* Extremely simple. Not bad. *Mary* by Deger, not much that I can see. Bambino is in a shirt. The girl who leads me about will light my cigar when I was going at the holy lamp. Yet she very modest. Pass the Rhine bridge and come back. At 4 o'clock by Schnellpost [express post] through Neuss to Viersen to visit Commercienrath [Councillor of commerce] Diergardt, whom I saw at Knoblauch's. At 9 o'clock at Viersen. Clean, comfortable bed as always here on the Rhine. Immense number of ports. People actually defend "Rock" Geschichte [story]. It is mere opposition to Prussia.

11 January, Saturday, Viersen. Diergart fetches me in the morning. He occupies about 3500 people. Excellent "Kranken-lage" [health benefits]. People work about 12 hours actually. Gain from 2 to 5 Thaler the week. Eat meat. Children in the silk weavers houses look very healthy. He makes velvet & velvet ribands [ribbons?]. Much for America, since about 10 years; so cloth on the other side of the Rhine Fabrikengericht [factory law court]. Very important, from Napoleon, "sonst hätten wir es nicht" ["otherwise we would not have it"] yet he is strong Prussian. Anecdote of Jacquard. He was attacked by the Lyons weavers & obliged to flee; now they erect him a statue because, as always with machine, thousands of hands more employed. Diergart decidedly for Publicity. Jury could never be abolished here. "Canal du Nord" of Napoleon unfinished, dried up. Bad demand of Prussian Government respect Savings banks of Solidarische Verpflichtung [joint obligation]. Hence in all Prussia only between 8 and 9 millions of Thaler in Savings Banks, while in Paris alone 140 or 160 millions. Nearly all Fabrikherren [factory owners] Protestant; workmen Catholic. Only a 1000 Protestant and 9000 Catholics in Viersen. The priests make now also difficulty. Level but fine country. Most excellent roads. Morality of girls better than in English manufacturing towns but worse than in America. Pregnator must marry pregnant girls; the priest obliges them. The savings bank at Aix la Chapelle alone 1 ½ million because its charter given before the present law. Dine at Dierbach's, frugal, simple. In his carriage to Gladsdorf. Here my mail to Neuss at 8. At 10 in Düsseldorf mail to Aix-la-Chapelle.

12 January, Sunday. Arrive at 5 at Aix. At 7 start on railway for Bruges. Find Spitta and at Verviers his companion asks: "Is Lieber yet in Europe?" It was Hitzig's son — odd finding [him] here. That fine piece of road to Liege. I saw long the Convent, my old hospital. Liege, Tirlemont, Louvain, Malines. Here one must wait 1½ hours; I start for town to see once more the fine Rubens. Yet now differently he & Raphael (Hampton Court) have treated the same subject. Fishing. See again my fine Gothic tower. Ghent. At 7 at Bruges. Terrible headache. Hôtel du Commerce. Comfortable, fine.

Bruges

13 January, Monday. Grande Place. Two houses, corners, together where Charles II lived in exile and Maximilian was kept prisoner by Bruges people (Craenenburg). Tower belfry, chime. Notre Dame. Beautiful coffins and monuments of Charles the Bold and Mary his daughter. The latter, the older, the finest. Very fine. Fine statue of *Mary & Child* attributed to Michel Angelo. I think worthy of him. Cathedral service, as yesterday afternoon at Malines, there archbishop, here bishop. Terrible long singing & responses. Hospital of St. John. The fine Memlings. Reliquary or *Chasse de St. Ursula.* Altar pieces. The small one the most [well] executed picture I have seen of Memling. Over the door a Van Dyck. *Mary.* Also a van Horst. At Hôtel de Ville the fine and very old ceiling. A portrait of Bonaparte as first consul, in red coat. Fine face by Vienue. Given by Napoleon to Bruges. A portrait of Joseph II. Curious Crypt of la Chapelle du Sang de Dieu, which is kept here (See as for other things Murray's Guide). Why don't they show this blood? More important than Christ's Coat. They do show it every Friday. Chimney piece at Maison de Justice. Academy. Van Eycks with [word illegible] Christs. Memlings here not so fine as at Hospital of St. John. To the Institute for the blind and deafmute under Abbé Carton. Especially considered Anna Temmermanns Deaf & Blind like Laura. About 23 years old and 5 here. Looks very brutish. See the work *Anna* par Carton, Gand, 1843, which I have not yet read but have bought it (2 francs). The Abbé was in the country, so La superieure leads me; a handsome young nun. They speak half by signs, half alphabetically to Anna, but could not say to her, she should thank me for a piece of money I had given her. At length she understood it. She does not cypher, has no [word illegible], etc., like Laura Bridgman, she stands much lower. Has strong sense of property. When her grandmother died, they told her she must die too; she distributed all her clothes except kerchief. When one of her friends died they made her touch her. She had no fear and said she must die too. But the Abbé said those who die must first have water poured over them. It was done and she gave up the idea. First passionate; now less so. Touched my hand much. Is not so delicate as Laura. She has no noises for certain companions. The deafmutes too invent signs continually to speak quicker, e.g., taking off hat for boy, and put hand vibrating to cheek for girl, signifying the flying cap. Anna speaks Flemish. She has in her box whole words which she composes. All seems to indicate that it is not half as delicately & shrewdly & deeply managed as by Howe. But I will read the book first. In the evening write to Matilda & Harriet and this journal. People in the street do not understand me speaking French. They are really handsome here — dark eyes, well-delineated faces and beautiful shoulders. More about Anna Temmermanns. She loves to hug, like Laura, especially young ones & the cat. She does not make so distinct a difference between the sexes as Laura does. She laughs very loud. She showed she would buy sugar plums for the money I gave her. She goes to bed of herself at very regular hours, never missing the time. They have taught her of God, through crucifix, whether she does not think that crucifix God? She prays the rosary. Taking her head between the hands is telling her to be attentive; a slight push means disapproba-tion, etc., as with Laura. —In the Academy were papers twisted over the mem-bers of statues, and paper pushed in between the legs of female statues.

England

14 January, Tuesday. Start at 7¾ from Bruges. At 9 at Ostend. Rowed out to steamboat, a slow substitute for regular one. Pay 10½ shillings sterling for second place to Dover. Pass Dunkerque, Calais, etc., White Coast — Albion. Dover castle. At 4¾ at Dover; might have been with regular boat at 2. Strange pass affair. Eat an exquisite mutton chop. Start at 6 o'clock. At 9½ at London Bridge. Excellent railway. I could sleep all the way. Very different from Belgium and Germany — and ours in the South! Hannover Square, Brunswick House. What tea! What plen-titude of comfort. I know the London roll of carriages. Could I but send some tea to Hamburg.

15 January, Wednesday. Fog of course. Breakfast. Large Times, good chops, strong coffee, muffin. To Putnam. A lawyer comes in and asks for Lieber's *Ethics;* see the 2 vols. of the U.S. Circumnavigation of the World. To Everett at home; to Lord Morpeth, not in town; to Hallam, long conversation; to Joseph Parkes, Great George Street, leaving word I would dine there at 7 o'clock; to Hambro, whether letter, old man kind & nice as ever. Invites me to dine tomorrow with him. Port-land Street. Parkes, dine, exquisite old port. He insists upon my taking home with me an excellent Ecce Homo. I wrote today to James, to Clara Woodhouse, to Lord Morpeth, Crawford.

16 January. Putnam, writing. Bunsen not in town. Sir Robert Inglis, John Kenyon, Lockhart, home where I found a very sweet letter from Hamburg. God bless them all. —An enormous shop at Piccadilly with nothing but <u>pâtes</u> de truffes and such things. In Egyptian Hall model of battle of Waterloo at 1 o'clock chiefly la Haye. Hugemont not there. Dine at Hambro's. He tells anecdotes of Heyne, who must have been the most offhand banquier. Hambro insists upon my send-ing him my Gerard Report because Arnold had spoken so well of me.

NOTE: Francis Lieber's Journal ends abruptly at this point. Thomas Sergeant Perry (*The Life and Letters of Francis Lieber*, [Boston: James R. Osgood, 1882], p. 193) says that he spent part of the month of January in England and Scotland departing on the 19th. From Frank Freidel (*Francis Lieber: Nineteenth-Century Liberal*, [Baton Rouge: Louisiana State University Press, 1947], p. 219) we learn that Lieber embarked for his return trip to America aboard the Royal Mail

Steamer *Hibernia*, arriving after a 12-day voyage in Halifax, Nova Scotia. In another two days, he was in Boston and heading back south to resume his teaching position in South Carolina where he awaited the return of his family.

Appendix of Entries Largely in German

A. Conversation with the King, Entry of 23 July 1844

Early to the Schloss. In the waiting room pictures with their painters; neat boxes with pearl shells from the Isthmus of Panama; a cane chair with broken seat. (Everyone in common boots except myself.) At about 10 minutes the King came in in common undress, no star or order, (blue pants, spurs) his cap and kerchief in hand. (Everyone spoke to him with great ease and the Majestät was but sparsely <u>parsime</u>.) He looked at the picture accurately, praised it much and kindly; passed me with a very friendly bow to go to the shells, looked at some prints and then came to me and said: "Sind Sie Herr Lieber? Kommen Sie doch herein." He opened the door, which I ought to have done but forgot and went into his cabinet, the corner room I think of the bell etage to the Lange Brücke. The large table of plain oak-wood. The room was full. No luxe whatever, no grandeur, no soldiers (except quite outside on the corridor, one sentinel). He began by saying: "Es thut mir sehr leid dass Sie wieder fort wollen. Ich dachte Sie wollten sich wieder unter uns niederlassen. Das ist ja sehr schade, etc., etc." I replied: "Ihre Majestät, ich habe Weib und Kinder, kein Vermögen, und dort mein Gehalt." King: "Wie viele Kinder haben Sie denn." I: "3 Knaben." King: "Wo sind Sie her." I: "aus Berlin." King: "Aus Berlin? In der That." I: "aus dieser Breite Strasse." King: "<u>Ah</u>, das wusste ich nicht." —All these questions were made in the common tone of politeness and kindness, no brusquerie. He has small blue eyes and uses frequently [word crossed out] a glass to look at pictures, etc. He has a considerable beginning of a pot belly, low down, so that the waist coat — a black silk one, buttoned to the neck, makes the folds it always does with potbellied people. His sandy hair is a good deal gone. —He asked about my residence; about South Carolina. I told him of the Proprietory Government, <u>Sclaverei</u>, etc., and Charles II. King: "Sagen Sie einmal Karl II stiftete Ritter von Nova Scotia. Ich muss Ihnen gestehen, ich weiss nicht wo das liegt. Wo ist es." I explained. King: "Ah, also heisst es noch so, etc." At length, I wedged in my thanks for his pardon. First he really did not seem to understand me, and at length said: "Oh, da habe ich nichts als meine Schuldigkeit gethan. Man hat Ihnen unrecht gethan. Mir ist es nur lieb dass ich diese Dinge noch ordentlich kennen gelernt habe. Ich konnte gar nicht anders handeln. Man hat Ihnen sehr unrecht gethan. Übrigens hatten sie ein Zeugniss was nach dem Evangelio mir das höchste ist — des verstorbenen Niebuhr. Das war ein edler Mann, etc., Ich erinnere mich wie er liebend von Ihnen in seinem Buche spricht." My affairs led to Jahn, whom I called "einen der irudesten Menschen." King: "Er war ein gemeiner Mensch. Denken Sie sich, an einem der 18ten October hatte er ein Feuer, besonders für den König von Sachsen, etc." (I did not precisely understand it, but it was some gross vulgarity regarding the King of Saxony, who was then a prisoner. Jahn was always an eminently vulgar man.) I: "I have often been surprised at the high pension which is left him." King: "Ah, er hatte ja ein weit höheres Gehalt und man hat ihm nie etwas überwiesen. Er hat auch gewiss nie etwas arges gewollt." I introduced the subject of commerce, the new treaty, and told him that I feared it would be thrown overboard, and why. King: "Ah, glauben Sie." This led me to say how the Americans were the chief people worth courting in a commercial point of view; I told him how they are the most consuming people on earth, and how this increases, of emigration, etc. [and] gave him data on Congress. He was astonished and listened attentively. At length came Penitentiary [reform]. He declared himself for [the] Pennsylvania [system], "aber," said he, "die Leute hier sind dagegen. Sie glauben nicht die Schwierigkeiten die man mir macht, und das alles mit unter von Leuten die es aus Philanthropie nicht wollen. Es ist merkwürdig. Einsam einsperren wollen sie die Leute nicht, aus Menschlichkeit, aber wie Hunde wollen Sie sie peitschen. Wahrscheinlich braucht das System modificationen für die Deutschen, der wie man sagt leichter im Gemüthe afficirt[?] wird, etc." I: "Ich glaube nicht viel. Der Deutsche ist schwererer, verzweifelnder Natur. Er ist leicht traurig; aber ich habe nie gesehen dass er leichter vom Pennsylvania System in übler Weise afficirt wird. Der Deutsche ist ein Schwierigkeitsfinder." King: "Ja wohl, und wir im Norden noch Schlimmer als im Süden. Und es nimmt immer zu." I: "Wie kommt es?" King: "Das weiss ich nicht." (But I did know it, I believe perfectly well. It is the natural consequence of the two causes, German character and the absence of all public, oral life and liberty of practical discussion.) We continued. I said: "Man sagt dass ein so mechanisches Mittel wie 4 Mauern nicht ein so geistiges Resultat wie die Besserung eines Menschen hervorbringen könne, indess ist ein Stück Brot auch mechanisch und doch hat es den spirituellen effect mein Denken zu befördern, oder wenn ich es nicht habe vielleicht den Gedanken des Stehlens hervorzubringen. Alles ist mit mechanischem zusammenhängend so lange wir leben. Die erste grosse Frage bei diesem Gegenstande ist: hat der Staat in welcher Lage es sei, ein Recht, einen Menschen schlechter zu machen als er schon ist? Doch gewiss nicht." King: "Nein wahrlich nicht. Das ist sehr klar dargestellt." I: "Nun aber macht sich der Staat dieses Vergehens geradezu schuldig wenn er Menschen in eine Lage bringt in der sie den ewigen Gesetzen der Ethik gemäss schlechter werden muss; Denn es ist ein festes Gesetz das Menschen von demselben Gedanken, Impuls oder Leidenschaft oder Bemühen bewegt, sich gegenseitig bestärken und befördern wenn sie in contact gebracht werden. Die Frommen werden frommer; die muthigen, muthiger; die bösen, böser und wenn man 6 Verbrecher zusammen bringt die 6 Grad schlecht sind, so verlassen sie das Gefängniss 12 Grad schlecht, etc, etc." King: "Das is sehr gut, sehr brav, sehr wahr." I told him yet much, of instances especially of the German I lately saw, etc. He then said: "Kennen sie Humboldt" Gehen Sie ja zu ihm. Er wird sich freuen Ihre Bekanntmachung zu machen. Sprechen Sie mit ihm darüber. Und sehen Sie doch General Thile. Ein äusserst braver, reiner Mensch, aber er ist dagegen. Sie müssen ihn bekehren. Da war ein Herr Tellkampf hier, auch jetzt ein Amerikaner. Der schien mir für das Pennsylvania System zu sein aber die Herrn sagen, er war es nicht besonders. Indess Sie sehen, diese sind selbst dagegen. Sie mögen sich täuschen. Kennen Sie Dr. Julius? Was halten Sie von ihm." I gave him my sincere opinion. —We talked of German books, and I said, "Das grösste Unglück scheint mir in Deutschland zu sein dass die gelehrte Aristocratie die Wissenschaft für entwürdigt hält, wenn man ihr einen Zweck beilegt, etc." King: "Das ist vollkommen wahr; so ist es auch. Mir ist das nie so klar erschienen aber ich fühlte dies immer. Die Engländer verdicken alles zu sehr, aber bei uns schreibt man als wenn es sich um Luftwesen handle," etc. —Toward the end, he said: "Es thut mir sehr leid, dass ich Sie verlassen muss. Die Minister warten auf mich. Könnte ich Sie doch nur noch einmal sehen, aber es ist ganz unmöglich. Ich habe dem Kaiser von Osterreich versprochen nach Wien zu kommen, wenn ich die Königin nach Tichel bringe und dann muss ich nach Preussen, etc. Wenn wir uns aber irgendwo kreuzen so lassen sie sich ja anmelden. Ich danke Ihnen aufrichtig für die sehr, sehr lieben Augenblicke die Sie mir bereitet haben." Before he said: "Ich muss sehen ob Sie nicht beim Gefängniswesen ankommen können. Ich muss doch wirklich daran denken, etc. I also said: "Lassen mich Eure Majestät ein Gegenstand berühren der sehr wichtig ist und den ich viel studiert habe. Jetzt sind Sie bei einer Gesetzreform, schaffen Sie doch die scandalösen öffentlichen Hinrichtungen ab." King: "Denken Sie sich. Bei der letzten Hinrichtung waren hier 40,000 Menschen, tobend, etc. Ein Kerl errichtete Gerüste. Man vorbot es ihm und der 'infame Racker' geht um 4 Uhr des Morgens doch hin mit Wagen und Brettern und errichtet einige Gerüsste. Ich habe jetzt wenigstens den Befehl gegeben sie nach Spandau zu verlegen. Vor einiger Zeit sagte man dass eine Hinrichtung bei Spandau statt finden würde, was gar nicht wahr war; dennoch war eine Unzahl von Menschen dort."

B. Letter from Julia Ward Howe; Extract from Entry of 3 August, 1844

August 1844
Julia's Letter, Züllichau, August 1844

Blumen schickst Du zu Annie, lieber Lieber, und mir wolltest Du Dornen schicken — ganz richtig denn bin ich nicht seine kleine Wespe und habe // I continue copying in Karnow's garden, Saturday 10th August // dich immer und immer fort geplagt und doch bin ich dir von Herzen gut und in meiner Gegenwart soll niemand von dir was unrechts sagen, denn dein Bild ist, ich weiss nicht wie, mit der Erinnerung meiner alten Tage verknüpft. Damals als ich dich zuerst kannte, lebte ich im Himmel und bei mir der liebe schöne Engel der nun zu seinem eigenen Paradies zurück geflogen ist. Ach Gott, wie nah bringt er mich zu dir dass du Heinrich geliebt, dass du seinen Tod geweint hast. Heinrich war er nicht eine Engelsseele, eine wunderschöne Natur, welche Stärke des Verstandes, welche Zärte des Gemüthes. Und das alles musste sterben — was nun? Ich begreife es noch nicht. Gott hat mir vieles gegeben aber dieses nahm er weg und gab es nie wieder und konnte es nicht ersetzen — ich versichere dir, mein bester, ich bin von Herzen verändert — was ich auch scheinen mag, die alte Julia bin ich nicht mehr und wird es nie wieder. Einmal war ich stolz in meiner Seeligkeit, auf der Erde ging ich nicht. Flügel hat ich und schwebte ins goldne Morgenlicht und wurd bis am höchsten Himmel getragen und möchte ich den Kopf hängen und meine Thränen verbergen. Damals sagte zu allem "Komm mir nicht zu nah. — ich brauche deiner nicht, ich wohne allein mit meinen wehen Gedanken auch die Geister der unsichtbaren Welt bringen meiner Seele göttliche Nahrung," und nun sagt mein Herz "geh nicht so weit von mir, verlass mich nicht, spotte [word illegible] nicht über mich — gieb mir eine Thräne, ein verstehendes Wort, Mitleid und Mitgefühl, denn ich habe gelebt und gelitten! —Doch wozu das alles? Ich weiss es wirklich nicht, geschieht was so bei jedermann? Ich glaub beinahe denn was fehlt mir. Hab ich nicht ja alles? Mein Mann schläft, mein guter Howe, denn es giebt kein besserer als er. Mein Kind schläft auch und wie schön. Die kleinen Händchen sind [illegible word] ausgestreckt —der Rosenmund liegt halb offen als ob er einen Engelskuss empfangen sollte — auf der schönen Stirn herrscht die tiefste Ruhe, in jede kleine Züge lese ich dass dieses noch ein unverdorbner, ein glückliches Geschöpf sei. Gott sei Dank — mein Kind soll lieben und glücklich sein und alles schönes geniessen. Der Gedanke ist mir lieb. Aber wir, müssen wir denn sterben? Adieu, meine guter Lieber — Könntest Du mir ein vollkommnes Herder kaufen? und noch dazu Luther und Goethe? Ich begehre auch ein oder zwei Kinderbücher, die ich ins englische übersetzen will —sie müssen aber schöne sein. Doch plagen Sie sich nicht damit wenn es Ihnen unbequem ist. Grüsse deine Frau für mich und schreib mir von Herzen. Gott sei mit dir. Lebe wohl. Julie Howe.

C. Conversation with the King, Letter of 21 October 1844

I have your last line, my dear wife, which Dr. Julius brought me and a letter which I found the day before at this place, where I had hoped to find one just now —

or, rather not hoped, but it would have made me happy as every letter of yours does, when it speaks of love and the kindness of your soul. But let me give you a description of my last visit to the King on Saturday, Oct. 19. Minister Uhden had brought me word from Potsdam that on Saturday the King would come by the first train, so that I ought to be at the palace at ½ past seven in the morning but that the King would go first, perhaps to the Exhibition, in which case I must excuse the waiting and return at about 11 o'clock. I went and after some waiting it was announced the King had gone at once to the two Exhibitions with the queen. I took my coffee, therefore with Ernst, and returned at the proper time. Waiting a good while I had a long conversation with the Kämmerer and was surprised to find in how narrow a space his Royal Majesty moves. There is not one of the wealthier English noblemen or Commoners who has so little room. His audience room is his "work room," dressing room and all. Close by is a half lighted little chamber in whch he sleeps, has his washing stand, etc. At last he arrived and bowed again to us (generals, Räthe, counts who merely came to show themselves and a republican) with that smiling eye which is, so far as my knowledge goes, wholly peculiar to him. A lieutenant was first admitted. He remained about two minutes, after which the Flügel-Adjutant came and said: "Herr Lieber aus Amerika." I entered, when I found the King throwing himself into an armchair, quite exhausted, saying: "Entschuldigen Sie mich, aber ich bin so müde. Ich kann kaum mehr stehen. Es freut mich ausserordentlich, Sie wieder zu sehen. Wie geht es Ihnen, sind sie wohl?. Sie sehen sehr wohl aus." Ich: "Ich bin sehr wohl Ihre Majestät aber lassen Sie mich zuförderst Euer Majestät meinen späten aber innigen Glückwunsch zu Ihrer wunderbaren Errettung bringen." König: "Oh! Ah! Ich danke Ihnen herzlich. Waren Sie noch hier als der Tschech auf mich schoss? Sie gingen jawohl damals nach der Neumark, nicht wahr." Ich: "Ich war noch hier und war Zeuge des allgemeinsten Abscheus, etc. Ich bin, seitdem ich die Ehre hatte Eure Majestät zu sehen, in Paris, München, Wien und Dresden gewesen." König: "Das ist schön." Ich: "Das Gespräch das mir Eure Majestät gewährten hat natürlich oft meinen Geist angeregt und so entstanden Bruchstücke, die ich nun Ihnen zu Füssen lege." König: "Das ist mir sehr lieb. Ich wollte Sie darum bitten. Ich werde es aufmerksam lesen." Ich: "Ich bringe Euer Majestät auch ein Exemplar meines Auftrages gegen Hinrichtung auf offnem Felde. König: "So? Haben Sie den drucken lassen? Das ist mir lieb. (Und nun fing er, das Buch dicht vor den Augen haltend zu lesen an, las weiter und weiter, auch die Anmerkungen und fuhr so ungefähr 5 ganze Minuten fort als er wieder anfing) "Nun bestehen Sie denn auf den Ausdruck Extramuran." Ich: "Mir liegt nur daran dass jene Hinrichtungen nicht öffentlich sein denn sonst heisst es gleich dass wir, die wir nicht öffentliche Hinrichtungen wollen, für heimliche sind." König: "Der Gegenstand ist sehr wichtig auch wegen der Tatsache dass wir hier das infame Gesetz haben, dass kein Geistlicher den Missethäter begleiten darf." <u>Ich</u>: "Mein Gott, wie ist das möglich?" <u>König</u>: "Es ist, das steht gedruckt; ich kanns Ihnen aufschlagen. Sie wissen, als man früher Menschen auf allen Gegenden zusammenstahl und sie zum härtesten Militärdienst zwang, gab es viele Menschen die so lebenssatt waren, dass sie nichts lieber als den Tod wünschten. Auf der anderen Seite stellten unvorsichtige Geistiche die Folgen der Reue so das dass die Leute wirklich glaubten eines Missthäters Seele könne von diesen Geistlichen geradezu wie eine Bombe in den Himmel geschossen werden. Es fanden sich also viele Verirrte die ein Kind mordeten weil sie glaubten dadurch einen Engel in den Himmel zu senden und für sich selbst glaubten sie wären durch den Geistlichen gesorgt. Es wurde also befohlen den Missethätern keinen Geistlichen mit auf Schaffott zu geben. Durch Ihren Vorschlag wird für beides sehr wohl gesorgt." <u>Ich</u>: "Das ist doch grässlich." <u>König</u>: "Ja, aber um die Infamie noch infamer zu machen, sagt das Gesetz, das die Katholiken einen Geistlichen haben mögen, die Protestanten aber nicht." <u>Ich</u>: "Aber was könnte denn da wieder der Grund sein?" <u>König</u>: "Die Katholiken sagten eben jeder dürft das nicht. Deine Seele wird ewig verdammt, während die Protestanten, Staat und Kirche zusammenwerfen denn das ist der Sinn der Territorial-Theorie. Der glückseelige selbstzufriedene Staat der alles und alles ist. Man sagte der Staat der zugleich Kirche ist bleibt ja doch beim Missethäter. Oh, es ist schändlich. Nun, ich habe heut sehr viel zu thun, leben Sie wohl, ich hoffe immer noch es wird uns gelingen Sie zu acquisieren. <u>Meine</u> Schuld solls nicht sein, ich beschäftige mich viel mit Ihnen." Diener *exit*. Vorher noch hatte er gefragt: "Haben Sie denn noch nicht Thile gesehen?" <u>Ich</u>: "Ich war zweimal bei ihm, aber leider habe ich ihn noch nicht gefunden." <u>König</u>: "Nun wissen Sie was! Schreiben Sie an Thile, ich habe Ihnen gesagt, dass er mir gesagt habe, er wünsche sehr Sie zu sehen; denn er wünscht wirklich, Sie zu sehen, und fragen Sie ihn um welche Stunde Sie ihn sehen können." I have seen General Thile, to whom I have given a copy of those *Fragments*. He received me and dismissed me very kindly and told me that he would study my Ms. with the pencil in hand and then send for me and that I also should openly tell him what I wished.

—Yesterday, I dined at Minister de Savigny, who pressed me to see him in the evening as often as my time would allow. You may show my letter to whom you like, but do not let it go out of your hand. The conversation is literally correct but for that very reason I do not want it to leak out in a circuitous way perhaps in a paper. One cannot be too cautious with things of this sort. And what now? That I would still sink down in fervant prayer of thanks did I receive the news of a place, or the place in Cambridge. The home of my soul is I believe there if it be any where besides in your and my boys' hearts. Love to all. I may leave Berlin the end of this week but you see that this depends not wholy upon myself. Kiss Carry and [name illegible]. Frank. Pray keep this letter for your Frank. I shall put it in my journal, not having an account there.

D. Conversation with Humboldt, Letter of 29 October 1844

Yet a letter, my heart, instead of myself but I do not linger here because I like it. Still this will be the last letter you shall have. I have had no letter from you; no doubt you fear that it would no longer find me. I will briefly tell you what has happened and if I mention details which may be flattering to me it is because I want to fix these events and also because the letter is for my wife. On Sunday last I saw Thile, who I have no doubt is an honest, excellent man but so confused, so unfit to comprehend the present times! The decalogue is the true criminal code, only sin has so complicated human life at present, etc. —The saddest thing I have seen here is that <u>he</u> could rise so high and keep himself there. He, however, wishes me here, has taken my direction, asked how long after I should receive an appointment, I might leave there, etc. He was very friendly to me. Humboldt had written me to see him on Sunday. I could not but told him I would go to Potsdam on Monday. So I went yesterday — first to Tieck, who received me very cordially [and] said: "Sie sind ja sehr bei uns bekannt, es bedurfte keines Briefes; Sie sind beim König gewesen, etc., etc." Countess Finkenstein, with whom he has been living so long or who has been living with him so long, was sitting on the sofa, an old decrepit woman. I told the old man one fib — the only one I think which I have told here in Berlin. I said: "Ich habe auch neulich einen lieben alten Freund gesehen in den Sie Interesse nehmen." <u>He</u>: "Wer, wer?" <u>I</u>: "Den gestiefelten Kater." Now the fact was that I found it very tiresome and insipid. But he will not write anymore, so my opinion could not possibly injure his productions. I trust the fib will be pardoned. I then went to Humboldt, who received [me] friendly and flatteringly, spoke to me in a manner that if I were to print but a small part of that conversation it would be seized upon with greediness by the English papers and fall like a bomb here. Whence this confidence? Whatever opinion they may have of me nothing in a man's life is a guarantee for his perfectly gentlemanlike honour but a trial of itself and they never tried me. Let me give you some of his sayings as they occur to me, torn, of course, out of connection: "Sie sind der Deutschen Sprache in einer merkwürdigen Weise mächtig, wie Ihr Brief, den Sie gestern an mich im Bahnenhofe so hinwarfen, zeigt. Der König sprach gestern Abend viel und sehr liebenswürdig von Ihnen. Sie haben einen vorzüglichen Eindruck auf ihn gemacht. Man stritt sich was Sie dort seien. Der König sagte in einer sehr hübschen Weise, Sie seien wahrer Jurist dort, ob Sie Jura studiert hätten oder nicht sei gleichgültig. Kommen Sie doch her, wir brauchen Leute wie Sie sind, um des reinen und edlen Eindrucks willen auf den König, und Sie würden ihn immer haben. Ich beschwöre Sie, ehe Sie segeln, einen herzlichen Brief an den König zu senden und ihm offen Ihre Ansicht über öffentliche Gerichtsbarkeit und Geschwornen zu sagen. Ihre Ansicht wird viel Gewicht haben. Der König sagte wie ganz besonders schnöde man Sie behandelt habe. Gehn Sie doch noch zu Herrn von Bülow (Minister der Ausu.) und wenn die Dienerschaft etwas Umstände machen, so sagen Sie, Sie kommen von mir. Ja, ich habe schon 89 erlebt und die Welt ist noch nicht weiter als Sie sie finden. Eine Zeit kommt doch wo die Menschheit frei wird, aber es mag lange dauern. Die einzigen Minister, die freisinnig sind, sind der Kriegsminister und von Bülow. Die verachten Pressezwang etc. Herr von Bülow liebt Englische Freiheit ohne den Englischen Aristokratismus. Ja, Ihnen könnte wohl einsame Haft nutzen, denn Sie hatten <u>den</u> Funken. Ihre Seele hat das höhre Feuer. Minister Eichhorn — dessen Werke ich zu vertheidigen nicht unternehmen werde. Ich verlasse den König jeden Abend um 11 Uhr und schreibe dann immer noch bis ½ drei Uhr. Sie werden mich gewiss sehr verwegen nennen, denn obschon ich a man of seventy-five bin, so habe ich noch mein grosses Werk — den *Cosmos* unternommen. Ein Theil ist schon fertig. Hier ist ein Brief an Herrn Prenot. Ich habe viel Liebes von Ihnen gesagt. Sein <u>Ferdinand und Isabella</u> ist weit besser als <u>Cortes</u>. (You know what I have always said.) Prenot ist der geschmackvollste Historiker der jetzt lebt." I must conclude, lest I lose the time. <u>All</u> in <u>confidence</u>. This evening Savignys have invited me and in the afternoon I must sip coffee at old Mrs Herz's. Kiss all the children, kiss the sisters, kiss me when I come. I long so much and ardently for you. This morning Dieffenbach sent to Gustavus to know my house, to pay his repects to me. What the deuce can Dieffenbach want? Ever your true and faithful Frank. I see you pretty soon. Oh a cup of tea! It is so wretched here. Carry give me a nice one will you? Keep this for my Journal.

Thematic References by Entry Date

The arts

Painting: 17 April; 21 April; 29 April; 30 April; 1 May; 6 May; 13 May; 20 May; 21 May; 22 May; 10 June;12 June; 17 June; 18 June; 21 June; 22 June; 1 August; 18 August; 31 August; 3 September; 11 September; 13 September; 14 September; 15 September; 16 September; 17 September; 17[18] September; 18[19] September; 22[23] September; 26[27] September; 27[28] September; 7 October; 8 October; 10 January; 12 January; 13 January.

Sculpture: 15 March; 22 May; 4 June; 8 June; 12 June; 14[?] July; 19 July; 1 August; 2 August; 15 August; 17 August; 18 August; 27 August; 3 September; 6 September; 10 September; 11 September; 13 September; 14 September; 17 September; 17[18] September; 18[19] September; 24[25] September; 10 October.

Architecture: 17 April; 28 April; 29 April; 1 May; 16 May; 19 May; 21 May; 22 May; 23 May; 1 June; 4 June; 5 June; 8 June; 12 June; 17 June; 18 June; 12 June; 18 July; 14 August; 26 August; 27 August; 6 September; 9 September; 10 September; 14 September; 17 September; 19[20] September; 6 January.

Decorative arts: 30 May; 3 June; 12 June; 11 August; 31 August; 17 September; 22[23] September; 26[27] September; 9 October; 10 October.

Care for the handicapped: 22 May; 3 August; 10 October; 13 January.

Economics and political science: 3 May; 24 June; 14[?] July; 13 July; 14 July; 20 July; 23 July; 26 August; 27 August; 3 October; 8 January; 11 January.

Education: 14 July; 22 August; 11 December.

Etymology and language: 24 April; 28 April; 2 May; 19 May; 9 June; 16 June; 17 June; 14 July; 16 July; 31 July; 25 August; 8 September; 22[23] September; 27[28] September; 3 October; 20 December; 13 January.

Journalism: 9 May; 14[?] July; 29 October.

Literature: 24 April; 26 April; 30 April; 21 May; 24 June; 27 August; 2 September; 17 September; 29 October; 2 January; 10 January.

The Military: 22 April; 23 April; 4 May; 14 May; 15 May; 16 May; 30 May; 12 June; 16 July; 18 July; 15 September; 20[21] September.

Parks and zoos: 30 April; 1 May; 24 May; 12 June; 19 July.

Penology and the jurisprudence: 12 March; 22 April; 26 April; 2 May; 14 May; 16 May; 21 May; 25 May; 31 May; 10 June; 14 June; 12 July; 23 July; 18 August; 20 August; 9 September; 21[22] September, 24[25] September; 27[28] September; 1 October; 21 October; 26 October; 29 October; 11 December; 17 December; 21 December; 23 December; 11 January.

Politics

Austria: 19[20] September; 27[28] September; 1 October.

Belgium and Holland: 10 June; 16 June; 20 June.

England: 21 April; 23 April; 26 April; 27 April; 30 April; 6 May; 8 May; 9 May; 10 May.

France: 19 May; 20 May; 21 May; 22 May.

Germany: 14[?] July; 23 July; 31 July; 29 October.

Religion: 11 March; 22 April; 27 April; 30 April; 3 May; 9 May; 16 May; 21 May; 22 May; 31 May; 18 June; 21 June; 27 August; 3 September; 8 September; 16 September; 19[20] September; 10 October; 21 October; 1 January; 8 January; 11 January; 13 January.

Social customs and public mores (selected): 15 April; 18 April; 20 April; 21 April; 22 April; 25 April; 27 April; 28 April; 30 April; 2 May; 5 May; 9 May; 10 May; 11 May; 13 May; 16 May; 19 May; 21 May; 4 June; 21 June; 22 June; 23 June; 30 June; 15 July; 16 July; 17 July; 18 July; 20 July; 18 August; 22 August; 23 August; 26 August; 27 August; 28 August; 30 August; 1 September; 2 September; 4 September; 5 September; 8 September; 10 September; 17[18] September; 21[22] September; 25[26] September; 27[28] September; 3 October; 5 October; 11 December; 8 January; 11 January.

Technology, industry, and civil engineering: 11 March; 19 April; 7 May; 16 May; 16 June; 18 June; 24 June; 14[?] July; 14 August; 18 August; 28 August; 15 December.

Theater and music: 20 April; 21 April; 11 May; 19 May; 20 May; 5 June; 13 August; 14 August; 17 August; 3 September; 7 September; 13 September; 18[19] September; 20[21] September; 21[22] September; 22[23] September; 25[26] September; 27[28] September; 6 October; 8 October.

Travel and transport: 7 March; 18 March; 17 April; 18 April; 22 April; 27 April; 4 May; 7 May; 14 May; 15 May; 9 June; 18 June; 12 July; 16 July; 13 August; 15 August; 26 August; 27 August; 29 August; 1 September; 11 September; 2 October; 14 January.

Some of Those Met

Brief Biographies

Adshead. Joseph Adshead (1800–61), the leading British penologist, who promoted in England the Pennsylvania penitentiary system favored by Lieber.

Appleton. Fanny Appleton, daughter of cotton planter Nathan Appleton, who married the poet Longfellow in 1843 and who served as the model for his heroine in the *Hyperion.*

Arning. Karl Gottlieb Arning (1786–1862), Hamburg senator and son-in-law of Jakob Oppenheimer.

Austin. Perhaps Sarah Taylor Austin (1793–1867), the translator of German writings and wife of the British jurist John Austin; the Austins had befriended Lieber in England in 1826. Lieber dedicated his *Reminiscences of an Intercourse with George Berthold Niebuhr, the Historian of Rome* (London: Richard Bentley, 1835) to Sarah Austin.

Beaumont. Gustave de Beaumont (1802–66), who had met Lieber in 1831 when on a trip to the United States with de Tocqueville to study American prisons. His *On the Penitentiary System in the United States* was published in Philadelphia in 1833 (rpt. Carbondale, 1964).

Bodelschwingh. Ernst von Bodelschwingh (1794–1854), a Westphalian aristocrat, who served as the interior minister in the Prussian Civil Cabinet.

Bossange. Martin Bossange (1765–1865), the long-lived founder of a dynasty of French literary publishers.

Brooks. The family of this name met by Lieber in Paris in June of 1844 may be that of Senator Preston Brooks of South Carolina, who later assaulted Charles Sumner, or might be Lieber's Boston friend Fanny Brooks and her English husband.

Brougham. Henry Peter Baron of Brougham and Vaux (1778–1868), publisher and Whig statesman. He opposed the slave trade and was a supporter of both free trade and education reform; he was the author of the Reform Act of 1832. He was lord chancellor of Great Britain (1830–34). Lieber had met him in London in 1826. They were agreed in their condemnation of trade unions as being prejudicial to the natural order of commerce and the growth of capital.

Bülow. Heinrich Ulrich Wilhelm Freiherr von Bülow (1791–1846), Prussian statesman who served as foreign minister from 1842. He was an associate of von Humboldt.

Bunsen. Christian Carl Josias Bunsen (1791–1860), intellectual and diplomat who had served as Prussian minister to Rome (where he established the German Archaeological Institute) and, later, to Great Britain. Like Lieber he held a doctoral degree from Jena. He was a close associate of Niebuhr in Rome and would have known the young Lieber there. He also was a close friend of the king of Prussia and came to Berlin in the Spring of 1844 with liberalizing constitutional proposals.

Calderon. Frances Calderon de la Barca (b. 1818) was one of the Inglis sisters with whom Lieber had spent time in Boston in 1837. She later was to publish an account of her life in Mexico.

Chateauneuf. The Chateauneuf family had aided the young Lieber on his flight from Prussia in 1826. He stayed in their house in Hamburg (17–21 May 1826) and they even provided his mount as he continued his journey out of Germany. On this see Thomas Sergeant Perry, *The Life and Letters of Francis Lieber* (Boston: James R. Osgood, 1882), p. 64.

Choate. Rufus Choate (1799–1859), American lawyer, celebrated orator, and politician. He served as congressman (1830–34) and then senator (1841–45) from Massachusetts, completing the unexpired term of Daniel Webster, who had become U.S. secretary of state. He admired Lieber's *Hermeneutics*.

Crawford. Thomas Crawford (1813–57), the important sculptor, a pupil of Thorwaldsen and a leading American classicist based primarily in Rome. He executed sculptures for the U.S. Capitol. He married Louisa Ward, sister of Julia Ward Howe and, thus, became part of the Lieber circle. Crawford wrote a friend from Paris that he found Lieber to be "a hearty, sociable, good fellow." See Robert Gale, *Thomas Crawford: American Sculptor* (Pittsburgh, Univ. of Pittsburgh Press, 1964), p. 221n. 147. Lieber served as a pallbearer at Crawford's funeral.

Crawford. William Crawford (1788–1847), English philanthropist active in the abolition of the slave trade and in penal reform. He was sent to the United States in 1833 to study prison systems and became enthusiastic about the Pennsylvania System with its separate cells, also endorsed by Lieber. Appointed a prison inspector in England in 1835, he issued many reports and was largely responsible for instituting the single cell system there; he also had particular responsibility for the oversight of the Parkhurst Reformatory and the large Pentonville Prison.

Diergardt. Friedrich Diergardt (1795–1869), textile manufacturer based at Viersen with the largest factory in Germany. He was one of the leaders in the mechanization of industry.

Donner. Conrad Hinrich Donner (1774–1854), banker from Altona and a businessman financially connected to the Danish court. He was a friend of Danish king Christian VIII, who visited him at his estate in Altona-Neumühlen.

Duchatel. Charles-Marie-Tanneguy comte Duchatel (b. 1803), French statesman, holding various posts in the government, including that of interior minister from 1840.

Eichhorn. Friedrich Eichhorn (1779–1856), Prussian minister of religious and educational affairs (1840–48) and a principal force in the Prussian Customs Union.

Endlicher. Stephan Ladislaus Endlicher (1804–49), Austrian professor of botany and director, from 1840, of the Botanical Garden in Vienna.

Everett. Edward Everett (1794–1865), the American classicist, Harvard professor, governor of Massachusetts (1836–39), and U.S. minister to England (1841–45); later president of Harvard and then secretary of state and U.S. senator with staunch unionist and abolitionist views.

Fay. Theodore Sedgwick Fay (1807–98), American author and diplomat, editor of the *New York Mirror* in the 1830s, and author of such novels as *Norman Leslie* (1835), *Sydney Clifton* (1839), *The Countess Ida* (1840), and *Hoboken* (1843). He was appointed legation secretary in Berlin in 1837, moving to Switzerland in 1853 as the U.S. minister.

Friedrich. Friedrich Wilhelm IV (1795–1861), a romantic and Christian mystic, who began his reign as king of Prussia in 1840 as a reformer, advocating a return to medieval spiritual principles; after the failed Revolution of 1848, he turned in more conservative directions.

Gevers. Dutch Chargé d'Affaires in New York and brother of W. A. Gevers whom Lieber saw in Holland.

Graham. Sir James Robert Graham (1792–1861), whig politician and home secretary in the Peel Government (1841–46) during which time he dealt with the Scottish Church Question and the trial of the Irish Catholic politician, Daniel O'Connell.

Guizot. Francois Guizot (1787–1874), French lawyer and statesman who supported the monarchy of Louis-Philippe. He served as minister of public instruction (1832–37) and was a major power in the conservative government of Soult from 1840.

Haller. Ferdinand Haller (1805–76), Hamburg lawyer and city senator in 1844 and later city treasurer (1860) and several times mayor. He was married to Adele Oppenheimer (1807–73), the daughter of businessman Jacob Amschel Oppenheimer (1778–1845) and Emilie Elisabeth Heckscher.

Heckscher. A friend of Lieber's from New York. His brother, Johann (1797–1865), in Germany, later achieved prominence in the Frankfurt National Assembly which attempted to create national unity in 1848. Edward Heckscher may have been another brother, resident in Paris. The Heckscher family was connected to that of the Oppenheimer by marriage.

Hildebrandt. Ferdinand Theodor Hildebrandt (1804–74), born in Stettin but associated with the Düsseldorf School of Painting. He became an instructor in the Düsseldorf Academy in 1832.

Hillard. George Stillman Hillard (1808–1879), Boston lawyer, admirer and devoted friend of Lieber whose *Political Ethics* he edited. His travel book, *Six Months in Italy* was published in 1834.

Hilliard. Henry Washington Hilliard (1808–92), professor at Alabama University, then state representative before taking his post as Chargé d'Affaires in Brussels (1842–44) and U.S. Congressman (1845–51). He opposed Alabama's secession and later was U.S. minister to Brazil (1877–81).

Hitzig. Julius Eduard Hitzig (1780–1849), leading Prussian jurist and cabinet figure who had befriended the young Lieber in Berlin in 1825.

Howe. See under Ward.

Hudtwalcker. Martin Heinrich Hudtwalcker (1787–1865), Hamburg lawyer and senator.

Hughes. Christopher Hughes (1786–1849) was a career diplomat known for his fluent dispatches and sense of wit. He had been a participant in the negotiations in Ghent ending the War of 1812 and later served in diplomatic posts in Sweden, Denmark, and the Netherlands. He was Chargé d'Affaires at the Hague from 1842 to his retirement in 1845.

Humboldt. Alexander von Humboldt (1769–1859), the great German naturalist and geographer who, despite his relatively liberal political and religious views, was an intimate of Friedrich Wilhelm IV and a member of the Council of State. Lieber had first met Humboldt in Rome in 1822, when the scholar had called on Niebuhr. His brother, Wilhelm, was a founder of the University of Berlin. On Lieber's estimations of and relations with Alexander von Humboldt, see the addresses he delivered on the geographer before the American Geographical Society in 1859 and when a bust of the scientist was unveiled in Central Park, New York City, in 1869 as given in *The Miscellaneous Writings I: Reminiscences, Addresses, and Essays*, ed. Daniel L. Gilman (Philadelphia and London: J. B. Lippincott, 1880), pp. 389–410.

Ingersoll. This may be either Charles Jared Ingersoll (1782–1862), the author and, in the 1840s, Pennsylvania Congressman and chairman of the Foreign Affairs Committee or the Joseph Ingersoll, who, in 1835, had introduced Lieber to Col. William Drayton of South Carolina, who, in turn, had set in motion Lieber's appointment at South Carolina College.

Inglis. Robert Harry Inglis (1786–1855), a leading conservative member of the English House of Commons and a strong churchman. He was both an opponent of the slave trade and a supporter of the Corn Laws. He was a popular member of the House of Commons, possessing a genial manner and the attitudes of a country gentleman.

Julius. Dr. Nikolaus Heinrich Julius (1783–1862), a Hamburg medical doctor and dedicated prison reformer. Raised in the Jewish faith, he converted to Roman Catholicism in 1809. In 1834, he was in America to study penal systems and became an advocate of the Pennsylvania system of single cell housing promoted by Lieber. He translated de Tocqueville and Beaumont's book on the American penitentiary system into German.

Between 1842–46, he published (together with Varrentrapp) an 11–volume annual on prison reform and attempted to introduce such methods into Prussia from his position as a cabinet advisor to the king.

Kenyon. John Kenyon (1784–1856), English poet and philanthropist. He was a friend of Tichnor and of the Brownings, having introduced Elizabeth Barrett to her future husband. One acquaintance described him has having "the face of a Benedictine monk and the joyous talk of a good fellow." Julia Ward Howe, in her *Reminiscences*, called him "a Maecenas of the period." Kenyon had entertained the Howes in London only shortly before he did the same for Lieber.

King. William Rufus King (1786–1853), congressman from North Carolina (1811–16) and senator from Alabama before resigning to become minister to France in 1844. He later served as Franklin Pierce's vice-president.

Knoblauch. George and Gustav Knoblauch were members of a Berlin family that had made its fortune in textiles and had a considerable political presence.

Lieber, Hamilton. Second son of Francis, he was born in Philadelphia in 1835. A Union army officer, he lost an arm at the Battle of Fort Donelson. He died in 1876.

Lieber, Matilda. Matilda Oppenheimer (b. 1807), the daughter of George Oppenheimer a prominent German merchant resident in England, met Francis in 1826 when he was retained as her tutor and came to the United States to marry him in 1829. Evidence indicates that her family was of Jewish origin although it had converted to Christianity. She used her multi-lingual talents to assist her husband in several translations.

Lieber, Norman. The youngest of the Lieber children, Guido Norman (1837–1923) was born in Columbia, S.C., received his education at South Carolina College and the Harvard Law School. He achieved distinction with the Union army in the Civil War and later assisted his father in organizing the captured Confederate Archives. Continuing both his military career and his father's interests, he taught military law at West Point and went on to become the judge advocate general of the United States.

Lieber, Oscar. Eldest of the Lieber children, Oscar Montgomery was born in Boston in 1830, was educated in Berlin, Göttingen, and Freiburg and fought with the revolutionaries in Berlin in 1848. Returning to the American South, he achieved distinction as a geologist in Alabama, Mississippi, and South Carolina and participated in an astronomical expedition to Labrador before his death at the Battle of Williamsburg in 1862 in the service of the Confederate army.

Lieber, siblings. Gustav, Ernst, Emil, Edward, Julius, whom Francis Lieber visited in Berlin and in the town of Züllichau. Most of the family, including Lieber's father, had moved to this town after Lieber's departure for America and a change in family focus from iron manufacturing to banking and stock trading.

Lockhart. John Gibson Lockhart (1794–1854), a noted British editor and biographer of Sir Walter Scott.

Macauly. Probably Thomas Macaulay (1800–59), the English historian and Whig politician, whose celebrated *Lays of Ancient Rome* had been published in 1842.

Mackintosh. Mary Appleton Mackintosh, sister of Fanny Appleton Longfellow, married to an Englishman in 1840.

McNeill. Sir John McNeill (1795–1883), medical doctor and diplomat serving as British emissary to Persia and involved with the complicated intrigues between that country, England, and Russia on the Afghan frontier.

Macollough. Probably John Ramsay McCulloch (1789–1864), Scottish statistician and political economist and a frequent contributor to the *Edinburgh Review* and other journals; he wrote the entry on political economy for the *Encyclopedia Britannica*. His *Dictionary of Commerce and Commercial Navigation* came out in 1832. He was appointed to the comptrollership of the stationery office in 1838. In 1843, he was made a foreign associate of the French Institute. Despite his long London residence he never lost his native accent.

Macready. Wife of the actor William Charles Macready (1793–1873), the Shakespearean actor and manager of the Covent Garden (1837–39) and Drury Lane (1841–43) theaters.

Mahon. Perhaps Philip Henry Stanhope (1805–75), viscount Mahon, a conservative MP, noted historian, and author.

Markoe. Francis Markoe, assistant to Secretary of State Abel P. Upshur and who enlisted Lieber's support in 1844 to promote a U.S. National Institute.

Mignet. Francois Mignet (1796–1884), the French historian and journalist who championed the overthrow of Charles X in 1830 and who was the author of a history of the French Revolution.

Milnes. Richard Monkton Milnes, Baron Houghton (1809–85), poet, author, and member of English Parliament. He was the first scholar to champion John Keats, Alfred, Lord Tennyson, and Algernon Charles Swinburne.

Mittermaier. Karl Joseph Anton Mittermaier (1787–1867), politician and professor of criminal law at Heidelberg University and correspondent with Lieber.

Morpeth. Viscount George (1773–1848), later Earl of Carlisle, and the brother of the Duchess of Sutherland. Morpeth had taken Samuel Howe and his wife Julia Ward to tour Pentonville Prison during their London visit in Spring 1843.

Murray. John Murray (1808–92), the third generation of a famous family of English publishers. His father, who had died in 1843, had established the publishing house at 50 Albemarle Street. While publishing a number of literary figures, the Murray House was particularly noted for its series of guidebooks, many of which the present John Murray had authored. Lieber used these guides on his European tour.

Napier. Sir Charles Napier (1786–1860), a distinguished English naval officer during the Napoleonic War and in various later expeditions in Portugal and the Mediterranean; he served as an MP in 1841.

Neander. Of Jewish parentage, the celebrated church historian Johann Neander (1789–1850) transferred from the University of Heidelberg to that of Berlin in 1815.

Niebuhr. Marcus Niebuhr (1817–1860), the son of the historian Berthold Niebuhr. Lieber had been his tutor in Rome, 1822–23. Marcus Niebuhr was highly religious, a confidant of the King of Prussia and his informal secretary. He served as Prussian privy councillor in 1851 and was a cabinet counselor in 1853.

Northampton. Spencer Joshua Alwyne Compton (1790–1851), second marquis of Northampton, whig politician, poet, and president of both the Geological Society and of the Royal Society (1838–49). He was associated with Sir James Mackintosh as a criminal law reformer.

Oppenheimer. The family of Francis Lieber's wife, Matilda, with whom the Liebers stayed in Hamburg. Some members were merchants in the West Indies, others in England. The family was of Jewish origin but most had converted.

Parker. Mrs. Parker, the daughter of Joseph Priestly (1733–1834), the English Unitarian theologian and scientist, who had discovered several gases, including oxygen, and had emigrated to the United States in 1794.

Parkes. Joseph Parkes (1796–1865), Birmingham lawyer and politician of radical views, who, at one point, even was an advocate of revolution. From 1833, he was secretary of the commission on municipal corporations and a parliamentary solicitor. His house at 21 Great George Street, Westminster, was a gathering place for Whig MPs.

Phillips. Perhaps Sir Thomas Phillips (1801–67), the former mayor of Newport, wounded by chartist rebels in 1839 and queen's counsel since 1842.

Quentelet. Lambert Adolphe Jacques Quentelet (1796–1874), Belgian astronomer, meteorologist, and statistician with a career as a professor at Brussels and as the director of Belgian Royal Observatory.

Rauch. Christian Rauch (1777–1857) was most famous as a sculptor for his equestrian statue of Frederick the Great in Berlin (1836–51) and his Blücher Monument of 1823–26. The 1854 edition of the *Encyclopedia Americana* describes Rauch as "distinguished for accuracy of execution."

Roebuck. James Arthur Roebuck (1801–1789), a politician born in India and educated in Canada. He was a disciple of both Bentham and John Stuart Mill. Of radical disposition, he was a member of the Reform Club created to promote interaction between Whigs and radicals.

Rogers. Samuel Rogers (1763–1855), inherited a banking business but was known for his biting wit and his poem *The Pleasures of Memory*, published in 1792, as well as for his literary gatherings.

Savigny. Friedrich Karl von Savigny (1779–1861), a great legal scholar and the minister for legal revision in Prussia from 1842–48.

Schnorr. Julius Carolsfeld von Schnorr (1794–1872), painter of religious and historical compositions; a member of the Nazarene group of German artists in Rome before going into service in 1821 for King Ludwig I in Munich, where he also was a professor and, then, director of the Art Academy. In 1835, Schnorr had provided Lieber with a drawing of Niebuhr to illustrate his (Lieber's) *Reminiscences of an Intercourse with George Berthold Niebuhr*.

Sieveking. Karl Sieveking (1787–1847), Hamburg city councillor. Lieber had met Sieveking in London in 1826. See Perry, *Life and Letters of Francis Lieber*, p. 65.

Stockton. Probably Robert Field Stockton (1795–1866), the naval officer involved in the settlement of Liberia (1821), the construction of the Delaware and Rariton Canal (1828–38), and who later served as Governor of California (1846) and Senator from New Jersey (1851–53).

Story. Judge Joseph Story (1779–1845), influential jurist, Harvard law professor and Associate Justice of the U.S. Supreme Court (from 1811) and strong anti-slavery advocate who was a constant supporter of Lieber's career.

Sumner. Charles Sumner (1811–74), the abolitionist lawyer, Harvard lecturer and later U.S. senator from Massachusetts (1851–74). He was assaulted by Preston Brooks on the Senate floor in 1856 over the slavery issue. He was a protegé and close friend of Lieber but did not feel he was sufficiently abolitionist in his conduct while at South Carolina College. George was his brother; Mary his sister.

Sutherland. Duchess of Sutherland (1806–68), daughter of the Earl of Carlisle and sister of George Morpeth; known as "the Great Duchess," she was an intimate of Queen Victoria.

Swinton. Possibly James Swinton (1816–88), the fashionable English portrait painter.

Temmermanns. Anne Temmermanns, celebrated Belgian deaf mute and a counterpart to Laura Bridgman in the United States, whom Samuel Gridley Howe treated and whose speech pathology Lieber studied. In an 1850 essay on Bridgman, Lieber contrasted the American with the "course and painful appearance of Anne Temmermanns." In this passage, Lieber says she was 24 at the time of his visit to Bruges. See Lieber's *Miscellaneous Writings I*, p. 494.

Thayer. Probably Eli Thayer of Boston (1819–99), the abolitionist and later Massachusetts "free soiler," who during the 1850s sponsored the relocation of anti-slavery settlers into the Kansas territory.

Thiers. Adolphe Thiers (1797–1877), French statesman and historian, the author of *History of the French Revolution* (1823–27) and *History of the Consulate and Empire* (1845–62). He promoted the monarchy of Louis-Philippe and served as his premier in 1836.

Tichnor. George Tichnor (1791–1871), author and educator who had studied at Göttingen in 1815 and had become a Harvard professor of languages in 1819. From 1835–49, he worked on his history of Spanish literature.

Tieck. Ludwig Tieck (1773–1853), the romantic poet and one of the literati closest to the King of Prussia. He also staged theatrical productions for the court, including *Antigone* in 1841 and *A Midsummer Night's Dream* in 1843.

Thile. Ludwig Gustav von Thile (1781–1852), Prussian adjutant general and cabinet minister and hero of the War of Liberation. He was a religious zealot and head of the First Department of the king's Civil Cabinet

Tocqueville. Alexis de Tocqueville (1805–59), the French politician and author of *Democracy in America* which had been translated by Lieber, as well as the *Systeme Penitentiare*, both the result of the tour of American penal institutions he had made with Gustave de Beaumont. He was a believer in political democracy and social equality.

Uhden. Karl Albrecht Alexander Uhden (1798–1878), Justice Minister, who had been a Prussian cabinet councillor and was given ministerial rank in 1844.

Varrentrapp. George Varrentrapp (1809–86), a Frankfurt penologist and collaborator on related projects with Dr. Nikolaus Julius. His *Annals of Prison Reform* was noted by Lieber in a letter to de Tocqueville dated 26 November 1844, given in Perry, *Life and Letters of Francis Lieber*, p. 192.

Villiers. Perhaps George William Villiers, Earl of Clarendon (1800–70), diplomat and politician.

Visconti. Louis Tullius Visconti (1791–1853), an Italian-born architect active in France; his most significant project was the design for Bonaparte's Tomb.

Ward. The Boston family of Samuel Ward (1814–84) and his three sisters in whose home Lieber was a frequent guest. Sam Ward achieved celebrity as a congressional lobbyist and was the suspected author of the anonymously written "A Public Man," published in the *North American Review* in 1879. One of the sisters, Julia Ward Howe (1819–1910), was an especial favorite of Lieber. She married Dr. Samuel Gridley Howe, with whom Lieber collaborated in the treatment of the blind and deaf mute Laura Bridgman. Howe, like Lieber, was a veteran of the Greek Revolution. Julia Ward Howe achieved prominence as both poet and philanthropist, advocating both negro emancipation and women's suffrage; she gained lasting fame as the author of the "Battle Hymn of the Republic" and was the first female member of the American Academy of Arts and Letters. Her sister, Louisa, married the sculptor Thomas Crawford and, after his death, the painter, Luther Terry.

Webster. Daniel Webster (1782–1852), one of the most celebrated American orators and statesmen of the 19th century. As U.S. senator from Massachusetts (1827–41), he played a crucial role in most of the debates of the day. His strong unionist position allied him with Lieber. On the occasion of this meeting, Webster had only recently left office as secretary of state under the Harrison and Tyler administrations (1841–43).

Wellington. Arthur Wellesley, Duke of Wellington (1769–1852), the British hero of the Napoleonic Wars and the victor at Waterloo. The "Iron Duke" later proved a staunch Tory who distrusted democratic institutions. In 1842, he had been made commander-in-chief of the British army for life and in 1844, he was serving as minister without portfolio in the government of Robert Peel.

Wheaton. Henry Wheaton (1785–1848), American lawyer and translator of the *Code Napoleon*, then diplomat in Denmark and U.S. minister in Berlin (1835–46). He was author of *Elements of International Law* (1836), *History of the Law of Nations* (1845), as well as of a book arguing that the Norsemen and not Columbus were the first Europeans in America (1831). He applauded Lieber's 1840 essay on the need for international copyright.

Wilberforce. Archdeacon Samuel Wilberforce (1805–73) was an Anglican priest and later bishop of Oxford (1845) and Winchester (1869). He was the author of a history of the American Episcopal Church (1844).

Commentary by Entry Date

7 March. The Preston mentioned here may be Dr. William C. Preston, former U.S. senator from South Carolina and then president of South Carolina College. The drawing by Mary McCord was the one presented later to Alexander von Humboldt in Berlin, as Lieber recounted in an 1859 address on Humboldt to the American Geographical Society: "The drawing of a beautiful live-oak near Charleston, which a fair friend had made for me, was taken by Humboldt to that circle [a regular evening discussion group convened by the king of Prussia] where it attracted so much attention that he begged me to leave it." See Francis Lieber, *The Miscellaneous Writings I: Reminiscences, Addresses, and Essays,* ed. Daniel L. Gilman (Philadelphia and London: J. J. Lippincott, 1880), p. 394. Mary McCord may have been a relative of Col. David J. McCord. Col. McCord was the head of the Columbia branch of the Bank of South Carolina. He praised Lieber's *Civil Liberty* in a review published in the *Southern Quarterly* and Lieber wrote an introduction to his wife, Louisa's, translation of Bastiat's *Sophisms of the Protective Tariff* (1848). Both of these McCords were staunchly pro-slavery.

8 March. Lieber's overnight train trip from Charleston brought him into central North Carolina by morning. Smithfield lies just off the present-day Interstate 95, some 30 miles southeast of Raleigh. Goldsboro (in Lieber's day called Goldsborough) lies on the Neuse River 20 miles east of Smithfield. The town was quite new when Lieber took his meal there, having been founded in 1840 to serve the recently opened Wilmington & Raleigh Railway. At its completion this track, 161 miles in length, was claimed to be the longest railroad in the world. Weldon, just east of Roanoke Rapids, lies due north of Goldsboro along another railroad line, running south from Richmond, Virginia. This small North Carolina community, about 10 miles south of the Virginia line, began to assume importance after railroad links to Virginia had been established in 1832–34. With changing transportation habits, Weldon has once again decreased in size and significance.

9 March. Lieber's Petersburgh is the modern Petersburg, Virginia; his Potomac bay is the Potomac River. He apparently took a river steamer up the Potomac to Washington from near Fredericksburg. The reference to Ashburton is probably to Alexander Baring, Baron Ashburton, who, together with Daniel Webster, concluded the Webster-Ashburton Treaty of 1842 which resolved the Northwest Boundry Dispute and U.S.-Canadian border claims along the Great Lakes and in Maine. It also led to the suppression of the slave trade.

10 March. Markoe was promoting the concept of a national institute. Abel Parker Upshur (1790–1844) was secretary of navy from 1841–43 and, then, Secretary of State. He was killed when a cannon exploded on the battleship *Princeton* (see entry comments for 11 March). He was from Virginia and was pro-slavery. Apparently if he had lived, Lieber would have begun his travels to Europe in an official capacity. On the *Orpheus* (a statue by Thomas Crawford), see entry for 15 March.

11 March. John Ericsson (1803–89) was the Swedish naval engineer and inventor who came to the United States in 1839 at the urging of Captain Robert Stockton to work for the navy. His designs for a steam frigate were realized in 1844 with the launching of the *U.S.S. Princeton*, the first screw-propelled ship of war. One of its two 12–inch guns, built by Stockton, exploded in the ship's trials, killing the secretaries of state and navy. Ericsson's reputation was redeemed with his *Monitor* of Civil War celebrity. The mention of "Jack Downing" refers to "Major Jack Downing," the pen name of the American newspaper publisher and humorist, Seba Smith (1792–1868), whose political satire and comic, rustic speech brought him great popularity through a series of published letters, essays, and other writings. "Jack Downing" is discussed by Lieber in his *The Stranger in America*, vol. 1 (London: Richard Bentley, 1835), pp. 253–60. The "Mr. Middleton," who donated the painting of Columbus, was likely a member of the important South Carolina planter family, and possibly the expatriate artist and collector, John Izard Middleton (1785–1849). For information on this Middleton, see: *The Roman Remains: John Izard Middleton's Visual Souvenirs of 1820–1823*, eds. Charles R. Mack and Lynn Robertson (Columbia: University of South Carolina Press, 1997), pp. 3–16. One source (Alicia Hopton Middleton, *Life in Carolina and New England During the Nineteenth Century . . .* [Bristol, R.I.: n.p., 1929], p. 68) reports, without any reference, that John Izard Middleton had spent time in Spain. The Library of Congress, then in the U.S. Capitol building, displayed two portraits of Columbus, both destroyed in the fire of 1851. On Preston, see the entry commentary for 7 March.

15 March. Ferdinand Freiligrath (1810–76) was a German nationalist and poet who published his *Confessions of Faith* in 1844, a collection of radical, liberal verse. Thomas Crawford's *Orpheus and Cerberus* was finished in 1843 and is now in the Museum of Fine Arts, Boston. Longfellow called it "a beautiful work of art; with more life in it than any modern statue I remember (Robert L. Gale, *Thomas Crawford: American Sculptor* [Pittsburgh: University of Pittsburgh Press, 1964], p. 208n. 52).

The *Orpheus* was later damaged in transit to Boston much distressing Crawford, who heard the news in Rome. Lieber wrote to him to "be of good cheer" (Gale, *Thomas Crawford*, p. 207n. 31). Considering Lieber's evaluation of the piece, this would seem to have been tongue-in-cheek encouragement.

16 March. Benjamin Marshall (1782–1858) was the English-born merchant and textile manufacturer, who relocated to America in 1803, where he acquired a successful shipping business. He was part owner of a line of packet ships that in 1818 initiated the first regular monthly passenger service between New York and Liverpool, the famous Black Ball Line. He sold his share to his brother, Joseph (to whom Lieber had written), in 1833.

18 March. This was Lieber's forty-sixth birthday; hence the presents.

14 April. Lieber's account omits discussion of his ship passage as well of as his first days in England. An allusion in his entry for 19 May suggests that his ship docked in Liverpool from where he would have traveled southwards to visit friends in Herefordshire. Leominster, where Lieber resumes his narrative, lies some 12 miles north of Hereford on the rivers Lug, Arrow, and Pinsley. In 1867 it was described in John Murray's *Handbook for Travellers in Gloucestershire, Worcestershire, and Herefordshire* (London: John Murray, 1867), p. 151, as a "neat market and borough town" with a population of 5700. According to Murray, the Priory of the 12th-century Leofminstre monastery in Leominster "forms part of the union workhouse." Henry Hallam (1777–1859) was the English historian and Whig philosopher who authored the *Constitutional History of England* in 1827 and *View of the State of England during the Middle Ages* in 1818. It was Hallam to whom Lieber had dedicated his *Political Ethics* in 1837.

15 April. Lying some few miles northwest of Leominster, the medieval Croft Castle contained on its grounds the remains of an early British fort called Croft-Ambrey of "elliptical form, and named after Ambrosius, a celebrated British hero (Murray, *Gloucestershire, Worcestershire, and Herefordshire,* p. 154). Berrington was described by Murray (p. 160) as being "a handsome stone mansion with portico on W. front, erected in the last century by Mr. Harley." Lord George Rodney (1719–92) was the British naval hero who had bested a Spanish fleet before Gibraltar in 1780 and a French one in the West Indies two years later.

17 April. Lieber's Oxford itinerary should be compared to that given in Murray's *Handbook for Travellers in Berks, Bucks, and Oxfordshire* (London: John Murray, 1860), pp. 133–82. Located on High Street near Queen's College, "the Angel Hôtel, opened as the first coffee-house in Oxford, for 'such as delighted in noveltie,' by one Jacob, a Jew, in 1650" (p. 158). Elsewhere Murray's guide (p. 142) notes that "there is great room for improvement in most of these inns [in Oxford] on the score of cleanliness, comfort, and moderate charges." Lieber's visit to the Bookseller was probably to that of "Mr. Parker's in Broad-street . . . [where] will be found one of the largest and best collections of modern books in the kingdom" (p. 182). The chapel at Magdalen College had been restored by Cottingham in 1833 (p. 161). Lieber attributed its altarpiece of *Christ Carrying the Cross* to Morales; Murray, however, assigned it to Ribalta, noting that it was installed in 1702 (p. 161). Brasenose College takes its name from an earlier building on the site which boasted a door knocker in the shape of a ring passed through a brazen nose (Murray, p. 166). Lieber's sense of Oxford's past is echoed by Murray (p. 142), who notes that "a general air of antiquity . . . pervades the whole, and this effect is not lessened . . . by the palatial colleges or Gothic halls and chapels, varied by the tall towers and spires, whose delicate pinnacles stand out brightly against the sky, while the grey masses below are broken by the brilliant green of the solitary trees or luxuriant gardens, which even more than its buildings are a chief characteristic of this ancient city." Lieber's final recollections of Oxford are of the monuments to "the Bishops Nicholas Ridley and Hugh Latimer [who] were cited to appear for examination [in the Divinity School];

when Ridley at first stood bareheaded, but as soon as he heard the Cardinal named and the Pope's Holiness he put on his cap" (Murray, p. 167). Lieber saw the monument to the three martyred bishops in St. Mary Magdalen Church which "retains rudely carved portraits of Cranmer, Latimer, and Ridley." By 1851, a monumental gothic cross with three statues of the bishops had been erected to commemorate the spot of their death (Murray, p. 173). While the Murray guide to London of 1868 (John Murray, *Handbook to London as it is* (London: John Murray, 1868) does not mention Lieber's London hotel by name, it does note that there are "numerous . . . hotels in Jermyn-street," adding that "house-rent in this quarter is expensive, and the terms are accordingly high." (Murray, *London,* p. 38*). Jermyn Street intersects St. James Street south of Piccadilly.

18 April. Belgrave Square would have been one of London's new sights for Lieber. It was laid out between 1826–33 by George Basevi, surrounded by classically-designed residential ranges. (Murray, *London,* p. 301) The square formed part of the new Belgravia district, "or the southern wing of the West End . . . whose houses, palatial in character and size, denote the high social position of their occupants. Regularity and largeness of proportion are the leading characteristics of this fashionable neighborhood" (Murray, p. 13*). According to Murray (p. 15*), "'The City' is, *par excellence* the head-quarters of the trade and commerce of the country. Here everything is brought to a focus, and every interest has its representative."

19 April. The Thames Tunnel between Rotherhithe and Wapping was a marvel of engineering. Situated two miles below London Bridge, work on it was initiated in 1825 under the direction of Sir Isambard K. Brunel and opened to the public in 1843. "The Tunnel consists of two arched passages, 1200 feet long, 14 feet wide, 16½ feet high, separated by a wall of brick 4 feet thick, with 64 arched openings in it. The crown of the arch is 16 feet below the bottom of the river. The descent and ascent are by stairs winding round cylindrical shafts 38 feet wide and 22 feet deep. The toll is one penny each passenger." (Murray, *London,* pp. 46–47). Lieber had seen the Tunnel on 7 July 1826 and described it in his diary then as "a most remarkable work, worthy of the Romans" (see Perry, *Life and Letters of Francis Lieber,* p. 66). Gas, produced by burning coal, began to be used in England for lighting purposes in 1810; by 1815 many streets and buildings throughout London were illuminated by this method.

20 April. Bolton Street, in which Lieber took up his London residence, runs into Piccadilly at Green Park and leads to Berkeley Square. The observations on American women made here might be compared to those offered in 1835 in Lieber's *The Stranger in America,* vol. 1, pp. 124–26. The opera *Semiramide* was written in 1823 by Gioacchino Antonio Rossini (1792–1868) for the Theater of La Fenice in Venice. On Fanny Elssler, see Ivor Guest, *Fanny Elssler* (Middletown, Conn.: Wesleyan University Press, 1970) and Albert Terhune, *Wonder Women in History* (London: Cassell, 1918). Terhune (p. 277) repeats this contemporary description of the seductive Fanny Elssler: " The perfection of grace attended every attitude; the airiness of gossamer every step. All that can be imagined of lightness indefinable and of movements seemingly effortless was displayed in her various pantomimes; and in these important requisites she has eclipsed every dancer known to the American stage. In person she is tall, but of exquisitely womanly proportions; and her German cast of features is set off by a complexion of delicate whiteness, contrasting charmingly with the rich glossiness of her classically braided chestnut hair. Fascinating beyond description is Fanny Elssler." Lieber's allegiance to Fanny Elssler was longstanding and deep. He was clearly infatuated, if not obsessed by her. On this see Frank Freidel (*Francis Lieber: Nineteenth-Century Liberal*, [Baton Rouge: Louisiana State University Press, 1947], pp. 205–6). See also Lieber's remarks in the entries for 11 and 20 May. Interestingly, only a year earlier, Lieber's good friend, Julia Ward Howe, while she was in London with her husband, saw several of these same performers and left her own impressions in her *Reminiscences:* "I saw Grisi in the great role of Simiramide . . . and Fornasari, a basso whom I had longed to hear in the operas given in New York." Giulia Grisi (1811–69) was an Italian dramatic soprano who was enjoying the height of her fame in the period 1834–49, when she was the *prima donna* of both the London and Paris opera. Her sister, Carlotta Grisi (1819–99), one of the most admired ballerinas of her day, danced in London and at the Paris Opera, where she was under contract since 1841. Luigi Lablache (1794–1858) was an Italian-born bass, who was a favorite in Paris and London; he sang at Beethoven's funeral in 1827 and taught voice to Queen Victoria.

21 April. Kenyon, with whom Lieber was in frequent company during his London stay, lived in one of the terrace houses along the south side of the Outer Circle which ran about Regents' Park. York Terrace was designed ca. 1812 by the architect Decimus Burton (Murray, *London,* p. 31). The Corn Law of 1815, limiting the import of grain, was designed to keep agricultural prices high. The lower classes objected but it was industry that forced repeal in 1846. William Johnson Fox (1786–1864), the Unitarian preacher and politician, was editor of the Unitarian journal *Monthly Repository* which served as an advocate for political and social reform, as well as literary criticism. Fox had a reputation for eloquent discourse on morals and politics; he opposed the Corn Laws. Nell Gwyn refers to the actress (1650–87) and mistress of Charles II.

22 April. Sir William Henry Maule (1788–1858) was justice of common pleas and was regarded as possessing a rare combination of legal expertise and common sense. William Ellery Channing (1780–1842) was the American Unitarian pastor at the Federal Street Congregational Church in Boston. Channing was a bitter foe of Calvinism (a sympathy Lieber would have shared based upon his conflicts with South Carolina Presbyterians) and an opponent of both war and slavery. The Prescott mentioned is William Hickling Prescott (1796–1859), the American historian who had achieved international stature with his several histories of Spain and the conquest of Latin America. Lieber was especially fond of him since Prescott had complimented him on his writing style in 1838. George Canning (1770–1827), the statesman and orator, was a protege of Pitt and later minister of foreign affairs. His reputation was made in the Parliament in the 1790s through his speeches against the slave trade. His bronze statue by Richard Westmacott is in the Palace Yard at Westminster Hall.

23 April. The Reform Club on the south side of Pall Mall was founded by the Liberal Members of Parliament at the time the Reform Bill was passed in 1830–32. "The house was built from the designs of Sir Charles Barry, R.A. The exterior is greatly admired. The interior, especially the large square hall covered with glass, occupying the centre of the building, is in excellent taste." (Murray, *London,* pp. 230–31). James Weir Hogg (1790–1876) was a politician closely tied to both the East India Company and the conservative government; he staunchly supported free-trade. Sir Robert Peel (1788–1850) was prime minister from 1841–46. He was the Tory leader and architect of the Conservative party. He had switched from supporting the Corn Laws (favoring the interests of Tory land owners) to advocating their repeal. Lord Edward Stanley of Derby (1799–1869) was originally a leader of the Whigs but was serving as colonial secretary in the Peel government. Lord John Russell (1792–1878) was the Whig opposition leader.

24 April. Samuel Rogers resided at 22 St. James Place in London (Murray, *London,* p. 259). His house was a favorite gathering place for London intellectuals.

26 April. According to Murray (*London,* p. 148), Pentonville was a model prison, located on Caledonian Road near the new Cattle Market. "The prison contains 1000 separate cells. The inmates are detained for two years and are taught useful trades; a most merciful and charitable provision, which it is to be hoped may prove successful. The cost of each prisoner [in 1868] is about 15s a week. The first stone was laid 1840, and the building completed in 1842. The total cost was 84,168£. 12s. 2d." Edward Law, Earl of Ellenborough (1790–1871) was several times the president of the Board of Control of the East India Company and also the governor general of India from 1841–44. John Singleton Copley, Baron of Lyndhurst (1772–1863), the American-born son of the artist, was a Tory member of Parliament and three-time lord chancellor and member of the House of Lords. The Dissenters' Chapel Bill of 1844, sponsored by Lyndhurst, provided that endowments not specifying forms of worship should remain in the hands of trustees for a period of 25 years.

27 April. The Courvoisier Trial refers to the celebrated trial of the murderer of Lord William Russell. It is discussed in Lieber's *Miscellaneous Writings I,* pp. 254–56.

28 April. The lawyers' church, Temple Church, is a circular structure dating back to 1160, with 13th-century additions. "The restorations and alterations, made 1839–42, at a cost of 70,000£., amounting nearly to the re-construction of the Choir, are in correct 12th and 13th century taste" (Murray, *London,* pp. 118–19). In 1868, Murray (p. 36*) reported that "Omnibus Routes traverse London not only N. and S. and E. and W., but in all directions through the central parts, to and from the extreme suburbs. There are about

1500 different omnibuses, employing nearly 7000 persons. The majority commence running at 8 in the morning and continue till 12 at night, succeeding each other during the busy parts of the day every five minutes. . . . The 'bus' is subject to the inconvenience of heat and crowding; and in wet weather the steam from wet great coats and umbrellas is very oppressive. Add to this, it is not infrequently chosen by pickpockets to carry out their operations. The seat on the roof, *vulgo,* 'the knife-board,' is free from those objections, provided you can climb up to it, which for females and infirm persons is not possible." Lieber caught his bus in the City at the Bank of England. Holland House, in front of which Lieber's bus passed, was in Kensington some two miles to the west of Hyde Park. It had been erected in 1607 and was a popular "meeting place for Whig politicians, for poets, painters, critics, and scholars" (Murray, p. 20). Among its residents were writer Joseph Addison and the politicians Henry Fox and his son Charles James Fox. The park still exists, although the house is in ruins, having been bombed in 1940.

29 April. Concerning Stafford House, located in St James' Park, between St. James' Palace and the Green Park, Murray (*London,* pp. 13–14) says: it "was built for the Duke of York, (second son of George III.), with money advanced for that purpose by the Marquis of Stafford, afterwards first Duke of Sutherland (d. 1833). The Duke of York did not live to inhabit it, and the Crown lease was sold in 1841 to the Duke of Sutherland, for the sum of 72,000£, and the purchase-money spent in the formation of Victoria Park. The upper story was added by the Duke of Sutherland. This is said to be the finest private mansion in the metropolis. The great dining-room is worthy of Versailles. The internal arrangements were planned by Sir Charles Barry. The pictures, too, are very fine; but the collection distributed throughout the house is private, and the admission is obtained only by the express invitation or permission of the duke." Murray notes the Murillos but does not mention the Thorwaldsen. The Danish sculptor, Albert Thorwaldsen (1770–1844) was ranked with Antonio Canova as the leading neoclassicist of the day and was a tremendous influence upon a whole generation of artists, many Americans among them. His works were to be found throughout Europe and Lieber's Journal is replete with his mention. Portraits and mythological subjects in the neo-classical style were his forte, although his *Memorial Lion* in Lucerne, Switzerland, is, perhaps, his most enduring work. Many of the American sculptors of the day were trained in his studio. Of Thorwaldsen, the 1854 edition of the *Encyclopedia Americana* says that he was "since 1826, president of the academy of St. Luke at Rome, the most distinguished of living sculptors, who has shed a new lustre upon the fine arts, and whose works would be considered as masterpieces in any age. . . . While the works of Canova are distinguished for loveliness and grace, those of Thorwaldsen exhibit a calm conception of true beauty, a simplicity and truth, which seem caught from the ideals on which the works of nature are formed, and which belong only to genius of the highest order. A sculptor like Thorwaldsen can dispense with the minor attractions to which inferior talent resorts to win the favor of the multitude; for the power of such striking genius is felt even by the most inexperienced judges." Lieber had met Thorwaldsen in Rome in 1822; on this see Lieber, *The Stranger in America*, vol. 1, pp. 134–35. For conflicting estimations of Thorwaldsen's merits made by Niebuhr and the young Lieber, see Francis Lieber's *Reminiscences of an Intercourse with George Berthold Niebuhr, the Historian of Rome* (London: Richard Bentley, 1835), pp. 136–37. Canova appears to have held onto his fame, while that of Thorwaldsen has diminished. The paintings listed by Murray as being in the Stafford House collection in 1868 were attributed to Raphael, Guido Reni, Parmigianino, Zurbaran, Velasquez, Dürer, Honthorst, Watteau, Rubens, Van Dyck, Titian, Tintoretto, Guercino, Poussin, Teniers, Lawrence, etc. The paintings of Boccaccio's women that attracted Lieber's attention were by Winterhalter. The reference to Cornelius is to Peter von Cornelius (1783–1867), the Munich painter also active in Düsseldorf and, since 1814, in Berlin. He was a leading exponent of the Renaissance revival in Germany and one of the most influential painters of his century and had been a member of the Nazarene group in Rome. He was a leading fresco painter, espousing subjects of an elevated religious or historical theme; Lieber would have approved his use of Raphaelesque motifs. Philipp Veit (1793–1877) was the Berlin-born and Roman-schooled painter, who assumed the directorship of the Frankfurt Academy in 1830. Like Cornelius, Veit practiced a neo-Renaissance style and established a reputation for historical and religious frescoes. The Order of the Swan, mentioned by Lieber in connection with Bunsen, was a fantasy of Prussian King Friedrich Wilhelm IV, who attempted to revive this 15th-century order dedicated to Christian good works and charitable service.

30 April. Murray (*London*, pp. 31–32) describes Regent's Park as enclosing 472 acres and having been laid out in 1812 after plans by John Nash. The name was derived from the prince regent (later George IV). The park included a Zoological Garden in its upper quarter, an observatory, and several villas. "Around the Park runs an agreeable drive nearly two miles long. An inner drive, in the form of a circle, encloses the Botanic Gardens." The reference to James Mackintosh is to Sir James (d. 1832), who had supported parliamentary reform.

1 May. The Houses of Parliament at Westminster was a work in progress when Lieber visited it. This neo-Gothic structure was designed by Charles Barry to replace the old Royal Palace burnt in 1834. The cornerstone of the Parliament buildings was laid in 1840. "In its style and character the building reminds us of those grand civic palaces, the townhalls of the Low Countries . . . and a similarity in its destination renders the adoption of that style more appropriate than any form of classic architecture" (Murray, *London*, p. 35). When Lieber was in London the building's signature Victoria Tower, with its celebrated "Big Ben," was not yet erected and would not be until 1857. The engraving of Westminster inserted into the Journal by Lieber shows the tower and is an artist's conception of the completed building. Murray (p. 190) describes the Zoological Gardens as belonging to "the Zoological Society of London, instituted in 1826, for the advancement of Zoology, and the introduction and exhibition of the Animal Kingdom alive or properly preserved. The principal founders were Sir Humphry Davy and Sir Stamford Raffles. . . . These Gardens are among the best of our London sights, and should be seen by every stranger in London. They contain the largest and most complete series of living animals in the world."

3 May. Bernard Gilpin (1517–83), the "Apostle of the North," was a clergyman famous for his hospitality and whose rectory was open to every traveler. Henry Phillpotts (1778–1869), the bishop of Exeter from 1830, was a member of the House of Lords opposed to Catholic emancipation and to the Reform Bill.

4 May. The docks to which Lieber refers are probably those of St. Katherine. George Oppenheimer was the father of Matilda Lieber, who had employed Lieber as his daughter's tutor. Concerning the location of Lieber's nostalgic meal, Murray (*London*, p. 42*) has this to say: "Simpson's at the Divan Tavern, 103 Strand, —The great saloon is fitted up like a French Restaurant; fresh joints are cooked every quarter of an hour, between the hours of 5 and half-past 7, and the dish is wheeled round to the diner, that the carver may cut to his liking; charge, exclusive of stout or ale, 2s [in 1868]"

5 May. The sculptor Shobal Vail Clevenger (1812–43) came from Ohio and established a reputation for his many portrait busts. While in New York, he had executed portraits of both Samuel Ward and his daughter; it was upon this occasion that Lieber probably met him. Clevenger was in France and Italy between 1840–43, dying of consumption on the return voyage to America.

6 May. Bedford Square and the home of Sir Robert Inglis lies just to the west of the British Museum. It is surrounded by three-story brick terrace houses with round-arch doorways, fitted out with fan-lit windows, balconies and stucco decorations in the pediments. The Disraelis were among the square's distinguished residents. William Wilberforce (1759–1833) was a British politician and humanitarian opponent of the slave trade.

7 May. As an American citizen, Lieber would have been especially pleased to see the telegraph system in operation, its practical method having been invented in 1837 by Samuel F. B. Morse.

8 May. Henry Warburton (1784?–1858), was a philosophical radical and MP from 1826–47; he was instrumental in founding London University and active in medical reform, the repeal of the duties on corn and newspapers, and in establishing the penny postage.

9 May. The Duke of Cambridge was Adolphus Frederick (1774–1850), the seventh son of George III and a professional soldier. The humorous and satirical weekly *Punch* first appeared in 1849. Merchant Tailors' Hall was the meeting place of the company which was incorporated in 1466. The Hall, itself, was constructed after the Great Fire. Murray (*London*, p. 245) notes that the corporation "has the honour to enumerate among its members several of the kings of England and many of the chief nobility" and that "here, in 1835, a grand dinner was given to Sir Robert Peel, at which the whole body of Conservative Members of the House of Commons were present, and Sir Robert announced the new principles of his party."

10 May. Lord Ashley was Anthony Ashley Cooper, Earl of Shaftsbury (1801–85), a social reformer who sponsored acts prohibiting the use of women and children in the mines and supporting care for the insane. His Factory Act of 1844 promoted a 12–hour per day limit in the working hours for women and children with the proviso that children under 13 would be worked no more than six and a half hours and that some limited schooling should be provided for them. Lord Howick was Charles Grey (1764–1845), the viscount Howick and Baron Grey, who served as Whig prime minister from 1831–34. After much maneuvering he had managed to pass a Reform Bill; he favored severe enforcement of the Irish Coercion Act of 1833.

11 May. The reference to the Niger Expedition may be to that which Captains H. D. Trotter and William Allen led up the Niger River in 1841. Lieber's disappointment in the performance of Cerrito was in the 1811 play of the water nymph who had no soul by Friedrich Heinrich Karl, Baron de la Motte-Fouque (1777–1843), the German poet, novelist, and playwright. Julia Ward Howe had seen Cerrito in London a year earlier: "All these [operatic] occasions gave me unmitigated delight, but the crowning ecstasy of all I found in the ballet. Fanny Elssler and Cerrito were both upon the stage. The former had lost a little of her prestige, but Cerrito, an Italian, was then in her first bloom and wonderfully graceful. Of her performance my sister [Annie Ward] said to me, 'It seems to make us better to see anything so beautiful.' This remark recalls the oft-quoted dialogue between Margaret Fuller and Emerson apropos of Fanny Elssler's dancing: — 'Margaret, this is poetry.' 'Waldo, this is religion.'" When Lieber was in London, Elssler was not; his own first-hand comparison of the two dancers would have been interesting.

12 May. Basil Montagu (1770–1851) was a writer on legal issues, especially bankruptcy, and other matters and a friend of both the poets Coleridge and Wordsworth. Sir Samuel Romilly (1757–1818) was the great English legal reformer much influenced by the philosophy of the Enlightenment. The Duke of Wellington's London residence since 1820 was at Apsley House at Hyde Park Corner (Murray, *London*, p. 10). The "loss" by Miss Priestly and Mrs. Austin probably refers to the 1839 failure of Nicholas Biddle's Bank of the United States of Pennsylvania which contributed to an economic depression lasting until 1843.

14 May. Carisbrooke Castle, a mile south of Newport, was the medieval fortress in which Charles I was kept for a year prior to his return to London for trial in December of 1648.

15 May. In Lieber's day, Havre (Havre de Grace) had a population of some 70,000 (John Murray, *Handbook for Travellers in France: Being a Guide to Normandy, Brittany; the*

Rivers Seine, Loire, Rhone, and Garbonne; the French Alps, Dauphine, Provence, and the Pyrenees; their Railways and Roads, 5th ed. [London: John Murray, 1854], p. 62) and was "one of the most thriving maritime towns of France." The situation may have changed somewhat due to the political events of 1848, but in 1854, Murray (p. 63) reported that the port was "the point of communication between the Continent of Europe and America; a great trade is carried on with the United States. The Declaration of Independence formed the groundwork of the present good fortune of Havre. A line of American steamers runs twice a month to New York. Here also a great number of emigrants, many from Germany, annually embark for the New World." Of the French diligence of the sort Lieber encountered on his journey from Havre to Rouen, Murray (pp. xxv–xxvi) has this to say: "The French stage coach or diligence is a huge, heavy, lofty, lumbering machine, something between an English stage and a broad-wheeled wagon. It is composed of three parts or bodies, joined together: 1. the front division called *Coupé,* shaped like a chariot or postchaise, holding 3 persons, quite distinct from the rest of the passengers. . . . The fare is more expensive than in the other parts of the vehicle. 2. Next to it comes the *Interieur,* or inside, holding 6 persons, and oppressively warm in summer. 3. Behind this is attached the *Rotonde,* 'the receptacle of dust, dirt, and bad company,' the least desirable part of the diligence, and the cheapest except the *Banquette* . . . an outside seat on the roof of the coupe, tolerably well protected from rain and cold by a hood or head, and leather apron, but somewhat difficult of access until you are accustomed to climb up into it. It affords a comfortable and roomy seat by the side of the conductor, with the advantages of fresh air and the best view of the country from its great elevation, and greater freedom from the dust than those enjoy who sit below . . . the French do not like to travel outside; and few persons of the better class resort to it, except the English, and they for the most part prefer it to all others. . . . The diligence is more roomy and easy, and therefore less fatiguing than an English stage: but the pace is slow, rarely exceeding 6 or 7 m. an hour. . . . The coach and its contents are placed in charge of the *Conducteur,* a sort of guard, who takes care of the passengers, the luggage, the way-bill, and the mecanique, that is, the break or leverage, by which the wheel is locked. . . . He is generally an intelligent person, often an old soldier, and the traveller may pick up some information from him. The large 1st class three-bodied diligences carry 15 passengers inside, and 4 out, including the conductor. . . . They are drawn by 5 or 6 horses, driven by a post-boy, from the box, instead of the saddle, as was formerly the case." The town, whose name Lieber forgot, where the road met the Seine, was probably Harfleur.

16 May. Ten years later, Murray's guide (*France,* p. 34) gave the population of Rouen as 92,083, making it the fifth city of France, and stated that it "yields to no provincial city of France in its majestic and venerable aspect, in historic associations, and in magnificent buildings, the triumph of the ecclesiastical and civil architecture of the middle ages" and noted that it "is a focus of trade, and the chief seat of the cotton manufacture of France." The Church of St. Ouen also impressed Murray, who stated (p. 37) that it "surpasses the cathedral [of Rouen] in size, purity of style, masterly execution, and splendid but judicious decoration. . . . It is beyond doubt one of the noblest and most perfect Gothic edifices in the world." Lieber's poor opinion of the Cathedral of Rouen was shared by an authority quoted by Murray (p. 34): "It is viciously florid, and looks like a piece of rock-work, rough and encrusted with images and tabernacles, and ornamented from top to bottom." According to Murray (pp. 39–40), the Palais de Justice shared in the flamboyant characteristics of the Cathedral, yet remained "a very interesting specimen of civic Gothic architecture, which may vie with some of the town-halls of the Low Countries." The Place de la Pucelle, according to Murray (p. 40), "serves to record the fate of the heroic and unfortunate Jeanne d'Arc, . . . who was burned alive here as a sorceress 1431, on the spot marked by the contemptible modern statue placed upon a pump, which bears her name, but the outward aspect of Bellona!" That the nearby church served as a stable seems to have been a common fate for, as Murray notes (p. 39): "There are perhaps a dozen suppressed churches in Rouen, most of them converted into warehouses." The Rue de la Grosse Horloge, mentioned by Lieber, is described in Murray (p. 40) as being not far from the Palais de Justice and as being "one of the narrowest and most picturesque in Rouen, . . . so called from the antique clock gatehouse, built 1527, by which it is spanned, adjoining the tower of the Beffroi, when the curfew is still tolled every evening." Concerning the railway line to Paris and its English "origins," Murray notes (p. 30): "This railroad was commenced in 1841, and opened May 1843. Its engineer is Mr. Locke, who executed the London and Southampton Railway; many of the shareholders are English capitalists of Lancashire; and even most of the workmen were English. . . . The rails are of French iron . . . but the locomotives, though made in France (Rouen), are executed by an English company, established there expressly to supply this railroad."

17 May. Of the Place de la Concorde, Murray (John Murray, *Handbook for Visitors to Paris*, [London: John Muray, 1868], pp. 93–94) says: "near the spot occupied by the obelisk, the Guillotine was erected, Jan. 21, 1793, for the execution of Louis XVI. . . . After a brief removal to the Place du Carousel, the guillotine was again raised here permanently, from May 1793 to June 1794, during which time 1235 persons were executed here." The obelisk of Rameses the Great was erected in the square by King Louis-Philippe in 1833. Lieber's antipathy to the spot reflects his repugnance at all forms of absolutism, including the democratic and revolutionary. The lively polka had originated among the peasants of Bohemia ca. 1830 and had spread rapidly in popularity. The modern dance is much more sedate; that witnessed by Lieber on his European travels would have involved feet tossed in the air and intricate turns by couples in close embrace.

20 May. The mention of the Texas Correspondence and Henry Clay may refer to that statesman's opposition to the annexation of Texas due to his presidential ambitions and his desire to eliminate Texas as a political issue. Around the perimeter of Place de la Concorde "are ranged 8 colossal statues of French cities — Lille and Strasburg by Pradier, Bordeaux and Nante by Calhouet, Marseilles and Brest by Cortot, Rouen and

Lyons by Petitot" (Murray, *Paris*, p. 95). The Chamber of Deputies (or House of Commons) met in the Palais Bourbon at the end of the Pont de la Concorde. Its elegance is described by Murray (p. 100): "The interior consists of lofty halls, passages, &c., some adorned with statues, bas-reliefs, &c., others painted and gilt under Louis Philippe. . . . The hall where the Chamber of Deputies sat . . . was begun in 1828 and finished in 1832. It is semicircular, or in the form of a Greek theatre, surrounded by Ionic columns, and lighted from above. The president's chair is considerably elevated, and in the centre of the semicircle, facing the members, who occupy crimson velvet seats rising as in an amphitheatre. . .the Corps Diplomatique, &c., have separate tribunes, like boxes in a theatre." The Opera Francais, on the Rue Lepelletier near the Boulevard des Italiens, was erected in 1821 in temporary fashion. This, says Murray (p. 237) "is distinguished for the splendour of its scenery and ballets." The Opera was given a new building, its current seat, during the Second Empire. The comparison of the dancing to that of Fanny Elssler recalls his long-standing admiration for this Austrian dancer (the prototype of Jenny Lind), whom he had first seen perform in Boston in 1840. On Lieber's fascination with Elssler, see the entry for 20 April, pp. 205–6. Lieber's mention of Raphael's *Madonna del Sisto* predicts his lengthy discussion of the painting in his entry for 8 October.

21 May. Lieber's comments on the visit to the Louvre, on this occasion, are curious both for what he omitted to mention and for what seems to have caught his attention. See his more amplified descriptions when he came back to Paris at the end of August. His visit to the Naval Museum, on the second floor of the Louvre, is, however, consistent with his interests in transportation, evidenced throughout the *Journal.* Murray (*Paris,* p. 177) says that this collection of ship models and naval equipment was a recent addition to the Louvre. Lieber's reference to St. Germain-L'Auxerrois and the "greatest crime in history" is to the Massacre of St. Bartholomew which took place in 1572 when thousands of Huguenot Protestants were slaughtered in accordance with a royal plan. The signal for the assault was the peeling of bells from this much-remodeled medieval church opposite the east gate to the Louvre. The church of St. Eustache, according to Murray (p. 111), at the "end of Rue Montmartre, where it opens into the Place des Halles" was "a church of late Gothic or Renaissance style, the largest in Paris after Notre Dame, attached to the largest and richest parish. The present edifice was commenced in 1532, but was not finished until 1641." The Halle au Blé, or Corn Market, stood nearby. Murray (p. 129) says that "the original roof was of wood, but was burnt in 1802, and the present dome of iron and copper, 125 ft. across, was raised in 1811, and well deserves examination; for the time when it was built it was a marvel." The Luxembourg Palace, begun in 1615 for the Italian Queen Marie dei Medici, in a style reminiscent of the Palazzo Pitti in Florence, was being used as the meeting place of the Peers' Chamber. The Théatre du Palais Royal, which was sold out on this evening, opened in 1831. Murray (p. 238) comments that "it is one of the most amusing in Paris and supported by excellent actors; but many of the pieces (vaudevilles and farces) abound in slang, and require a thorough knowledge of French to enjoy." The interior had been transformed by Chalgrin, the architect of the Arc de Triomphe, while the exterior was enlarged between 1836–41 by Alphonse de Gisors. Today it is the meeting place of the French Upper House, the Senate.

22 May. Lieber's comments concerning the Modern Gallery at the Luxembourg may refer to the Gallery of Living French Artists which had been initiated in 1818 (Murray, *Paris*, p. 180). The private apartments of Marie dei Medici were "still little altered, the panels and furniture having been taken down and concealed during the Revolution, and in point of exquisite work and lavish gilding they have scarcely been exceeded even at the present day. The paintings on the panels are attributed to Poussin and to P. de Champagne; those on the ceiling to the school of Rubens." The Chamber of Peers, furnished during the reign of Louis-Philippe, "is like a lecture-room, the president in the middle, the members sitting in a semicircle on rising seats in front of him." Victor Cousin (1792–1867) was the philosopher and educational reformer, who became minister of public instruction in 1840 and advocated the philosophical freedom of the universities. The church of Ste. Genevieve, called the Pantheon, was built between 1758–89 after the designs of Soufflot. It is "the largest and finest ch. of the Italian style in Paris; the dome is a very conspicuous object. . . . In 1792 it was converted into a 'Pantheon' to 'perpetuate the memory of illustrious citizens,' according to the inscription placed upon its frontispiece. . . . In 1822 it was re-converted into a ch.; in 1831 to a pantheon." The Hôtel Dieu was the oldest and largest hospital in Paris. The reference to the murder of Coligny is to the St. Bartholomew Day (1572) assassination of the Huguenot leader, the Admiral Coligny.

23 May. The Arc de l'Étoile, or Arc de Triomphe, is "the largest triumphal arch in the world; seen from and commanding a view over nearly all Paris" (Murray, *Paris*, p. 52). It was designed for Napoleon in 1806 by Chalgrin and finally completed in 1838. Murray (p. 53) agrees with Lieber concerning the sculptures of the Fames: "The four figures of Fame in the spandrels of the great arch are by Pradier, but not good."

24 May. The Jardin de Plantes, or Botanical Garden, was initiated as early as the reign of Louis XIII (1626), and "combines large botanical and zoological gardens, connected with which are most interesting collections of natural history in every department, and comparative anatomy" (Murray, *Paris*, p. 145). Murray agrees with Lieber concerning the superiority of the London facility.

25 May. Murray (*Paris*, p. 230) tells us that "the most important of all the learned Societies of France is the Institut, which possesses the Mazarin palace on the Quai opposite the Louvre, and on the S. side of the Seine. The Institut consists of 5 Academies — the A. Francaise. . .; the A. des Inscriptions et Belles Lettres. . .; the A. des Sciences. . .; the A. des Beaux Arts. . .; and the A. des Sciences Morales et Politiques, — law, jurisprudence, moral philosophy, statistics, &c. Each academy meets once a week, with a general meeting. . .once a year." De Tocqueville secured a corresponding membership in the French Institute for Lieber in 1851. Count Simeon was Joseph-Jerome Simeon

(1749–1842), the French statesman and jurist, who was entrusted by Napoleon with organizing the new German Kingdom of Westphalia in 1807, applying the new French civil code which he had helped to draft.

30 May. The Laffitte Funeral, which seems to have been quite an occasion, was for Jacques Laffitte (1767–1844), an important financier and speculator, who in 1818 had purchased a château and estate near St-Germain-en-laye and divided the property into residential lots (the town of Maisons Laffitte). Of Sèvres, Murray (*Paris*, p. 229) says: "A prettily situated village on the Seine, where the hills close on each side; it is chiefly celebrated for its Porcelain Manufactory, supported by the Government at considerable expense. . . . The magnificent and unrivalled productions of Sèvres must be familiar to every one; much of their value is derived from the exquisite manner in which they are painted." Murray (p. 27) says that "several of the houses in the Palais Royal, and a large proportion of the Boulevards, are occupied by Restaurants of the first class, and amongst these the principal difficulty is to make a selection, all being good."

31 May. Lieber's visit was to the site of the Bastille. Concerning the column and the elephant, Murray (*Paris*, p. 62) says: "The site was levelled [after the destruction of the Bastille], and a huge model in plaster of an elephant, designed to be ultimately cast in bronze, stood there under a shed for many years. In 1831 Louis Philippe laid the foundation of the present Column of July, dedicated to the memory of the French citizens who fought in the three days of the Revolution of the preceding year. . . . The column (154 feet high) is entirely of bronze, not merely a bronze case like that in the Place Vendome, and has some well-carved lions round it. On the pedestal are the names of 615 citizens who fell in July, 1830." The figure topping the column is actually of Liberty and not Fame. Pére-la-Chaise, then a three-mile drive Northeast of the city, according to Murray (*Paris*, pp. 209–12), is "the oldest and largest extramural cemetery in Paris. . . . The N.E. extremity of the Rue de la Roquette, leading to the cemetery . . . is filled with makers of sepulchral monuments, dealers in wreaths to decorate the tombs, crosses, &c. . . . The ground now occupied by the cemetery was given to the Jesuits in 1705, and received its name from Pére la Chaise, confessor of Louis XIV. . . . On the expulsion of the Jesuits in 1763 it was sold and passed through several hands, until, in 1804, it was purchased by the municipality to be converted into a cemetery. Up to this time the dead had been buried in churches or churchyards within the city, and the idea of making a cemetery outside the walls seems to have originated in Frankfort, and thence to have been introduced by Napoleon into France, as since 1842 into England." Murray (p. 211) notes the "handsome monument of Casimir Perier (died 1832)" and the Tomb of Abelard and Eloise, tracing the course of this latter funeral monument from the 12th century and the final transferal of their tomb furniture to this cemetery in 1817. Perier (1777–1832) was a financier and statesman, who served as a minister under Louis-Philippe and then as his premier. He had died rather heroically while personally aiding cholera victims. Baldomero Espartero (1793–1879) was the Spanish general and victor over the Carlist forces in Spain; he later was the ruthless regent of Spain from 1841–43, when he was driven into exile. The Philadelphia Riots of 6 May-8 July 1844 were incited against Catholic immigration and left 20 dead and 100 injured.

1 June. The funereal theme of the previous day was continued when Lieber visited the Invalides and the proposed tomb of his national nemesis Napoleon Bonaparte. The tomb, in 1844, was a "work in progress" and was not completed until 1861. Meanwhile the body of the emperor, brought back to Paris from St. Helena in 1840, lay either under the cupola or in the St. Jerome Chapel of the Church of St. Louis des Invalides. Following the completion of the monument, Murray (*Paris,* p. 141) could write: "Beneath the dome, a circular marble balustrade surrounds a depression 19 ft. deep, in the centre of which stands the sarcophagus of Napoleon I. The effect of this is very good, and that of the entrance to the tomb is exceedingly fine and grand." Of the artillery on which Lieber remarked, Murray (p. 141) says: "In front of the grand court [of the Invalides] . . . are ranged a battery of trophy guns, 'the cannon of the Invalides,' fired . . . on great occasions. . . . Some of these are Austrian, captured at Austerlitz, some Prussian." Preston's letter was from the hand of the future president of South Carolina College, William Preston.

2 June. The Mabille was a "nightclub": "The Bal Mabille opens out of the Allée d'Antin, just beyond (on l.) the great Rond Point or circle, with a fountain" (Murray, *Paris,* p. 80). Here Lieber experienced not only the Bohemian polka (see entry for 9 May) but its rival in dancing popularity, the French cancan, which also originated in the 1830s. The high kicking steps of this social dance were to be incorporated into the dance revues made famous in the posters of Toulouse-Lautrec at the end of the century. Jacques Offenbach's cancan-based music was not yet composed but may serve to give us some idea of the source of Lieber's headache.

3 June. Brumaire was the name of the second month (beginning on 22 October) of the French Revolutionary calendar, as established in 1793. On 18 Brumaire of Year VIII (9 November 1799) Napoleon overthrew the Directory and established the Consulate which led to his assumption of imperial power. Louis de Bourrienne (1769–1834) was Napoleon's private secretary and a counselor of state; he later supported the Bourbon restoration and King Charles X. He published his memoirs between 1829–31.

4 June. Lieber apparently devoted the first part of this day to securing his place on a diligence for his further travels to Belgium. According to Murray (*France,* xxvi): "Two great companies, whose head-quarters are at Paris, the Messageries (Royales) Nationales and the Messageries Generales (Laffitte, Caillard, et Compagnie) furnish diligences on the great roads of France and correspond with provincial companies who 'coach' the more distant and cross roads. . . . The two chief Messageries are equally good, and, generally speaking superior to any of the minor companies; indeed, they manage to keep down their rivals, by a mutual understanding with each other." Although he makes no mention of it, one must wonder if Lieber, on his visit to Versailles, remembered that it was there in 1783 that the independence of the American colonies was formally recognized. The great palace at Versailles was essentially abandoned with the French Revolution and, says Murray (*Paris,* p. 247), "remained unoccupied until Louis Philippe had the courage to undertake the task of repairing and restoring the palace, and making what we now see — a museum for works of art illustrative of the history of France. He spent altogether £900,000 upon it."

Modern-day criticism agrees with Lieber that this effort was inappropriate and actually did considerable damage to the historical integrity of the palace. Lieber's reference to Galignani is to the daily paper *Galignani's Messenger* which, according to Murray (*Paris,* p. 83) provided the visitor to Paris with information on "what exhibitions, reviews, theatres, &c., are open for that day, besides . . . the usual news, home and foreign." The doors of the Hospital of the Knights of St. John at Rhodes were in one of the baronial rooms in the Salles de Croisades suite on the ground floor of the north wing (Murray, ibid., p. 252). Murray adds that they had been given to King Louis-Philippe by Sultan Mahmoud in 1836. The statue of Jean d'Arc was sculpted by Princess Marie d'Orleans in 1836. Based on the overall themes of battles and victories, it is little wonder that Lieber would remain suspicious of latent French militarism. The Theatre Francais, in the Rue Richelieu, "is the seat of the French regular drama, tragedy and comedy; besides the classic works of Racine, Corneille, Moliere, &c., modern plays are also performed by the best actors . . . (Murray, p. 237). Rachel was the stage name of Elisa Felix (1821–58), a celebrated tragic actress during the 1840s. Some of this material, including Lieber's impressions of Rachel and his conversation with de Tocqueville and Mignet on the next day, are discussed in a letter written to Matilda on 11 June, an extract of which is given in Thomas Sergeant Perry, *The Life and Letters of Francis Lieber* (Boston: James R. Osgood, 1882), p. 183.

5 June. The Roman baths and medieval Hôtel de Cluny had recently been acquired by the government and were in the course of a vigorous restoration; hence Lieber's need for a special entry permit (Murray, *Paris,* p. 88). The Musée Duppuytren, according to Murray (p. 105), featured "a large collection to illustrate pathological anatomy, begun by the celebrated surgeon whose name it bears." It was located in the refectory of a Franciscan monastery in the Rue de l'École de Medicine and was "open to gentlemen only." The singing pathologists were to be seen in the École d'Anatomie Pratique (dissecting-rooms) adjoining the School (Murray, p. 108). At the École des Beaux Arts, Lieber found "a school and museum of architecture . . . where in 1795 M. Lenoir collected the tombs &c., out of the churches desecrated during the Revolution. . . . These were mostly sent back to their churches after the Restoration, and that part of the present building which faces the Rue Bonaparte was erected between 1820 and 1830 for a School of Art; it deserves to be more generally known and visited" (Murray, p. 106). The ballerina Maria Taglioni (1804–84) achieved her initial fame in 1832 in her father's *La Sylphide.* Six years older than Fanny Elssler, Taglioni was her greatest rival. On the Howes' stay in Paris see the comments for the 7 June entry. Julia Ward Howe also describes her impressions of Taglioni's abilities in her *Reminiscences.*

7 June. The Abbé de l'Epee, whose tomb Lieber visited in the church of St. Roch, had founded the Institut National des Sourds-Muets, an asylum for the deaf and dumb, in 1770. Lieber's particular interest in such matters recalls his philological studies of Laura Bridgman (See Freidel, *Francis Lieber,* pp. 182, 183, 207, 221) and his visit to Anna Temmermanns in Bruges (see Entry for 13 January 1845). He could have compared notes that evening with Samuel Gridley Howe, who, together with wife, Julia Ward, infant daughter, Julia Romana, and sisters-in-law, Annie and Louisa Ward, was on his way back to New York from a stay in Rome. While in Paris, Louisa almost eloped with sculptor Thomas Crawford, whom she later was to marry. On Julia Ward, see comments for the 3 August entry. See additional comments on the Howes in the commentary to entry for 3 August.

8 June. Construction of the church of la Madeleine was begun in 1764, halted with the Revolution, resumed in 1806 under Napoleon (who desired that the building become a Temple of Glory), given religious reaffirmation in 1816, and finally completed in 1842. The italianate Palais d'Orsay was begun by Napoleon and given its internal decorations under Louis-Philippe. The reference to the "Venetian Palace" is to the 15th-century Palazzo Venezia in Rome, built for the Venetian Pope Paul II and which later served as the embassy of the Venetian Republic; it is a classic example of the Roman architectural style of the Early Renaissance. The Hôtel Mirabeau was in the Rue de la Paix. Hiram Powers (1805–73) was one of the most noted neo-classical American sculptors, whose *Greek Slave* of 1843 achieved a world-wide reputation.

9 June. Lieber's reference to the Battlefield of the Spurs is explained in John Murray, *Handbook for Travellers on the Continent: Being a Guide to Holland, Belgium, Prussia, Northern Germany, and the Rhine from Holland to Switzerland,* 9th ed. (London: John Murray, 1853), p. 113: "Under the walls of Courtrai was fought the famous *Battle of Spurs,* 1302 . . . gained by an army of 20,000 Flemings . . . under the Count de Namur, over the French. . . . 700 gilt spurs (an ornament worn only by the French nobility) were gathered on the field from the dead, and hung up as a trophy in the church of the convent of Groenangen, now destroyed."

10 June. The silly anecdote about the Ghent Belfry given in Murray is probably the following (*Continent,* p. 128): "Charles V, when recommended by the cruel Alva to raze to the ground this town, whose rebellion had given him so much trouble, took him to the top of the Beffroi [the Belfry], and showing him the vast city spread out beneath, asked, '. . . How many skins of Spanish leather would it take to make such a glove?'— thus rebuking the atrocious suggestion of his minister." Lieber's mention of the iron cannon of Ghent is given elaboration in Murray (p. 132): "In a street close to the Marche [au Vendredi — the Square of the Friday Market], called the Mannekens Aert, is an enormous cannon, one of the largest in existence, being 18 ft. long and 10 ½ in circumference, named *De dulle Griete,* or Mad Margery; it is of hammered iron, was made in the days of Philip le Bon, and used by the Gantois at the siege of Oudenard, 1382, and again in 1452." The Beguinage, or convent community, is now a delightfully secluded museum of Flemish culture. Murray's description (p. 134) was of a still active institution, being "one of the few nunneries not suppressed by Joseph II., or swept away by the torrent of the French Revolution. It is of great extent, with streets, squares, and gates surrounded by a wall and moat. It is certainly worthy of a visit. At the hour of vespers . . . strangers should repair to the chapel, where they will have an opportunity of seeing the whole sisterhood assembled. They amount to more than 600, and many are persons of wealth and rank. The sight of so large an assemblage, all in black robes and white veils . . . has a picturesque effect. . . . The sisters live generally in separate houses. On the doors are inscribed the names, not of the tenant of the house, but of some saint who has been adopted as its protectress. . . . The Beguines are bound by no vow; they may return into the world whenever they please. . . . They attend to the sick in the Beguinage, as nurses, and are constantly seen at the Hospital." Lieber's Maison de Force is the same as the Maison de Detention — the penitentiary — described in Murray (p. 135) as being "an octagon building of vast extent, begun 1772, and finished 1824. A prison truly is an object which an Englishman can see frequently enough in his own country, but this is particularly well managed; it was held up as a pattern by Howard the philanthropist, and has served as a model for many others, not only in Europe, but in America." The picture in the Cathedral of St. Bavon discussed by Lieber is the celebrated *Ghent Altarpiece* of ca. 1430 by the brothers Hubert and Jan van Eyck. Lieber's criticism of this masterpiece of the early Northern Renaissance echoes that given in Murray (p. 129): "Considering the period when it was painted, this picture is remarkably free from the stiffness of the early school: the finish of the faces is most elaborate, and the strength and freshness of the colours in a painting 400 years old is truly wonderful." In Lieber's day, several of the panels of this great poliptych were in the royal collections in Berlin. Murray further notes that "The 2 exterior lower wings [actually upper wings] are said to be still in the possession of the chapter, but are shut up from motives of false delicacy, because they represent Adam and Eve in a state of nature." The city of Malines is also known in Flemish as Mechelen. The Hôtel de l'Europe in which Lieber lodged while in Brussels received a "good" rating in the Murray guide of 1853 (p. 155) and was located in the Place Royale. J. J. G. Foelix was a writer and legal scholar.

12 June. The eighteenth-century palace of Laeken, three miles outside of Brussels, was "handsomely furnished, but there is nothing to distinguish it from other kingly residences, of which a traveller may see enough in a continental journey" (Murray, *Continent*, p. 155). While residing at Laeken, Napoleon planned his disastrous Russian Campaign of 1812. Murray (p. 156) notes that "Brussels abounds in English in search of cheapness, which their presence has banished. From the long sojourn of so many of our countrymen, the English language is very generally spoken, from the landlord of the hotels down to the shoeblack in the streets." Murray (p. 158) describes the Hôtel de Ville in the Grande Place as "the grandest of those municipal palaces which are found in almost every city of the Netherlands, and nowhere else of the same splendour. . . . The market-place, in front of it, is lined with picturesque old houses, most of which were the halls of various Corporations and Guilds. Here the Counts Egmont and Horn were beheaded, by order of the cruel Alva, in 1568." The Brussels Museum, the Palais des Beaux Arts, was housed in the Old Palace near the Place Royale and received little better praise in Murray (pp. 156–57) than that given by Lieber: "The number of pictures here exceeds 300: the bad preponderate much over the good; and the whole collection is far inferior to that at Antwerp." The Aremberg Palace, according to Murray (p. 160) was "furnished with great splendour [and] contains a small but choice gallery chiefly of Dutch and Flemish masters . . . and is well worth seeing."

13 June. Lieber's experiences in the Waterloo campaign and its aftermath, as recalled in an 1833 essay, are given in his *Miscellaneous Writings I,* pp. 151–75 and in the more detailed account given in *The Stranger in America,* vol. 1, pp. 155–208. Lieber's visit to the scene of the allied victory over Napoleon took place almost 29 years to the day since he had taken part in the great campaign. Lieber's guide at Waterloo was dead at the publishing of Murray's *Continent* in 1853, but was recalled in the Waterloo Museum "formed by the late Serjt. Cotton opposite the Hôtel de la Colonne, which contains some really interesting objects" (ibid., p. 162). He had been succeeded in his duties by a Sergeant Munday of the 7th Hussars, who was recommended to the English traveler, who would find the fields of Waterloo a tourist destination where "he will be assailed by guides and relic-venders, claiming the honour of serving him in the capacity of guide." Murray devotes a lengthy description to the Waterloo Battlefields (pp. 162–63). Mont St. Jean was the village lying a mile behind the allied lines at Waterloo. Hougoumont was the farm château lying just beyond the right flank of the allies and a pivotal point of contention between the two armies. The Mound of the Belgic Lion was a matter of some controversy: "The mound . . . [is] by far the most conspicuous object in the field of Waterloo. . . . It marks the spot which may be considered the centre of the conflict . . . . It is a vast tumulus, 200 ft. high, beneath which the bones of friends and foes lie heaped indiscriminately together. A flight of steps leads up to the top. The lion was cast by Cockerill of Liege, and is intended to stand on the spot where the Prince of Orange was wounded" (Murray, pp. 163 & 165). Quatre Bras lies along the road between the Waterloo and Namur battlefields; it was so called because four major roads intersected at this spot. It was the site of an important engagement fought between English and French forces on 16 June, 1815.

14 June. The Battlefield of Sombreffe and Ligny was the site of Napoleon's repulse of Blücher's Prussians (including the young Lieber) two days before the decisive Battle of Waterloo. Despite the appearance of a French victory, Blücher fought heroically and "in spite of his defeat . . . maintained his communications with the English, and made good his retreat to Wavre; no beaten army ever rallied quicker" (Murray, *Continent,* p. 169). The mill mentioned by Lieber was that of Bussy from which Blücher directed his forces. The village of Fleurus lies four miles southwest of Sombreffe. Namur, at the confluence of the Sambre and Meuse, was a town of some 22,000 famous for its cutlery; the Hôtel d'Harscamp was one of two in the town rated as "good" by Murray (p. 170).

16 June. According to Murray (*Continent*, p. 171): "Steamers ply on the Meuse, when there is water enough, between Namur and Liege. In going to Liege the voyage of about 45 m. is performed in 4 hrs. . . . During the summer 2 steamers a day leave Namur for Liege, — one at 6 A.M., the other at 3 P.M. The banks of the Meuse between Namur and Liege are hardly surpassed in beauty by any river scenery in N. Europe. . . . The Meuse affords a pleasing mixture of cultivation and wildness, of active industry and quiet nature, smoking steam-engines and naked and abrupt cliffs of limestone, ruined castles and flourishing villages, with huge many windowed mills and factories, which give an agreeable variety." The citadel at Huy was an impressive work, having been "repaired and strengthened on the most approved plans of modern fortification, under the direction of skilful English engineers, since 1815" (p. 171). Seraing was a landmark of Europe's new age of industry. "This colossal establishment," according to Murray (pp. 172–73), "was formed by the enterprising manufacturer the late John Cockerill, 1816. It is perhaps the largest manufactory of machinery in the world; and occupies the former Palace of the Prince Bishops of Liege, which now serves but as the facade or vestibule of the other vast constructions since added to fit it for its present purpose. . . . Amidst the smoke and flames issuing from its 40 or 50 tall chimneys, its palatial and ecclesiastical character have alike nearly disappeared . . . where iron is wrought into articles of all sorts from penknives up to steam-engines and locomotives. . . . Mr. Cockerill was originally in partnership with the late King of Holland; but after his expulsion from Belgium, in 1830, Mr. C. purchased his share. Mr. C. died at Warsaw in 1840, and Seraing has since been disposed of to a company, styled 'La John Cockerill Societé,' by whom it is now worked." Nearby Liege was certainly influenced by all this industrialism. "The clouds of smoke usually seen from a distance hanging over it proclaim the manufacturing city, —the Birmingham of the Low Countries; and the dirty houses, murky atmosphere, and coal-stained streets. are the natural consequences of the branch of industry in which its inhabitants are engaged. The staple manufacture is that of firearms; Liege is, in fact, one great armoury" (p. 173). Lieber's infatuation with the lovely Julie Lessoine is treated by him in an 1833 essay and presented in his *Miscellaneous Writings I*, pp. 169–70 and in *The Stranger in America*, vol. 1, pp. 193–94.

17 June. Neerwinden was actually the site of two significant engagements. In the first, fought in 1693, the English under William III were routed by the French; in the second, in 1793, the French Revolutionary army was defeated by the Austrians. Lieber's derogatory opinion of the Town Hall (1448–69) of Louvain is challenged by that given in Murray (*Continent*, p. 183) where it is described as "one of the richest and most beautiful Gothic buildings in the world." The paintings in the Cathedral of St. Peter mentioned by Lieber were (p. 184): "2 altar-pieces by Hemling [Memling] — the *Martyrdom of St.*

Erasmus, a horrible subject, but treated with great propriety by the painter, and the *Last Supper,* a work of high merit. A *Holy Family,* by Quentin Matsys, in a side chapel at the back of the high altar . . . considered the great ornament of the church." Of the Vandenschrieck collection, Murray (p. 185) says that it was "one of the most select now in the Netherlands as regards native masters." In Malines (Mechelen), Lieber visited the Church of Notre Dame near the railway station which "contains behind the high altar the *Miraculous Draught of Fishes,* by Rubens, painted for the Guild of Fishmongers, and considered one of his most masterly works (p. 154)" and the Cathedral where he commented on the Van Dyck *Crucifixion* said by Murray (p. 153) to be "considered as one of the first pictures in the world, and gives the highest idea of Vandyck's powers: it shows that he had truly a genius for history painting, if he had not been taken off by portraits." Lieber noted that the Van Dyck appeared "spoiled" but, in fact, "the picture was carefully cleaned in 1848, and seems to have been little retouched" (p. 153).

18 June. Lieber's high opinion of Rubens' *Descent* in the Antwerp Cathedral is not contradicted by Murray (*Continent,* p. 139), who says "This picture, of all the works of Rubens, is that which has the most reputation." Lieber's distaste for the Cathedral's mighty tower is not evident in Murray's description (p. 142) but much of his information concerning it is dependent upon that guide, including the story of Napoleon, who "compared it to Mechlin lace" and the information that it should not be "regarded as a structure solely of stone, but rather as a framework of iron bars, with bits of stone strung upon them like beads, held together by copper bolts, the gaps and interstices being filled up with plaster, and the joints partly covered with lead." The Antwerp basins which attracted Lieber's interest were those created by Napoleon, who "laboured unceasingly to make Antwerp the first seaport and naval arsenal of the N., to render it the rival of London in its commerce, and of Portsmouth as a naval establishment" (p. 149). After the fall of Napoleon, "the two basins were allowed to remain for commercial purposes, and form a chief source of prosperity to the city. In 1843, 1560 vessels entered here." The Ottoveniusses of Lieber is Otto van Veen. The Antwerp citadel of the 16th century, its site now occupied by the city's art gallery, "was remarkable for the siege which it endured in 1832 [during the revolt of Belgium from Holland]" The siege is described in some detail in Murray (p. 149–50). The Dutch defenders were led by General Chasse and were besieged by the French allies of the Belgians under Marshal Gerard. After a two-month resistance, the citadel capitulated on 23 January 1833.

19 June. Murray (*Continent,* p. 143) regarded St. Jacques as "a very handsome church, even more splendid than the cathedral in its internal decorations of marbles, painted glass, carved wood and fine monuments." The picture that would have most attracted Lieber's attention would have been Rubens' *Holy Family* over the artist's tomb. According to Murray (p. 86) the trip by diligence from Antwerp to Rotterdam took twelve hours, including the passage of the Hollands-Diep, the Merwe, and the Maas by steamboat ferries. Dort is better known as Dordrecht and Lieber's reference to the city being of "Calvinistic memory" refers to it having been the site, in 1618–19, of the Synod of Dort.

The outcome of this theological gathering was "to declare the Calvinistic doctrines respecting predestination the established faith, and to condemn Arminius and his followers as heretics" (Murray, p. 81). Considering the Episcopalian Lieber's problems with local Presbyterians back home, this would have been of considerable interest to him.

20 June. Murray (*Continent*, pp. 5–6) informs us that "There is not, perhaps, a country in Europe which will more surprise an intelligent traveller than Holland," adding that "Holland may be considered in many respects as the most wonderful country, perhaps, under the sun: it is certainly unlike every other. What elsewhere would be considered impossible has here been carried into effect, and incongruities have been rendered consistent." Murray (p. 3) describes the diligence coaches of Holland as "roomy and convenient, travel at the rate of about 6 miles an hour, and are usually drawn by 3 horses yoked abreast." The roads "connecting the principal towns and villages of Holland are paved with bricks, and are excellent." In the Dutch capital of the Hague, "the Chambers of the States General or Dutch parliament, and several of the public offices, are situated in the Binnenhof [the inner court of the old Count's palace]. The public are freely admitted to the debates of the Second Chamber" (p. 30).

21 June. Murray (*Continent*, pp. 31–35) presents a detailed description of the Picture Gallery and Museum situated in the Maurits Huis (named after Prince Maurice of Nassau). Murray commences the itinerary with the painting that attracted Lieber's eye, the *Young Bull* by Paul Potter, calling it "his masterpiece, remarkable as one of the few examples in which the artist painted animals as large as life" and then launching into a lengthy and evocative description of this painting. It is curious, however, that Lieber's Journal ignores many of the great paintings then in the gallery, including Rembrandt's *Anatomy Lesson of Dr. Tulp,* Rubens' portraits of *Isabella Brant* and *Helena Forment,* as well as works by Poussin, Brueghel, Ostade, Dürer, Velasquez, Steen, etc., all of which are enumerated in Murray. See Lieber's entry for 22 June and commentary. Of the Japanese collection, Murray comments that "the rarities of Japan are unique, as the Dutch are the only European nation admitted into that country, and have therefore alone opportunities for curiosities. They give a most satisfactory insight into the manners and habits of that remote and highly civilized country." In the collection of historical relics, Lieber was especially taken by a portrait of van Spyke, "who blew up his vessel before Antwerp, 1831" and "the dress of William Prince of Orange on the day when he was murdered at Delft by Balthazar Geraarts. It is a plain grey leathern doublet, sprinkled with blood, pierced by the balls, and showing marks of the powder. By the side of it is the pistol used by the assassin, and two of the fatal bullets." Lieber's reference to "that brutal exhibition of breasts at the window" alludes to the still continuing presentation of prostitutes in the "red-light" districts of the cities of Holland and Belgium. Of the death of the De Witts, Murray (p. 30–31) notes "Between the Buitenhof (Outer Court) and the Vijverberg is an old gate-tower, called Gevangepoort (prison gate), remarkable as the place in which Cornelius De Witt was confined, 1672, on a false charge of conspiring to assassinate the Prince of Orange. The populace, incited to fury by the calumnies circulated against him and his brother John . . . broke into the prison . . . dragged them forth, and literally tore them to pieces, with ferocity more befitting wild beasts than human beings." Again, Lieber would have reflected on the dangers of an unbridled democracy gone to mob rule.

22 June. It is noteworthy that the paintings to which Lieber was most attracted, even when surrounded by great works of the Flemish Renaissance and Dutch Baroque, were those of the Italian masters of the Renaissance. Many of the paintings discussed in this entry are no longer at the Hague, e.g., the panels by Dirk de Haarlem (Dieric Bouts) are now in Brussels. The *trekschuit* by which Lieber traveled to Delft (some four miles from the Hague) was a canal barge pulled by a horse. According to Murray (*Continent*, p. 4) these barges "are nearly filled by a long low cabin, divided by a partition into two parts; the fore-cabin . . . appropriated to servants and common people; and the after-cabin, set apart for the better classes. . . . The barge is more commodious for night travelling and less fatiguing than the diligence, and the traveller may enjoy a comfortable sleep, provided the gnats permit." The funeral monument of William of Orange is in the New Church of Delft. The play attended by Lieber in the Hague would have been performed at the Schouwburg where "French pieces are performed 3 times a week, and Dutch twice; German are given but rarely" (p. 35).

24 June. "Polder is the name," writes Murray in *Continent*, p. 13, "given to a piece of ground below the level of the sea or river, which having once been a morass or lake . . . has been surrounded by embankments, and then cleared of water by pumps." Lieber's trip to the Haarlemer Meer allowed him to see the largest such project yet undertaken. The Lake of Haarlem no longer exists and the technological marvel that Lieber inspected caused its disappearance. According to Murray (p. 47–48): "Since the 15th cent. the body of water called the Lake of Harlem has spread itself over, and, in fact, swallowed up, a large portion of the districts known as the Rijn and Amstel-land. . . . The States General of Holland have sanctioned a plan for converting the bed of the lake into arable and pasture land. Operations were commenced in the spring of 1840, by forming a watertight double rampart or dyke and ring canal round the lake, into which the water is pumped up, to be discharged through the Katwijk, the Spaarne, and the sluices at Halfweg into the sea. . . . Three enormous pumping engines have been erected. . . . The engine called the Leeghwater (in honour of a celebrated Dutch engineer, who first proposed to drain the lake in 1623), which is near Warmond, was the first erected." Murray notes that the engines first went into operation in 1849 and provides a further technical description of the project that might be compared with the observations given in Lieber's *Journal*. Jean Baptiste Say (1767–1832) was the French economist, who published his *Treatise on Political Economy* in 1803 popularizing on the continent many of the theories of Adam Smith and stressing the importance of capital to production. Lieber used Say's text in his classes on political economy.

26 June. The Baumhaus marked the entrance to the inner harbor of Hamburg. Droschke were horse-drawn taxis or open hackney coaches. 13 Esplanade was the residence of the Lomnitz Family, with whom the Liebers were staying. On this see the addresses of the letters sent from Berlin by Lieber on 21, 26, and 29 October 1844. They likely were Oppenheimer relations.

29 June. The Free City of Hamburg, with a population of some 150,000 in Lieber's day, was a city rebuilding itself. "By the dreadful fire of 1842 Hamburg sustained a calamity unequalled in extent except by the fire of London. . . . Hamburg has profited to a certain extent by the calamity in the improvements introduced in laying out the new buildings, the widening of streets, the establishment of water-works, the construction of sewers, and the filing up of stagnant ditches" (Murray, *Continent*, p. 320).

30 June. Lieber evidently returned from his walk rather late and found the town gates barred (torsperre). "The gates of Hamburg are shut every evening at dusk, and a toll, increasing progressively every hour till 12, is demanded, after which persons may pass and repass all through the night, upon payment of 1 mark each" (Murray, *Continent*, p. 322). About the German traveling journeymen or Handwerksburschen, Murray (p. 217–18) says: "By an ancient regulation prevailing very generally throughout Germany and Switzerland, no apprentice can obtain his freedom and become a master until he has passed a certain number of years in travelling, and in exercising his calling in foreign parts . . . that he should gain experience in his craft, and learn the methods practiced in other countries besides his own, as well as some knowledge of the world" and "the characteristics of the class are, a pipe in the mouth without fail, and generally a stick in the hand, with an enormous knapsack on the back, from the sides of which a pair of boots are usually seen to project. These are wandering journeymen; they are often not undeserving objects of charity." The popular German song "Happy Wanderer" recalls this former tradition. They are still to be seen in Germany, usually wearling black corduroy pants and vests and large-brimmed, black hats. On the Vierländer costumes, Murray (p. 321) says: "The objects chiefly calculated to attract a stranger's attention are, first the Costumes seen in the streets of Hamburg. . . . The peasants who frequent the market wear a very picturesque attire; they are chiefly natives of a part of the Hamburg territory bordering on the Elbe, called Vierland [four lands or four villages], which is principally laid out in gardens, and supplies the market with vegetables." In a later passage (p. 330), Murray notes the Vierländers "are believed to be the descendants of a Dutch colony."

14[?] July. Lieber's reference to *Reminiscences* is unclear; perhaps he was referring to his own book of conversations with Berthold Niebuhr published in 1835 but there were books by several authors with this word in their title. Now a part of Hamburg, Altona was a distinct entity in Lieber's time. "Altona, which joins Hamburg and from the river [the Elbe] seems to form a part of it, though within the Danish territory [part of the Duchy of Holstein]. It has risen to great mercantile prosperity, perhaps to the prejudice of its neighbour, so that the Hamburgers say that its name agrees with its situation, as it is All-zu-nah (All too near). . . . It is the most commercial and populous town in Denmark next to Copenhagen" (Murray, *Continent*, p. 319).

12 July. Lüneburg (in the famous heath country) is described in Murray (*Continent,* p. 329) as "a most interesting old town: though decayed and little visited, it was formerly the capital of a duchy, has still 13,000 inhab., and retains the aspect of its primitive antiquity. . . . Many of the gable-faced houses are fine specimens of domestic Gothic; many of them retain in front the ornamented posts, with coats of arms, which marked the residence of the magistrates." The inn at which Lieber and his son stayed was described by Murray as being "clean and moderate." The walk to the geologically interesting Kalkberg predicts Oscar Lieber's later career as a geologist.

13 July. Friedrich Christoph Dahlmann (1785–1860) was both a politician and historian.

14 July. Karl Ritter (1779–1859) was a German geographer holding professorships in Frankfurt and Berlin whose application of the principles of comparative anatomy to geography in his *Erdkunde* (2nd ed., 1822–28) was a landmark in the field.

15 July. Lieber does not seem to have objected to the waltz as he had to both the polka and cancan he had witnessed in Paris. The waltz, evolved from German folk dances, had gained popularity among polite circles in the late 18th century and its graceful movements dominated the ballrooms of Lieber's day through the popular compositions of Johann Strauss Senior and his son, who formed his own orchestra in 1844.

17 July. Lieber's revulsion at the displays of masculine affection he witnessed at Wittenberge might have been unwarranted. In his introductory comments concerning German manners, Murray (*Continent,* p. 215) notes that: "In thus recommending to travellers the imitation of certain German customs, it is not meant, be it observed, to insist on the practice prevalent among the German men of saluting their male friends with a kiss on each side of the cheek. It is not a little amusing [for the English visitor] to observe this, with us feminine, mode of greeting, exchanged between two whiskered and mustachioed giants of 50 or 60." Had Lieber forgotten the customs of his native land in two decades of American residence? The handholding incident observed by Lieber on the streets of Wittemberge is left unexplained in Murray. The Hôtel de Stadt Rom, where Lieber found his initial Berlin lodgings, was on the city's major east-west boulevard, Unter den Linden, leading from the Royal Palace (the Stadtschloss) to the Brandenburg Gate. "The Inns [of Berlin] in general," says Murray (p. 332), "are not good." The Friedenssaule, mentioned by Lieber, was the "Friedens Denkmal, a pillar of granite, surmounted by Victory, by Rauch, erected in 1840, to commemorate the Peace which had then lasted 25 years" (Murray, p. 348). This monument was set up at the end of the three-mile long Friedrichstrasse, outside the Halle Gate and just beyond the Belle-Alliance Platz (now Mehring Platz).

19 July. Of Berlin's great Tiergarten park, Murray (*Continent,* p. 348) says: "Immediately beyond the Brandenburg Gate commences the Park (Thiergarten), an extensive plantation, interspersed with flower beds, with open spaces here and there, and ponds, coffee-houses, &c., among them, and dull, except when thronged with people on a fine

Sunday afternoon." Lieber's apparent fascination with military decorations would seem peculiar but for Murray (p. 213), who tells us that "A fondness for titles, orders, and high-sounding forms of address, which was ever the characteristic of the Germans, though perhaps less intense than formerly, has by no means yet disappeared. The German is scarcely happy until he can hang a little bit of striped riband from his button-hole, and every effort of interest and exertion is made to increase the number of them, and of the crosses and stars which dangle from them. This is the eagerly coveted object of every placeman. 'There are two things . . . that a *Beamte* cannot avoid — Death and the third class of the Red Eagle.'" Despite his long Americanization and republi-canization, Lieber seems to have retained this interest.

20 July. "The Museum [now called the Alte Museum], facing the Lustgarten. —This very handsome edifice was finished in 1830, from the designs of the distinguished architect Schinkel. . . . The collection which the Museum contains consists of —1. The Antiquar-ium, on the ground floor. —2. The Sculpture Gallery, on the 1st floor. —3. The Picture Gallery, on the upper story" (Murray, *Continent,* pp. 338–39). After the Glyptothek in Munich, this is the oldest museum building in Germany; it was severely damaged in WWII but its collections, by then dispersed into other later buildings on Berlin's Museum Island, were saved, for the most part. The *Amazon,* deemed by Lieber to appear out of place, apparently is the sculpture described by Murray (p. 338): "At the rt. side of the staircase [to the Museum] is a magnificent group in bronze, representing the combat of an Amazon with a tiger by Kiss. On the l. side is a horseman contending with a lion, by Rauch." Of the ancient works in the Sculpture Gallery, Murray (p. 339) notes: "The antiquities are principally composed of the collection of Cardinal Poli-gnac. It may be premised that few of them are above mediocrity as works of art, and that a large part of them are so much indebted to modern restorers. There is, how-ever, at least one exception. *The Boy Praying* is one of the finest antique bronze stat-ues in existence; it was found in the bed of the Tiber." All of this, of course, was before the ambitious archaeological expeditions at the end of the century which created in Berlin one of the greatest collections of ancient art in existence, now housed adjacent to Schinkel's museum in the Pergamon Museum. Karl C. A. H. von Kamptz had been the Prussian justice minister to whom Lieber had addressed an angry letter once he was safe in England in 1826. Regarding his accommodations at the Rome Hôtel, Lieber seems to have forgotten the beds of his German youth. "One of the first complaints of an Englishman on arriving in Germany," writes Murray (p. 200), "will be directed against the beds. . . . A German bed is made only for one; it may be compared to an open wooden box, often hardly wide enough to turn in, and rarely long enough for any man of moderate stature to lie down in. . . . The place of blankets is sometimes supplied by a light puffy feather-bed, which is likely to be kicked off, and forsaken in his utmost need by the sleeper, who, on awaking in cold weather, finds himself frozen: should it remain in its position in warm weather, the opposite alternative is that of suffocation beneath it."

23 July. Much of this entry with Lieber's conversation with King Friedrich Wilhelm IV is given in German; the verbatim entry is presented in the Appendix A. An English translation is presented in Perry, *Life and Letters of Francis Lieber,* pp. 185–88. The King's Palace (Stadtschloss) has disappeared, having been severely damaged in WWII and, then, totally removed in 1950 to make way for Marx-Engels Platz and the Palace of the Republic (DDR) of 1973. At this writing, it is proposed to reconstruct this central feature of old Berlin. Thanks to a painting (see illus. 5) by Franz Krüger, we can enter the royal study with Lieber. Krüger's painting, *King Friedrich Wilhelm IV in his Study in the Königliches Schloss, Berlin,* was executed ca. 1846 and represents the Prussian monarch wearing his "common undress" uniform, casually leaning against his desk, a "large table of plain oakwood" in a vaulted chamber filled with small paintings and curios. The room and its furnishings were, in fact, designed by the great German architect Karl Friedrich Schinkel for the use of the then crown prince between 1824–26. Johann Louis Tellkampf was a German emigrant to America who would precede Lieber on the faculty at Columbia University.

31 July. The Knoblauch family house (built 1765 and now a museum) is one of the few buildings in central Berlin to have endured the destruction of WWII. It is located on Poststrasse near the old Molkenmarkt. On Raczynsky's collection, see the commentary for 1 August. The old Turnplatz at Hasenheide, recalling to Lieber his days as a lieutenant of Friedrich Jahn, was just to the south of the city, outside the Halle Gate. It is located just to the north of the present old city airport of Tempelhof (famous from the 1948 Berlin Airlift).

1 August. According to Murray (*Continent,* p. 345) Count Raczynsky's Gallery contained "interesting specimens of modern German art — the finished Sketch of Kaulbach's Battle of the Huns; a Sposalizio by Overbeck; Sohn's Two Leonoras; Leopold Robert's last work, &c.; Cornelius's Christ in Limbo. Also fine specimens of Bellini, Francia, Luini, Steinle, Bendeman, and Führich." Shortly after Lieber's trip, the gallery was relocated from Unter den Linden into new quarters in the Exercier-Platz, outside the Brandenburg Gate and adjacent to the studio of the artist Peter von Cornelius (1783–1867). Wilhelm von Kaulbach (1805–74) was court painter to Ludwig I of Bavaria from 1834 and a member of the Berlin Academy from 1842. His monumental historical compositions drew upon the literary themes of Goethe, Klopstock, and Wieland. On Cornelius, see the entry for 29 April. The site of this later Raczynsky Gallery and Cornelius' studio is now occupied by the German Reichstag, built 1884–94. Concerning the Humboldt villa outside Berlin, Murray (pp. 347–48) says "At Tegel, 7 m. beyond the Oranienburg Gate, is the seat of the late Wm. von Humboldt. In the garden is a monument to his wife, a statue of Hope upon a pillar, the work of Thorwaldsen." The Humboldts' Schloss Tegel was constructed by Schinkel between 1822–24; its park houses the tombs of both Wilhelm and Alexander von Humboldt marked by Thorwaldsen's monument of Hope. Added insight into Lieber's visit to the Humboldt villa can be found in his 1859 Humboldt memorial address, given in his *Miscellaneous Writings I*, p. 398.

2 August. A gavonoplastic copy makes use of electrolysis to reproduce sculptures by coating them with a thin layer of metal.

3 August. The University of Berlin (now the Humboldt University) was founded in 1809 at the instigation of Wilhelm von Humboldt. It was installed in the former palace of Prince Heinrich, the brother of Friedrich II, on Unter den Linden. In addition to his paintings, Cornelius also executed illustrations for both Goethe's *Faust* and the medieval *Nibelungenlied*. The often melancholic, Julia Ward Howe, whose letter Lieber transcribed, was fluent in German; in an 1844 letter, Lieber had noted that she "speaks German as if she had grown up near one of the 'lovely German mill-brooks'" (Freidel, *Francis Lieber*, p. 204). The complete German text of this letter is given in the Appendix B. Much of this letter was transcribed by Lieber on his visit to the Silesian town of Züllichau on 5–11 August. On the location of Züllichau, see comment for the 5 August entry. Julia's brother Henry (the Heinrich of the letter) had died of typhoid fever in October 1840. Julia had married Samuel Gridley Howe in April 1843 and the couple soon after set off for Europe, sister Annie in tow. They were joined later by another sister, Louisa, before Julia gave birth to Julia Romana in Rome on 12 March 1844. Johann Gottfried Herder (1744–1803), whose works Julia Howe requested Lieber to acquire for her, was a philosopher, theologian and literary critic, an associate of both Goethe and Kant; he was a collector of German folk songs and folk tales and in his later years challenged Kant's philosophical positions.

4 August. Crossen (now Krosno Odrzanskie) was in Lower Silesia, since World War II a part of Poland.

5 August. Züllichau (now Sulechów) was in East Brandenburg, since World War II a part of Poland. Apparently Lieber's parents and several of his siblings had relocated to this rural town. On his brother Edward's inability to immediately recognize him, see the entry for 26 August.

12 August. The Berlin residence of the Lieber family was an old building with a stepped gable located on the east side of Breitestrasse just down from the Marstall (the royal stables). These buildings were destroyed in World War II. The Breitestrasse which led to the gates of the Royal Palace was one of the primary streets of the old city. Four years after Lieber's visit, this street was the scene of bloody popular demonstrations before the royal palace; Oscar Lieber was among those who took part.

13 August. According to Murray (*Continent*, pp. 345–46), "the Gewerbe Schule, School for Trade, is an establishment of a kind only recently introduced into Great Britain. It is a school for instructing gratuitously promising young artisans in drawing, modelling, and other branches of the fine arts calculated to be of practical use in their trade, with a view of improving the designs of articles of furniture and patterns in stuffs of all sorts, and the like." It was located on Niederwallstrasse on the site of the present St. Joseph's Hospital. The Singakadamie, writes Murray (p. 346) "is a private association of from 200 to 300 amateurs, male and female, of the respectable and upper classes, who meet together to practice every week during the whole year, and give annually several delightful concerts, to which the public are admitted, in the tasteful Grecian building of the Academy, designed by Ottmar, behind the Grand Guardhouse [Neue Wache]. The performance of sacred vocal music is probably not carried to greater perfection in any part of Europe." The Singakademie building, now the Maxim Gorki Theater, was constructed in 1827.

14 August. The Köpenickerfeld is now occupied by the Neukölln district of Berlin. Lieber's complaint about the monument at Kreuzberg refers to the one standing on "a low sandhill [½ mile south of the Halle Gate] called the Kreutzberg, almost the only eminence near Berlin, and commanding a tolerable view of it. It is named from a Gothic Cross of cast iron, 160 ft. high, upon its summit, called Volks Denkmal (People's Monument), erected by the late king [Friedrich Wilhelm III] as a memorial of Prussia's recovery of independence from the French. . . . Schinkel designed it, and Rauch and Tieck executed the statues of Prussian warriors in the niches, and the bas-reliefs representing the principal victories gained by the Prussians" (Murray, *Continent,* p. 348). The production of *Midsummer Night's Dream* was probably that first staged Berlin in 1843 by Ludwig Tieck.

15 August. Of the Gustavus Adolphus memorial by which Lieber passed, Murray (*Continent,* p. 435) says: "About a mile out of the town [of Lützen], a rude unsquared block of granite . . . is set up, shaded by a few poplars, and further distinguished by a Gothic canopy of cast iron, raised over it in 1838. This is called the stone of the Swede (Schwedenstein), and marks the spot where Gustavus Adolphus fell, in the midst of the battle of Lützen, 6 Nov. 1632."

17 August. Lieber's tale of the miller of Hanau is explained in Murray (*Continent,* p. 428): it refers to the Battle of Hanau fought in 1813 against the Austrians and Bavarians by Napoleon on his retreat from Leipzig. "The loss of the allies exceeded that of the French; it would have been greater, but for the manoeuvre of a miller, who, observing the German infantry hard pressed by a body of French cavalry, suddenly let the water into his millstream, between the two parties, and thus secured the retreat of his own friends." In Frankfurt, Lieber saw "just outside the Friedburg Gate . . . the monument erected by the king of Prussia to the memory of the Hessian soldiers killed in the siege of Frankfurt, 1792" (Murray, p. 498). Johann Heinrich Dannecker (1758–1841), of whom Lieber became a great admirer, was a pre-eminent neo-classical German sculptor, a pupil of Canova and a rival of Thorwaldsen. Dannecker's *Statue of Ariadne on the Panther,* of 1804–14, which so captivated Lieber, has been destroyed. Dannecker's terracotta model for it is in the Staatsgalerie in Stuttgart (see illus. 6). The marble original merited a special paragraph in Murray (p. 498) where it was described as being "in the garden

of Mr. Bethman, near the Friedburg Gate," and as being "the great boast of Frankfurt, and [which] deserves to be ranked among the distinguished productions of modern art. The artist," adds Murray, "whose works are little known in England, was a
native of Würtemberg. The statue is placed in a pavilion built for its reception, and is
usually shown from 10 to 1 daily." In the 1854 edition of the *Encyclopedia Americana,*
it was noted that Dannecker was "professor sculpture at Stuttgart; one of the most eminent of modern sculptors" and that "after many other works, he at length began, in
marble, in 1809, his Ariadne riding upon a panther, as the bride of Bacchus; and in
1816, this was sent to Mr. de Bethmann, at Frankfort. It is one of the most beautiful
works of modern times." The Public Library, according to Murray (p. 498), is a handsome building, facing the Main [River], close to the Ober Main Thor. . . . In the
entrance-hall is a marble statue of Goethe, by Marchesi." Of the Goethe birthplace in
the Hirschengraben, Murray (p. 498) comments that "his father's coat of arms, which,
by a curious coincidence, bears the poetical device of 3 lyres, still remains over the door."
The opera which Lieber attended and found boring was *Fernando Cortez* composed
by Gaspare Spontini in 1809; it was a particular favorite of the former Prussian King
Friedrich Wilhelm III.

18 August. The Städel Museum is the great art gallery of Frankfurt. Lieber's comments
on Overbeck's *Christianity and the Arts* may have been partially derived from that given
in Murray (*Continent,* p. 497): "Considered a chef d'oeuvre of the artist: all the heads
are portraits of persons renowned as authors, divines, or artists. In this production of
elaborate pedantry the traveller will easily discover how much the artist has borrowed
from Raphael's School of Athens and Dispute of the Sacrament."

19 August. The Bergstrasse runs between Darmstadt and Heidelberg. Murray (*Continent,* p. 525) describes it as "celebrated for its beauty," and so called "because it runs
along the base of a range of hills, which form the E. boundary of the valley of the Rhine.
Its chief beauty arises from the fertility and high cultivation of the district it overlooks,
rich in its luxuriant vegetation of vines and maize, enlivened by glimpses of the Rhine,
and bounded by the outline of the Vosges mountains in France. . . . The villages and
towns are beautifully situated at the foot of the mountains, overhung by vine-covered
slopes, and embosomed in orchards, which extend in cheerful avenues along the road
from one town to another." No wonder that Lieber was distressed that his English traveling companion was too preoccupied to enjoy the scenery. The caps to which Lieber refers
were probably similar to those still worn by Amish or Mennonite women. Mittermaier,
with whom Lieber visited in Heidelberg, had sufficient celebrity to be mentioned in
Murray (p. 530): "It is as a school of law and medicine that Heidelberg [University] is
most distinguished. Many of the professors at the present time are men of great reputation: . . . Mittermeyer in criminal law." In a letter written to his wife on this date
(extract given in Perry, *Life and Letters of Francis Lieber,* pp. 188–89), Lieber bemoans
"Is there no escape from Columbia" and proceeds to outline the perils of a professorship in Prussia. He concludes by pleading, "Boston, I say, God grant me Boston." He

would have been very happy in Heidelberg, however, as we learn in a 2 February 1845 letter he wrote to Mittermaier shortly after his return to America. In it Lieber proclaims, "Would that I had received an offer from your dear Heidelberg! One sometimes falls in love with women at first sight; I thus loved Heidelberg" (Perry, *Life and Letters of Francis Lieber,* p. 194). It is small wonder that Lieber would dream of a position on the faculty. He would also have appreciated the assurance given in Murray (p. 534) that "Heidelberg is a cheap place of residence, provisions being moderate and abundant. An English gentleman, who resided here in 1834, states that his expenses for the year to have been but 380£., including horses, carriage, house-rent, and servants."

20 August. "As an edifice the University is not remarkable. It is a plain and not very large house in the small square (Ludwigs Platz) near the middle of the town" (Murray, *Continent,* p. 530). On the Woodhouse family, see the entry for 14 April.

21 August. Lieber's Kaiserstuhl was probably the Königstuhl described in Murray (*Continent,* p. 533) as "the highest hill in this district [which] lies behind the town and castle. The summit may be reached in 1 or 1 ½ hr.'s walk . . . and the view is the most extensive in the neighbourhood. A lofty tower has been erected for the convenience of visitors, who often repair hither to see the sun rise, and if possible to extend the limits of the panorama, which includes the valleys of the Rhine and Neckar, the Odenwald, Haardt Mountains on the W., the Taunus on the N.W., the ridge of the Black Forest on the S., with the Castle of Ebersteinberg, near Baden, and the spire of Strassburg Minster, 90 m. off. There is a small tavern near the top, called Kohlhof."

26 August. Lieber's "big tun" was that described in Murray (*Continent,* p. 531): "In a cellar under the castle is the famous Heidelberg Tun, constructed 1751; it is the largest wine-cask in the world, 36 ft. long and 24 ft. high; being capable of holding 800 hogsheads or 283,200 bottles, which is far less, after all, than the dimensions of one of the porter vats of a London brewer. In former days, when the tun was filled with the produce of the vintage, it was usual to dance on the platform on the top. It has, however, remained empty since 1769, more than half a century." Opposite the tun sits a sculpture of the court fool Perkeo, dating from ca. 1728. On Lieber's comments about recognition, see the entry for 5 August. Mannheim had been subject to numerous destructions in various conflicts with France. Lieber's low view of its present condition is echoed in Murray (pp. 515–16): "To the cause stated above the modern town owes its present rectangular and monotonous regularity. It consists of 11 straight streets, crossed by 10 other streets at right angles to them and, at equal distances, an arrangement which renders it difficult for a stranger to distinguish one part of the town from another. . . . Mannheim does not possess many objects of interest, and need not detain a traveller long."

27 August. Lieber offered a comparison between the beauties of the Rhine and the Hudson Valleys in *The Stranger in America,* vol. 1, pp. 270–77. Even before Wagner, Murray (*Continent,* p. 514) could observe that "the country round Worms was the favourite theme of the Minnesänger, who speak of it under the name of Wonnegau (Land of Joy). It is partly the scene of the Nibelungenlied." It is curious that the one work which Lieber wished to see in Mayence [Mainz] was the modern statue by Thorwaldsen. Actually, his reasons may have had more to do with the subject than the sculpture. Gutenberg would have special significance for a "publicist." It is, perhaps, for the same reason that the statue received comment in Murray (p. 293): "Mainz was the cradle of the art of Printing, and the birthplace and residence of John Gensfleisch, called Gutenberg or Guttemberg, the discoverer or inventor of moveable types. In 1837 a bronze statue of Guttemberg, modelled by Thorwaldsen, a Dane, and cast at Paris by a Frenchman, was erected in the open space opposite the Theatre. The expenses . . . were defrayed by subscriptions from all parts of Europe." At Biberich was "the Château of the Duke of Nassau, of red sandstone, with a circular projection in the centre . . . one of the handsomest palaces on the Rhine, though now somewhat dilapidated" (Murray, p. 289). According to the same source (p. 265), "the castle of Rheineck, consisting of an ancient watch-tower and a modern castellated residence adjoining, built at lavish expense, by Lassaulx, for Profr. Bethman-Hollweg, of Bonn. The architectural taste displayed in this edifice is very questionable." The University of Bonn had been established in 1818 by the king of Prussia and already had achieved a significant scholarly reputation. "Among those who have already filled chairs here, the most distinguished are Niebuhr and A. W. Schlegel, both dead" (Murray, p. 259). It was, of course, the memorial to his old mentor that demanded Lieber's attention and also a sentence from Murray (p. 260): "In the Churchyard outside the Sternen Thor, Niebuhr the historian is buried." The Latin quotation is from a poem to Virgil upon the death of Quintilus and is found in the *Odes of Horace*, 1.24.1–2. Of the Cologne (Köln) Cathedral, Murray (pp. 246–47) notes that "Had the original plan been completed . . . it would have been the St. Peter's of Gothic architecture. Even in its present state, it is one of the finest and purest Gothic monuments in Europe," adding that "from 1824 to 1842, 215,000 thalers had been laid out on the building by the late and present Kings of Prussia. . . . A fresh impulse was given to the works on the accession of the present King, who contributed more largely to its funds, and on the 4th Sept. 1842 laid the foundation stone of the transept."

30 August. Although Napoleon's celebratory column was left standing in Place Vendôme, his bronze statue had been pulled down and melted in the Restoration. It had been replaced by a figure of Victory, sculpted by Seurre, cast in 1831 from cannon captured at Algiers (Murray, *Paris*, p. 243). The celebrated Tuilleries Gardens, between the Louvre and the Place de la Concorde, according to Murray (p. 244) "have long been the favourite resort of Parisians of every class. At all times of the day children and their nurses swarm, and in the afternoon during spring and autumn, and in the evening during summer, the walks and chairs are filled with crowds of gaily dressed people, enjoying the fresh air and the pleasure of seeing and being seen."

31 August. Lieber's earlier visits to the Louvre in May had been cursory and this return finally brought him into contact with some of the greatest paintings in its collections.

1 September. Paris was left unfortified ever since Louis XIV had pulled down its constricting medieval walls. Newer fortifications were discussed but "nothing was however done until 1841, when under Louis Philippe £6,000,000 was voted for constructing a complete system of fortifications. . . . The works were executed in three years" (Murray, *Paris,* p. 117). On his 15–mile railway trip to St. Germain-en-Laye, Lieber passed through these installations.

3 September. The hospital for the blind, the Quinze Vingts, was located in the Rue de Charenton, in faubourg St. Antoine. Murray (*Paris,* p. 220) says: "Poor blind people with their families are maintained here, to the number of 300; and there are 4 times as many out-door pensioners. The original hospital of Quinze Vingts was established by St. Louis for 15x20 blind persons, and stood between the Palais Royal and the present Louvre. It was removed to its present site in 1780." The Opera Comique, on the Place des Italiens, is described by Murray (p. 238) as "a heavy building with a handsome saloon," featuring lighter operas, and furnished with "stalls, fauteuils d'orchestre or de galerie."

4 September. On the *Galignani's Messenger,* see the notes to the entry for 4 June. The Canadian Revolution refers to the 1837–38 revolts of the French citizens of Lower Canada and the simultaneous uprising against the governing officials in Upper Canada led by William Mackenzie.

6 September. Generally acknowledged as being the first example of the Gothic style, St. Denis was restored in 1813, but so inadequately that three years after Lieber's visit a new restoration was initiated under the direction of Viollet-le-Duc. Of these transformations, Murray (*Paris,* p. 102) says: "The restoration of the church was undertaken during the Restoration, but in such execrable taste that much of the work then done has since been removed. Louis Philippe repaired and restored it in better taste."

7 September. On the Théatre Francais and Rachel, see the commentary to the entry for 4 June.

8 September. The Messageries Royales, from which Lieber's diligence departed, was located on the Rue Notre Dame des Victoires. On these coach services, see the commentary for the entry for 4 June.

9 September. Of Nancy, Murray (*France,* p. 524) says: "It has been styled the prettiest town in France; it is, at least, clean and orderly, and is distinguished for the regularity and uniformity of its buildings and breadth of its streets." Concerning the Lesczynski monument, the guidebook notes (p. 524–25): "The Place Royale is . . . ornamented with a statue of Stanislas Lesczynski, ex-king of Poland, to whom Nancy is indebted for its modern aspect and architectural embellishments. After abdicating the throne of Poland (1735), he resided here many years as Duke of Lorraine and Bar until his death (1766), when these domains fell to the crown of France."

10 September. Lieber's shock at women doing field work should be compared with his comments in *The Stranger in America*, vol. 1, pp. 100–01. Strassburg, according to Murray (*France*, p. 527) had a population of 64,242 in 1854. Murray notes that "though it has now for a long time been united to France . . . yet it bears all the external aspect of a German town in the appearance of the streets and houses, and in the costume and language of its inhabitants. The statue of Clever mentioned by Lieber was probably that of General Kleber of Strassburg whose body was removed from the Cathedral "to a vault in the centre of the Place Kleber, and a monument has been erected over it" (Murray, p. 530). According to Murray (p. 529), "the statue of Guttemberg, on the Marche aux Herbes, now called Place Guttemberg, was modelled by David [d'Angiers], and it appears, on the whole, not inferior to the one in Mayence [see Lieber's comments for 27 August]." Murray's guide (p. 529) notes that "the earliest attempt at printing was made at Strassburg (about 1436) by John Guttemberg, who finally brought his invention to perfection at Mayence." The Cathedral or Münster, which seems to have disappointed Lieber on this visit, is described by Murray (p. 527) as "one of the noblest Gothic edifices in Europe, remarkable for its spire, the highest in the world, rising 474 ft. above the pavement; 24 ft. higher than the great Pyramid of Egypt, and 140 ft. higher than St. Paul's." Of the sculptures over the portal, which Lieber did not like, Murray says (p. 528): "Although the greater portion of these carvings are modern, the originals having been destroyed by the democrats of the Revolution . . . they have been restored with a perfect exactness, with great truth of sentiment, and good taste, by MM. Kirstein of Haumack. The group of the Deathof the Virgin is executed in a masterly manner." Lieber's protestant church was that of St. Thomas. The tomb of Marshal Saxe is described in Murray (pp. 528–29) as "erected to his memory by Louis XV, the masterpiece of the sculptor Pigalle, and the result of 25 years' labour. It represents the General descending with a calm mien to the grave, while France, personified in a beautiful female figure, endeavors to detain him, and at the same time to stay the threatening advance of Death. It is looked upon as a very successful effort of the chisel; though somewhat theatrical, there is a tenderness of expression about the female figure which is truly charming. The monument was saved from destruction at the Revolution by a citizen of Strassburg . . . who covered it up with bundles of hay and straw, the church having been turned into a straw warehouse." The retour coach that Lieber took to Stuttgart meant that he had to pay for its return journey (see Murray, *Southern Germany*, p. 3).

11 September. Lieber's hotel in Stuttgart, the König von England, is described in Murray, *Southern Germany*, p. 5, as being "fair." Concerning the Schiller monument, Murray (p. 7) says: "In front of the Stiftskirche, near the Old Palace, stands a colossal bronze Statue of Schiller, designed by Thorwaldsen and cast at Munich: it is rather stiff and heavy." Of the work of Dannecker, Murray (p. 6) comments: "The Hospital Church contains a statue (in clay) of Christ, by Dannecker." The physical situation of Stuttgart also attracted Murray (p. 6): "It is prettily situated in the small valley of the Nesen brook, surrounded by hills of no great height, entirely covered on their slopes with vineyards, and rising so close to the town as to impend over it. . . . Their vicinity is, indeed, injurious to the health of the town, preventing a free circulation of air, and allowing the exaltations from the valley to stagnate and produce a kind of malaria, at some seasons." The Fine Arts Museum was a new addition; in 1843, Murray simply said (p. 7): "A New Building (Kunstanstalten Gebaude) is in progress in the Neckar Strasse, to contain collections of works of art; among them a series of casts from the works of Thorwaldsen."

12 September. The Eilwagen of South Germany was a diligence and the equivalent to the Schnellpost of Prussia.

13 September. In Lieber's day, Munich had a population of almost 96,000. Murray (*Southern Germany*, p. 35) tells us that "Since the beginning of the present century, Munich has thrust out new quarters and suburbs beyond the line of its former walls, its population has nearly doubled itself, and the number of fine buildings, which have risen up on all sides within that period, have scarcely a parallel in another European capital. . . . There are few capitals in Europe N. of the Alps which will better repay the traveller for a visit, or hold out greater inducements for a prolonged stay, than Munich at the present time." Lieber was to spend six days in the city. The Hôtel Bayerischer Hof, in which Lieber lodged while in Munich, was located on Promenaden Platz and received a better than average review by Murray (p. 34): "new and good, and not extravagant, though not cheap: improved since its commencement, when complaints were justly made, especially of bad attendance [staffing]. It is an immense establishment, contains 123 rooms and nearly 200 beds, and is said to have cost 40,000£." Of the domestic architecture of the city, noted by Lieber, Murray (p. 34) says: "The houses were built in the quaint but not unpicturesque style . . . their fronts, crowded with windows, are ornamented either with stucco patterns and scroll-work, or with rude fresco paintings." The German Christoph Wilibald von Gluck (1714–87) composed two operas with the name Iphigenia in their title, *Iphigenie en Aulide* (1774) and *Iphigenie en Tauride* (1779) and it is unclear to which Lieber was referring.

14 September. Lieber spent most of his time in Munich inspecting its artistic offerings, both old and modern. According to Murray (*Southern Germany*, p. 35), "Munich owes its present prominent position, as the seat of the fine arts, mainly to one individual, the reigning monarch, Lewis of Bavaria. Himself a poet of no mean skill, he has made the study of art his favourite pursuit from early youth, and even while Crown Prince, had formed a first-rate gallery of sculpture . . . and a valuable cabinet of paintings; sparing neither pains nor expense in the accumulation of such treasures." Not only did Ludwig assemble worthy collections of ancient sculptures and old master paintings but he encouraged the arts of his own day. "There are, probably, not fewer than from 600 to 800 artists resident in Munich at the present time, either attracted thither from other countries, by the encouragement thus held out to them, or bred and educated on the spot. The Prince who has originated all this is not a solitary patron of art, since he has created a taste, or set a fashion, which has spread over his own country through all parts of Germany" (Murray, p. 35). Among the artists' studios open to visitors in Munich was that of Kaulbach in Tatenbacher Strasse in the suburb of St. Anna Vorstadt. On Kaulbach, see commentary to the entry for 1 August. Murray (p. 55) says that Kaulbach "confines himself almost entirely to oil-painting. One of his greatest achievements is the cartoon of the destruction of Jerusalem. . . . The studios of the painters Schnorr and Hess, and of Schwanthaler the sculptor, are equally interesting." "The Basilica of St. Bonifacius, in the Karl Strasse," according to Murray (p. 37), "nearly opposite the Glyptothek, founded 1835, to be finished in 1845, exceeds in size and splendour any of the modern ecclesiastical edifices of Munich. It is built in the Romanesque style, and resembles the Church of St. Paul (fuori delle Mura) at Rome." Of its fresco decorations, Murray remarks that "the lower series, devoted to the history of St. Boniface, are designed and painted by Hess and his pupils. The departure of the Saint from his native shore (England) is the work of the master himself; and for colour, feeling, and expression one of the finest frescoes of modern times." Concerning the works of Schwanthaler, Murray (p. 55) describes "The Bronze Foundry of Stieglmaier, 1 mile out of town, on the Nymphenburg road, [which] bids fair to become the most eminent in Europe. A temporary wooden building adjoining, at present contains the model of the colossal figure of Bavaria, 44 feet high, the work of Schwanthaler." The statue of Huss was, of course, that of John Huss (1373–1415), the Bohemian reformer and religious martyr, the precursor of Martin Luther. Ziska was John Zizka (1376–1424), the Hussite general and major figure in the Bohemian civil war during the reign of Wenceslaus IV; Ottakar probably refers to Ottakar II, son of Wenceslaus I, a famous and legendary Bohemian town founder, supporter of law and order, and encourager of German immigration. The sculpture of Jean Paul was probably a portrait of Jean Paul Richter (1763–1825), the romantic writer to whom Lieber had sent the manuscript of his "Wine Songs" in 1825; Richter's encouraging reply unfortunately went astray and Lieber, lacking the hoped-for support, gave up his poetical aspirations. The friezes for the building opposite the Glyptothek would have been for the present Antikensammlungen, begun as an exhibition hall in 1838 and completed in 1848. Murray provides a lengthy description of the Residenz Palace (pp. 37–39). The frescoes by Schnorr were in the Festbau portion of the palace, "representing the chief events in the lives of Charlemagne, Frederick Barbarossa, and Rudolph of Hapsburg" and covered the three halls preceding the throne room. That room was "decorated with 14 colossal whole-length statues in gilt bronze of the Electors and Princes of Bavaria, in the costume of the time in which they lived, 10 ft. high, designed by Schwanthaler and cast by Stieglmaier."

15 September. As Murray (*Southern Germany,* p. 56) points out, the technique of lithography was a Bavarian innovation, ca. 1800, "and the art still maintains great perfection here . . . [and] good specimens may be seen at the shop of Baron Cotta, the bookseller. . . . Promenaden Strasse." Murray gives (pp. 41–52) a detailed itinerary of the Alte Pinakothek, which opened in 1826.

It is interesting that Lieber's eye ignored the many masterpieces then attributed to Rubens, Giotto, Fra Angelico, Dürer, Cranach, Rembrandt, Murillo, Velasquez, Domenichino, Titian, Correggio, etc. and settled its attention on the Francesco Francia in the private cabinet of the king of Bavaria (Room IX). The stylistic resemblance of this artist's manner to that of the early Raphael may have occasioned this but Lieber, on this visit, seems to have ignored the several Raphaels in the museum, including the *Canigiani Holy Family* and the lovely *Tempi Madonna;* but see his reappraisals of 17 [18] September.

16 September. Lieber visited a different portion of the Royal Residence on this day — the yet to be completed New Palace to which the public was admitted at fixed hours. Murray (*Southern Germany,* p. 38) describes: "The ground floor consists of state apartments, whose walls are painted in fresco, with subjects from the ancient national epic . . . the Nibelungenlied. They are the productions of Julius Schnorr, and are masterly efforts of historical painting. Some years must elapse before they can be finished."

17 September. The All Saints Chapel lay behind the Residenz and had been constructed in the "Byzantine manner" by Leo von Klenze. In contrast to Lieber's dislike of the building's overly decorated interior, Murray (*Southern Germany,* p. 37) found it "entirely painted in fresco, on a gold ground, by Hess and his pupils . . . deserving of minute attention. The subjects are from the Old and New Testaments. . . . The effect of the gold ground is rich without appearing glaring, and notwithstanding the splendid character of the internal decorations, all that is not painting or gold within the building being marble or scagliola, its general character is solemn." On Lieber's return to the Stieglmaier Foundry, see the commentary for 14 September. "The Parish Church of Maria Hilf in the Suburb Au is a building in the pointed Gothic style, with high lancet windows, and reflects credit on the architect Ohlmüller. A chief ornament of this church are 19 large windows of modern painted glass, containing subjects from the Life of the Virgin, designed by living painters and executed under the direction of Hess" (Murray, p. 37). The Hofgarten, adjacent to the Residenz Palace, was "a square enclosure, planted with rows of trees [and] surrounded by an open Arcade lined with Fresco paintings by modern German artists. . . . One side of the Hofgarten is occupied by the Bazaar, which includes cafes, restaurants, shops, &c" (Murray, p. 39).

17[18] September. It is with this entry that Lieber loses a day in his reckoning, not recognizing his mistake until preparing to leave Vienna more than ten days later. Of all the treasures of Munich, the magnificent collection of ancient sculpture housed in the Glyptothek proved to have the greatest impact upon Lieber.

The temple-like Glyptothek, occupying the northern side of the Königsplatz "is a very chaste and classical edifice of the Ionic order, erected by Von Klenze for the present King [Ludwig I]; who, while Crown Prince, formed the very interesting and valuable collection deposited in it entirely at his own expense" (Murray, *Southern Germany,* p. 39). That the king continued a very personal association with his collection is made clear by the fact that "on Wednesday and Saturday it is closed, except when the King is out of town. No one is allowed to draw in the gallery without especial permission from the king." In Hall V, Lieber seems to have been particularly taken by the third-century BC *Barbarini Faun*, "a masterly production of ancient art," supposed by Murray (p. 40) "to have been executed by Praxitiles or Scopas." In Hall VI, he found the *Ilioneus* "wonderful" as did Murray (p. 40–41) who provided a discussion of this "gem of the gallery . . . thought to have belonged to the collection of Emperor Rudolph II. at Prag [Prague], dispersed after his death. It was accidentally discovered in the yard of a stone-mason who had provided it with a head and arms to fit." Interestingly, Lieber does not discuss one of the great glories of the Museum, the celebrated sculptures from the East and West Pediments of the Temple of Athena Aphaia at Aegina discovered by several Englishmen in 1811 and purchased for the Munich collection before they could be acquired for the British Museum. Of the modern interior decorations of the Glyptothek, Murray (p. 41) comments that "Rooms VII. and VIII. are decorated with modern frescoes by Cornelius, and his scholars Zimmermann and Schlottbauer. The subjects in the VIIth called the Hall of the Gods, are taken from heathen mythology; those in the VIIIth, the Trojan Hall, from Homer's Iliad." Lieber does not mention either the building of the Antikensammlungen or the lovely Propyläen which complete the architecture of the Königsplatz; the former was not completed until 1848 and the latter not until 1862. Lieber's return to the Pinakothek brought to his attention the Raphaels he had omitted earlier as well as a celebrated work by Titian. The Munich Loggia, in the Odeonsplatz west of the Hofgarten, was designed by Professor F. Gärtner as a copy of the Loggia dei Lanzi of Florence. "The Church of St. Lewis (Ludwigskirche)," according to Murray (pp. 36–37), "completed 1842, was designed by Professor Gärtner, in the style of Gothic called Byzantine or Romanesque, which is common in the N. of Italy. . . . A fine fresco of Cornelius, an immense painting of the Last Judgment, 64 ft. high, occupies the entire end wall." Obviously, Lieber's eye was more critical. The Follen who was with Lieber in Dresden 20 years earlier probably was Charles Follen (1796–1840), a student friend, whose liberal political views forced his flight to America in 1824. Follen preceded Lieber as director of the Boston gymnasium and then went on to a professorship in German at Harvard. His vocal abolitionist advocacy caused his dismissal and he turned to the Unitarian ministry. Follen died in a shipwreck.

18[19] September. "The Leuchtenberg Gallery of Pictures, formed by Eugene Beauharnois, Viceroy of Italy, afterwards Duke of Leuchtenberg, is a small but very choice collection, well worthy of attention. It is feared they may be removed to Russia. The gem of it, one of the most remarkable productions of the Spanish School is Murillo's Virgin and Child" (Murray, *Southern Germany,* p. 52). G. B. Salvi (1605–85), called Sassoferrato after his hometown in the Italian Marches, painted in a style which was related to that of Carlo Dolci and harkened back to that of Raphael. Murray does not mention the Sassoferrato that attracted Lieber's eye but he does note "two masterpieces of sculpture by

Canova, the Graces and the kneeling Magdalene." Gaspare Spontini's *La Vestale* was first performed before Napoleon in 1807. The composer later went on to serve Friedrich Wilhelm III of Prussia. It is likely that Lieber would have attended the opera in the Odeum concert hall, whose entrance was opposite that of the Leuchtenberg Palace. Despite his interest in penology, Lieber left Munich without paying a visit to the Zucht und Arbeits Haus (the Bavarian State Prison) in the Au suburb, to which Murray (pp. 56–57) devotes almost a page of description. Considering the importance of this prison, the growth of the University of Munich, and the progressive character of Bavaria's king, it is surprising that Lieber did not obtain an introduction to King Ludwig in an attempt to secure a meaningful position. Perhaps he was put off by the vanity he perceived in the monarch or counted too heavily on success in his native Berlin.

19[20] September. Of the Kapuziner promontory, Murray (*Southern Germany,* p. 199) says: "The view from the convent terrace, on the brow of the Capuzinerberg (about 10 minutes' walk from this churchyard [of St. Sebastian]) . . . extends over the town and castle to the colossal masses of the Unterberg . . . and Hohe Gohl . . . embracing the windings of the Salza." The Cathedral of Salzburg warrants little space in the Journal but receives approval in Murray (p. 198): "The Cathedral is a vast and imposing edifice in the Italian style, and of great architectural merit." Mozart, notes Murray (p. 198), "was born, 1756, in the third story of a house still standing (No. 225, opposite the University Church." Lieber apparently confuses his St. Maximus with Salzburg's St. Rupert (d. 623) whose "cell, cut in the rock, and now enclosed within St. Gile's Chapel (Aegidius Kapelle), is still pointed out" (Murray, p. 198). Lieber's frustration with the monetary system of Austria is clarified in Murray (p. 127) which discusses, at considerable length, a "good coinage, in which the florin or Gulden contains 60 Kreutzers. . . . This is called the Gulden Schwer, or Münz (heavy or good Gulden) . . . [and] a depreciated currency called Schein or Papier-geld (make believe or paper money). A Gulden Schein = only 24 kr. of the heavy currency; it is divided into 60 depreciated Kreutzers. . . . The copper money of the Schein currency is very puzzling; so that, whenever it is possible, it is well to decline receiving it in exchange, and to ask instead for Silber Münze. . . . Accounts are generally made out in Schein Gulden and Kreutzers, and it is possible that a dishonest innkeeper or tradesman might allow a stranger to pay in good Gulden an account made out in Schein Gulden." Concerning the police permits to use a coach, Murray (p. 130) says: "The passport must be presented, properly visé, before a place can be taken in a public conveyance."

20[21] September. Of the river journey to Vienna, Murray (*Southern Germany,* p. 146) says that "the descent of the Danube, from Linz to Vienna, is a most interesting voyage. . . . By the introduction of Steamboats, the navigation of this portion of the river is rendered much more easy and agreeable than formerly" [and p. 191] "Steamboats every day, (descending in 9 hours, ascending in 18 or 20.) — between Linz and Vienna, call at Grein, Yps, Pöchlarn, Mölk, and Stein. . . . The scenery of this part of the Danube is highly interesting, especially in the neighborhood of the celebrated Studel and Wirbel, at Mölk, and at Dürrenstein." Lieber seems to have been so occupied in his conversation with the countess that he missed many of the sights along the way. "Nussdorf is a small village . . . at the entrance of a branch channel of the Danube which flows past the walls of Vienna. . . . The passports of travellers are usually taken from them here. The steam-boat stops at Nussdorf and disembarks its passengers, who must proceed into the city, a distance of about 3½ miles, in a fiacre or other carriage which may be hired on the spot for 5 or 6 Zwanzigers. . . . At the outer lines or barriers leading into the suburbs of Vienna, 2 miles off, baggage is also liable to be searched by the officers of the municipal police. In addition to the articles prohibited on the frontier, edibles are here subjected to a tax" (Murray, p. 196). The "lines" specifically were, according to Murray (p. 154) "low ramparts, thrown up originally in 1703, to repel a threatened attack of the Hungarians." Leopoldstadt was the suburb just across a minor Danube tributary from Vienna (Murray, p. 185). It was here, rather than in Vienna proper, that Lieber decided to lodge. The Golden Lamb Hôtel, at 581 Prater-strasse, was an interesting choice. Murray (p. 149), who says of the inns of Vienna that "none [are] exceptionable on the whole," speaks in rather flattering terms of this hotel: "Goldenes Lamm, in the Leopoldstadt. The other inns are in narrow, confined streets, this in an open situation; it is a large house, it ranks among the best, and is free from smells, but is noisy and rather remote." Lieber seems to have wasted no time in attending a theatrical performance, concerning which Murray (p. 153) says: "Theatre an der Wien, in the Wieden suburb, the largest and most handsome house in Vienna, celebrated for melo-dramas and spectacles."

22[23] September. According to Murray (*Southern Germany,* p. 162), "the Archduke Charles's splendid Palace, . . . adjoining the Emperor's Palace, contains a library and one of the finest collections in Europe of Engravings and Drawings formed by the late Duke of Saxe Teschen, and much augmented by the present owner, his heir and son-in-law." The guidebook goes on to say, in keeping with Lieber's interest, that "among the drawings by the old masters (more than 15,000 in number), the most interesting is Raphael's own sketch of the Transfiguration. It was probably a study for the anatomy; since the figures, which occupy the same situation as in the painting, are all drawn naked; affording an interesting proof of the pains-taking and laborious exertions by which the greatest painter who ever lived attained to his eminence in art." Murray notes that there are 122 additional drawings attributed to Raphael in the collection, as well as 132 by Dürer and studies for the *Last Judgment* by Michelangelo. In Raphael's *Marriage of the Virgin* of 1504, the angry suitor appears on the right side; Lieber was recalling the reversed image in the print. Murray does not mention the Kugel Restaurant but does praise (p. 151) Viennese dining in general: "The Restauranteurs in Vienna are numerous, and cuisine excellent, not inferior to the Parisian, nor so expensive." The Theater in the suburb of Josephstadt was one of five mentioned in Murray (pp. 152–53), who noted that "the performances begin usually at half-past 6 or 7 o'clock, and are generally over soon after 9." The Botanic Garden adjoined the Belvedere Palace in the Rennweg (Murray, p. 171). The Imperial Arsenal (Kaiserliches Zeughaus) was in Renngasse and was open to the public on Monday and Thursday. Murray (p. 166) claims it to be "one of the richest and most extensive armouries in Europe," mentioning many of the flags and battlefield spoils from the Napoleonic campaigns but not the English banner that caught Lieber's attention.

23[24] September. The Polytechnic Institute, according to Murray (*Southern Germany,* p. 173–74), was "a handsome structure facing the Glacis, on the left in going towards the suburb called Wieden [and] was established by the late Emperor Francis in 1816, to afford instruction in the arts and practical sciences, as well as in trade, commerce, and manufactures, to 500 pupils. It is an interesting and useful establishment for the encouragement of national industry, which deserves to be seen." Of the Vienna Cathedral, Murray (pp. 157–58) says: "All that is lofty, imposing, and sublime in the Gothic style of architecture is united in the cathedral" of St. Stephen. Its tower, built between 1359–1453, "is a masterpiece of Gothic architecture, diminishing gradually from its base to its summit in regularly retreating arches and buttresses: it is 465 ft. high. It is well worth while to ascend it on account of the view. . . . The view extends not only over the city and suburbs, but across the Danube to the Marchfeld and over Napoleon's famous battle-fields of Lobau, Wagram, Asperne, and Essling."

24[25] September. Murray's *Southern Germany* does not discuss the Viennese prison in particular. It does say (p. 173), however, that "The public institutions of all kinds for the benefit of the people in Vienna are endowed and supported on a very enlarged and liberal scale. Few continental capitals can vie with it in the number and extent of its hospitals, schools, &c. The prisons, though less numerous and extensive than elsewhere, are well managed." Lieber, apparently, would have taken issue with that last sentence. The Esterhazy Summer Palace in the suburb of Mariahilf boasted a picture gallery which "includes no less than 50 examples of masters of the Spanish school, which are rarely found in other collections out of Spain" (Murray, pp. 172–73). In addition to its Velasquez, Zurbaran, and Murillo canvases, it also claimed works by Rubens, Correggio, Tintoretto, Rembrandt, Poussin, and Raphael. "The Sculpture Gallery contains some excellent works of modern artists; of Canova (bust of Napoleon), Thorwaldsen, Schadow, Bartolini, and others." Of Schönbrunn and its environs, Murray (pp. 179–80) says, "Schönbrunn, the palace of the Emperor, and his usual summer residence, situated about two miles from Vienna, was begun as a hunting seat for the Emperor Matthias, by Fischer of Erlach, and finished by Maria Theresa. . . . The building . . . possesses some historical interest, as having been inhabited by Napoleon in 1809, when the treaty of Schönbrunn was signed here. . . . Gloriette, a temple, with a colonnade of pillars, on the high bank immediately behind the palace, commands a fine view of Vienna. The spot seems better suited for a palace than that on which Schönbrunn actually stands. . . . Outside Schönbrunn Garden, a little way beyond the Botanic Garden, is the village of Hitzing, composed chiefly of villas and country houses, which on Sundays in inundated with the ruralising citizens of Vienna." Lieber does not say where in Hitzing he dined but it could have been in the Casino of Dommeyer which was "a house of entertainment, fitted up with the utmost magnificence, combining restaurant, cafe, billiard-tables, and a very splendid saloon for dining and music. . . . It is the practice of parties to come and sup here, listening to the attractive strains of Strauss's band." If so, hopefully it was Würth who paid for the occasion since "the admission is comparatively high." The Strauss noted by Murray in this 1843 description was probably Johann Sr., the orchestra of his son not having been formed until a year later.

25[26] September. This Thursday foray took Lieber into the mountainous Viennese surroundings, called the Wiener Wald (Vienna Woods) and essentially followed an itinerary set in Murray, *South Germany*, pp. 185–87. "No one should visit Vienna without exploring these heights and recesses." The Leopoldsburg offered a sweeping view of Vienna and the Danube, as well as a closer proximity to those Napoleonic battlefields Lieber had seen from the tower of St. Stephen. The Kahlenburg provided more views and the memory of the Polish deliverance of Vienna from the Turkish siege in 1684; it was here that Sobieski encamped before the battle. Kloster Neuburg was a large Augustinian monastery of largely 18th-century date. For such a country outing, according to Murray, transportation could be found when "quitting Vienna by the Nussdorf lines, where hackney-coaches and omnibuses (Stellwagen) may always be found." Vincenzo Bellini (1801–35) was one of the most important Italian operatic composers of the century. His *I Capuleti e i Montecchi* was one of his last works, performed first in Venice in 1830 and then in London and Paris in 1833.

26[27] September. The Ambras armor collection was in the lower Belvedere of the two-part royal palace "built by Prince Eugene of Savoy, who resided in it during the latter years of his life" (Murray, *Southern Germany*, p. 166). Murray (p. 167) says that the "Ambras Museum was formed in the latter part of the 16th century (about 1560) by Archduke Ferdinand II., . . . who, having a taste for art and antiquities, obtained from his friends and contemporary European monarchs suits of armour and other curiosities. . . . To many of them he wrote autograph letters; which together with the replies, have been carefully preserved, and serve to prove the authenticity of this the most interesting historical collection of ancient armour in Europe." The upper Belvedere housed the Imperial Picture Galleries, open Tuesdays and Fridays, and was given a lengthy description in Murray (pp. 169–71). The paintings were arranged in a didactic fashion, chronologically hung in galleries according to national school. This innovatively-organized collection was first opened to the public in 1781 — a dozen years before the Louvre, which required a revolution to open its doors. This was the collection that, today, forms the core of Vienna's celebrated Kunsthistorisches Museum, to which it was transferred in 1891. Lieber seems to have spent his time in Rooms III, IV, and V. devoted to the Italian masters of the Roman, Florentine, and Bolognese Schools. No. 52 was the famous *Madonna in the Meadow*. Lieber's reference to the Leuchtenberg Sassoferrato is found in his Munich entry for 18[19] September. Once again, Murray does not discuss this painting. The Antiken Cabinet adjoined the Royal Imperial Palace and was open on Mondays and Fridays. "It contains several very celebrated cameos and intaglios. . . . Among them the Apotheosis of Augustus [which] is perhaps the finest cameo in the world, remarkable alike for beautiful workmanship, historical interest . . . and for its large size. . . . It cost the Emperor Rudolph II. 12,000 ducats" (Murray, p. 164). Lieber's immediate mention of "Napoleon's head" might refer to the resemblance the portrayal of Augustus on this cameo has to the features of the young Bonaparte. The Antiquities Cabinet also contained a collection of 1200 vases and 134,000 coins and medals. Like the Picture Gallery and the Ambras Collection, this all is now part of the Kunsthistorisches Museum.

27[28] September. "The Picture Gallery of Prince Lichtenstein," according to Murray (*Southern Germany,* p. 171–72), in his uninhabited summer palace in the Rossau, is most liberally thrown open to the public every weekday at any hour but that of dinner. . . . It consists of 1484 pictures, among which are valuable specimens of almost every school of art, and many of the very first excellence," but adds Murray, "they are not well arranged, and there is no printed catalogue." The Kärnthner Thor Theater was "the Opera-house of Vienna, close to the Carinthian Gate. Operas and ballets are got up here in a very splendid style, not surpassed by any theatre in Germany, and the orchestra and singers are usually of first-rate excellence" (Murray, p. 153). Both Lieber and the general tourist seem to have had concerns about the Austrian police. According to Murray (pp. 133–34), who felt it necessary to devote considerable space to this issue, "were the English traveller to put implicit confidence in all the exaggerated accounts that have been written of that Argus-eyed monster the Austrian police, he would perhaps, in the first instance, be deterred from entering the country at all. . . . But it is equally certain that the police regulations are not more oppressive than in most other continental countries, and the officers by whom they are administered are invariably distinguished for the civility and politeness with which they treat strangers."

28[29] September. Most of this Sunday excursion into the scenic environs around Vienna is covered in Murray, *Southern Germany,* pp. 181–84. Mödling was a village lying among the vineyards at the entrance to the valley of the Briel. "A day may be very agreeably spent in wandering about the beautiful valley of the Briel, and visiting the various points of view in these grounds" while "Baden, a town of 4500 inhabitants, on the Schwächat, lies in the midst of vineyards, at the foot of the Styrian Alps, about 14 miles from Vienna" Murray points out that "during the life of the late Emperor, while the court was at Baden, the concourse of people was so great, that it was prudent to bespeak apartments beforehand. It is now comparatively deserted in consequence of the dislike the present Emperor has taken to it since an attempt was made by a madman to assassinate him. Still on Sundays and holidays from 10,000 to 12,000 strangers sometimes assemble here from Vienna."

2 October. "The Northern Railroad, or Kaiser Ferdinand's Nord-Eisenbahn," according to Murray (*South Germany,* p. 407), "is completed from Vienna to Brünn, and to Olmütz, and is intended to be continued to Cracow and Bochnia, a distance of 276 miles, and thus to connect the Danube with the Vistula. Even in its present stage it is the first and greatest undertaking of the sort completed in Germany. . . . Trains go 2 or 3 times a day, taking from 4 ½ to 5 ½ hours to Brünn." The inn at which Lieber stayed at Brünn (the modern Brno) was probably the "Kaiser von Österreich; new and well-fitted up, and close to the railroad" (Murray, p. 408). Lundenburg (51 miles from Vienna) was a stop on the route to Brünn.

3 October. Lieber was thwarted in his desire to visit the Castle of Spielberg due to construction. His interests in the place were penological. Murray (*South Germany,* p. 408) says that "since its fortifications were destroyed by the French, [it was] converted into a prison, in which state criminals, conspirators, and political offenders are confined. . . . By the clemency of the present Emperor, however, the tenants of its dungeons on account of political offences have all been set free." From Brünn to Prague, Lieber was forced to make use of a horse-drawn mail coach.

5 October. Lieber's Ratchin, of which he was uncertain, may be identical with Hradschin, one of the four city quarters of Prague; it lies on the left bank of the Moldau. The Hradschin (meaning "steep hill") is the site of the medieval palace of the Bohemian kings.

6 October. Murray (*South Germany,* p. 383), says that "a very small but neat Steamer, resembling those on the Thames above London-bridge, navigates the Elbe from Dresden to within 20 miles of Prague; omnibuses convey passengers over the intermediate distance." Inclement weather and spirited conversation appear to have distracted Lieber from one of the most scenic river voyages in Europe, through the sandstone hills of "Saxon Switzerland" and on past the mighty mountaintop fortress of Königstein. Lieber was familiar with Dresden, having lived briefly in the city in 1820, following his doctoral studies at Jena. According to Murray (*Continent,* p. 440), Lieber's hotel in Dresden would have been in the Neumarkt (New Market Square), near the Picture Gallery, and was described as a "very good inn."

8 October. *Oberon* was written by Carl Maria von Weber (1786–1826). This play may have had a special significance for Lieber since he had called on Weber in London on 4 June 1826, when the composer was there to oversee the production of this opera; Weber died the next day. The Painting Gallery of Dresden was housed in the former Riding Stables (the Stallgebäude or Johanneum), now the Transportation Museum, adjacent to the New Market Square. In 1856 the collection was transferred to the Zwinger Palace and installed in a wing especially built for it by Gottfried Semper (See the old installation description and commentary on individual paintings in Murray, *Continent,* pp. 445–50). A plan of the galleries as Lieber knew them is given in Murray (p. 446), and in greater detail (but with different arrangements) in Friedrich Matthaei, *Königlich Sächsichen Gemälde-Galerie zu Dresden.* Dresden: Gästner'schen Buchdruckerei, 1835, II. The gallery in which the Raphael and its companions hung is depicted in a print of 1830 reproduced in Angelo Walther, "Zur Hängung der Dresdener Gemäldegalerie zwischen 1765 und 1832," *Dresdener Kunstblätter* 25 (1981): 79. It is interesting to compare

Lieber's description of this encounter with Raphael's *Sistine Madonna* with that which he had had, as a young romantic, in the summer of 1820, when he recorded that "I saw some pictures but irresistibly I was drawn on until I stood before the *Madonna del Sisto*. I stood surprised — overcome — and wept, and looked again, amazed and touched — and so I stood from nine to one, when the gallery was closed and I walked down those stairs another being — I felt at once, my soul was wider" (as quoted in Freidel, *Francis Lieber,* pp. 28–29). Lieber's praise of the painting is also close to that he had used in his biographical entry on Raphael in the *Encyclopedia Americana* of 1832: "The loftiness, dignity and sublimity, combined with a sweetness, grace and beauty,which reign in this picture, render it inimitable." Many of the same overwhelming sentiments had been felt by the indefatigable English traveler Mrs. Anna Jameson a decade before Lieber's return to Dresden. In her *Visits and Sketches at Home and Abroad* (London: Saunders & Otley, 1834), Mrs. Jameson described the *Sistine Madonna* as "that divinest image that ever shaped itself in palpable hues and forms to the living eye!" Jameson found the painting a "revelation of ineffable grace, and purity, and truth, and goodness!" Interestingly, Lieber first wrote in his Journal of the Christ Child being "*in* her arm" and then crossed the word out in favor of "*on* her arm." Much the same feeling had been expressed by Mrs. Jameson, who had said that the Child "seems not so much supported as enthroned in her arms." Both writers implied a hovering relationship to the Madonna. Raphael's *Sistine Madonna* was still on Lieber's mind at the end of his life when he wrote an essay on the U.S. Constitution. See his *The Miscellaneous Writings II: Contributions to Political Science* (Philadelphia and London: J. J. Lippincott, 1880), p. 63. In this context, Lieber says that it was as unfair to the memory of Columbus to name the continents he discovered after Vespucci as it would be to disassociate the *Sistine Madonna* from Raphael. Among the other paintings in the Gallery, Lieber mentioned as being of especial interest to him were three canvases by the Italian Baroque master Carlo Dolci (Lieber's *Judith* is actually a *Salome*), Titian's *Tribute Money* and a workshop copy of his *Venus Before a Mirror,* Palma Vecchio's *Venus Resting,* and, probably, Giorgione's celebrated *Sleeping Venus,* then attributed entirely to Titian's hand. Some five Correggios were in the Museum and it is difficult to determine which one caught Lieber's especial attention; perhaps it was his beautiful *Night Nativity.*

9 October. Lieber spent the day across the Elbe at the Japanese palace (designed 1727–37 by Pöppelmann) which housed collections of antiquities, porcelains (oriental, Meissen, etc.) and a library of rare books and manuscripts. Fresh from the great collection in Munich, Lieber found the Antikensammlung of Dresden disappointing, a sentiment shared by Murray (*Continent,* p. 454–55): "A traveller fresh from the galleries of Rome and Florence may perhaps be disposed to despise this collection [of ancient art], which indeed ranks after that at Munich, &c., and has moreover suffered both from the ignorant mutilations of a barbarous age, and from the reparations and restorations of a more enlightened period." The porcelain collection was of greater value. According to Murray

(p. 456) "Dr. Klemme, the intelligent director, has taken great pains in the arrangement of this collection in its present place." That collection is currently at the Zwinger and the Japanese Palace now houses a museum of prehistory and ethnography.

10 October. A collection of plaster casts was installed beneath the Picture Gallery of the Stallgebäude. "They are called the Mengsischen Abgüsse, having been made by and under the superintendence of the celebrated artist Raphael Mengs. . . . Amongst other interesting objects is a group representing Menelaus carrying away the body of Patroclus, put together and restored from antique fragments in the Pitti Palace at Florence [now exhibited in the Loggia dei Lanzi on the Piazza della Signore]" (Murray, *Continent,* pp. 449–50). The Royal Palace (largely destroyed in WWII) "possesses a great attraction for the lovers of modern art in the frescoes, by Bendemann, in the Thronsaal. A series of scenes painted on gold grounds, representing the various conditions of life, its occupations and labours from the cradle to the grave, form a frieze round the room. . . . At the lower end are figures of heroes and great men; at the upper four large compositions from German history. . . . These paintings are superior to most of the modern German frescoes. The Ball-room is painted with subjects from mythology and private life of the ancient Greeks" (Murray, pp. 442–43). The largely ethnographic collection in which Lieber took particular interest appears to have been that housed at the Zwinger Palace (see description in Murray, p. 453). Lieber saw the statue of Beethoven a year before its installation in Bonn where "a bronze statue by Hänel was erected to him in 1845, in the Münster-platz" (Murray, p. 260).

11 October. Even in Lieber's day Leipzig was celebrated for its great fairs but Murray (*Continent,* p. 436) cautions that "during the fair the charge for a room is double the ordinary price." Lieber would have been in Leipzig at the end of the city's Michaelmas Fair when "every hotel and lodging-house is filled to overflowing; the streets are thronged with strange costumes and faces; Jews from Poland, Tyrolese, Americans, and even Persians from Teflis, Armenians, Turks, and Greeks, are mingled together as in a masquerade, and most of the countries of Europe send representatives hither with their produce" (Murray, p. 436).

21 October. The text of this letter dealing with Lieber's second interview with the Prussian monarch is partially given in German and is presented in its original form in the Appendix. An attempt on the King's life had been made by Heinrich Ludwig Tschech on 26 July 1844. There were no political motives; the would-be assassin seems to have been mentally unbalanced and to have blamed the King for his personal problems. His shots went wild and he was arrested. Despite the King's inclination towards leniency, his counselors persuaded him to allow Tschech's execution in December, the result being an evaporation of previous public sympathy for the King. Perry (*Life and Letters of Francis Lieber,* pp. 190–91) presents some of the content of this letter but in much abbreviated form and synthesized with some of the content of the letters of 26 and 29 October.

29 October. The text of this letter is partially given in German and is presented in its original form in the Appendix D. A visual reconstruction of Lieber's conversation with the great geographer can be imagined through the colored lithograph of *Alexander von Humboldt in his Study*, ca. 1845, by Paul Grabow in the Kupferstichkabinett of the Germanisches Nationalmuseum in Nuremberg (Kapsel 1338a, HB 25382/L3260). The print is inscribed "A true picture of my study as I work on the second volume of my *Cosmos*," and has been reproduced in *Berlin: Die Ausstellung zur Geschichte der Stadt*, ed. Gottfried Korff and Reinhard Rürup (Berlin: Nicolai, 1987), p. 134. For additional information on Lieber's visit with the great geographer and his interest in penology, as well as the assistance he rendered Lieber, see Lieber's 1859 Humboldt address given in his *Miscellaneous Writings I*, p. 395.

11 December. Lieber had returned to Hamburg by the beginning of November when he was writing letters to de Tocqueville, mailed from that city on 7 November and on 26 November. Extracts of these letters are given in Perry, *Life and Letters of Francis Lieber*, pp. 191–93. The Rauhes Haus (loosely, "Hard Times House") was apparently a poor house near Hamburg. Count Christian von Bernstorff was the former Prussian minister for foreign affairs in whose family Niebuhr had secured Lieber a position as tutor in July 1825.

15 December. On the sewers of Hamburg, see the commentary for 29 June.

21 December. The *Fragments* by Lieber was published in Hamburg in 1845 as *Bruchstücke über Gegenstände der Strafkunde besonders über des Eremitensystem* (n.p., n.d.).

23 December. Lieber discussed the Prussian offer and his having to refuse it in a 2 February letter to Mittermaier (Perry, *Life and Letters of Francis Lieber*, p. 194).

6 January. By 1853, the Nicolai Church was nearing completion (Murray, *Continent*, p. 321): "The churches [of rebuilt Hamburg] have little architectural beauty, excepting St. Nicholas [Nicolai], in the Hopfenmarkt, a noble modern Gothic structure, with a tower and spire at the W. end, of open work, which will be a beautiful building. It is designed by the English architect G. G. Scott, who built Camberwell Ch."

8 January. The "Apostles" to which Lieber referred are in the early fifteenth-century Town Hall of Bremen: "In a particular compartment of the cellars beneath it, shown only by permission of the burgomaster, are casks called the Rose and the 12 Apostles, filled with fine hock, some of it a century and a half old" (Murray, *Continent*, p. 375). Lieber's *Roland* was to be found in the market square in front of the Rathhaus: "a stone statue of a man 18 ft. high, a symbol of the rights and privileges of the town, erected 1412 in the place of a wooden one. The drawn sword and the head and hand at the feet of the figure refer to the power of life and death in criminal cases enjoyed by the magistrates" (Murray, p. 375).

9 January. The Justus Möser monument was in the Cathedral Square in Osnabrück according to Murray (*Continent*, p. 374), who offered no help to Lieber as to the identity of the sculptor. The Gothic cathedral in which Lieber offered his prayers for the family was similar in style to that of Cologne. The Schnellwagen (Schnellpost) was the Prussian version of the postal diligence.

10 January. According to Murray (*Continent,* p. 234), "Düsseldorf, though a neat town, contains nothing remarkable at present except its school of living artists, who occupy the Palace near the Rhine. . . . It contained, down to 1805, the famous collection of pictures now at Munich. . . . The old pictures which now fill the gallery are not good for much. Tasso and the 2 Leonoras by Carl Sohn is a charming modern work." Of the other works that Lieber inspected, Murray mentions only the painting by Deger, which actually was in the Church of the Jesuits: "In the ch. of the Jesuits is a good specimen of Deger's painting. It is over the altar in the S. aisle, and represents the Virgin standing on clouds, supporting the infant Saviour" (p. 234). Lieber would have mentally compared this modern treatment of a subject familiar to him from his beloved *Sistine Madonna* by Raphael. Schlemiel refers to the fanciful *Peter Schlemiels wundersame Geschichte* of 1814 by the Prussian botanist/poet Adelbert von Chamiso, whom Lieber had met in 1825 during salon evenings in the Hitzig home in Berlin.

12 January. Lieber mistakes the author of the Van Dyck *Crucifixion* in the Cathedral for Rubens; see comments from Murray to entry of 17 June.

13 January. The "Venice of the North," Bruges today is a Belgian Williamsburg, overrun with tourists. In Lieber's day it was otherwise. "This city," writes Murray (*Continent,* p. 121), "the Liverpool of the middle ages, which was rich and powerful when Antwerp and Ghent were only in their infancy, is now reduced to 49,437 inhab., of whom 15,000 are paupers. . . . At present it wears an air of desolation; the people in its streets are few, and it has lost the indications of commercial activity. Its appearance is the more mournful from its great extent, and the size and unaltered splendour of many of the public buildings and private houses, —vestiges of its former wealth and prosperity." Lieber's notation concerning Charles II and Maximilian is explained in Murray (p. 125): "On the S. side of the square [the Grande Place] . . . is the house inhabited by Charles II during his exile from England . . . the opposite corner . . . now occupies the site of the Craenenburg, historically remarkable as having been the prison of the Empr. Maximilian, 1487–8, when his unruly Flemish subjects, irritated at some infringement of their rights, rose up against him, seized his person, and shut him up in this building, which they had fortified, and converted into a prison by barring the windows." The quick mention of "tower belfry, chime" alluded to Les Halles on the same Grande Place. "The tower or belfry in its centre is an elegant Gothic structure, imposing from its height. . . . The Chimes from the tower are the finest in Europe and almost incessant: they are played 4 times an hour by machinery" (Murray, p. 125). Elsewhere, Murray (p. 97) informs us that "Chimes, or carillons, were invented in the Low Countries; they have certainly been brought to the greatest perfection here, and are still heard in every town. . . . So fond are the Dutch and Belgians of this kind of music, that in some places the chimes appear scarcely to be at rest for ten minutes, whether by day or night. . . . Chimes were in existence at Bruges in 1300." In the church of Notre Dame, Lieber admired the "Tombs of Charles the Bold, Duke of Burgundy, and his daughter Mary, wife of the Empr. Maximilian, the last scions of the house of Burgundy, and the last native sovereigns of the Netherlands. The effigies of both father and daughter, made of copper, richly gilt, but not displaying any high excellence as works of art, repose at full length on slabs of black marble. . . . The Monument of Mary of Burgundy was erected in 1495, and is far superior to the other." The *Bruges Madonna* in the same church is now firmly attributed to Michelangelo, dated to 1503, and regarded among his most significant works. In Lieber's day, there was some doubt. "In a chapel in the S. side of the Ch. is a statue of the Virgin and Child, said to be by Michael Angelo, and is believed by Sir Joshua Reynolds to have certainly the air of his school. There is a grandeur about the upper part of the Virgin's figure, and in the turn of the head and in the features, which resemble some of M. Angelo's works. . . . Horace Walpole is said to have offered 30,000 fl. for it" (Murray, p. 122). Murray continues his itinerary of Bruges by noting that "close to Notre Dame is the Hospital of St. John, an ancient charitable institution, where the sick are attended by the religious sisters of the house," and which "also contains the celebrated pictures, the pride of the city and admiration of travellers, painted by Hans Hemling, or more correctly Memling, and presented by him to the hospital out of gratitude for the succour which he had received while a patient in it, suffering from wounds received in the battle of Nancy, 1477" (Murray, pp. 122–23). Murray went on to laud, as did Lieber, the famous *Shrine of St. Ursula* and to note the presence of a *Holy Family* by Van Dyck. Of the Chapel of the Blood, Murray (p. 124) says: "There is a Gothic chapel in the corner of the Square at the opposite end of the Town House . . . called La Chapelle du Sang de Dieu, from some drops of our Saviour's blood, brought . . . from the Holy Land . . . and now deposited in a richly jewelled and enamelled shrine of silver gilt. . . . The crypt called the Chapel of St. John, is the oldest building in Bruges, perhaps of the 9th cent." As it was for Lieber, a principal attraction of the Palais de Justice was "a magnificent chimney-piece, occupying one side of the room [Magistrates Chamber], carved in wood (date 1529), including statues as large of life and well executed, of Charles V, Mary of Burgundy and Maximilian, Charles the Bold and Margaret of York, his third wife, surrounded with coats of arms of Burgundy, Spain, etc. It is also decorated with marble bas-reliefs representing the story of Susannah" (Murray, p. 124). In the Academy of Painting, the van Eyck that would have most attracted Lieber's eye would have been the celebrated *Madonna of Canon van der Päle* of 1436. It is interesting that even in their museum setting, the religious works in the Academy still prompted the devotional messages of the faithful.

Select Bibliography

Barclay, David E. *Frederick William IV and the Prussian Monarchy, 1840–61.* Oxford: Clarendon Press, 1995.

Becker, Peter Wolfgang. "Francis Liebers wissenshaftliche Leistungen in den U.S.A." In *Franz Lieber und die deutsch-amerikanischen Beziehungen im 19. Jahrhundert.* Ed. Peter Schäfer and Karl Schmitt, 31–44. Jenaer Beiträge zur Politikwissenschaft no. 2. Weimar/Cologne/Vienna: Böhlau Verlag, 1993.

Brown, Bernard Edward. *American Conservatives: The Political Thought of Francis Lieber and John W. Burgess.* New York: Columbia University Press, 1951.

Dorfman, Joseph, and Rexford G. Tugwell. "Francis Lieber: German Scholar in America." *Columbia University Quarterly* 30 (1938): 159–90, 267–93.

Farr, James. "Francis Lieber and the Interpretation of American Political Science." *Journal of Politics* 52 (1990): 1027–49.

Freidel, Frank. *Francis Lieber: Nineteenth-Century Liberal.* Baton Rouge: Louisiana State University Press, 1947.

————. *Franz Lieber: ein Vorkämpfer des nationalen Denkens und des internationalen Rechts.* Bad Nauheim: Ludwig Wagner for the Franz-Lieber-Haus, Bad Godesberg/Rhein, 1957.

Harley, Lewis R. *Francis Lieber: His Life and Political Philosophy.* 1899. Reprint, New York: AMS Press, 1970.

Holls, Friedrich Wilhelm. *Franz Lieber: Sein Leben und seine Werke.* New York: E. Steiger & Co., 1884.

Kennedy, Thomas J. "Francis Lieber (1798–1872): German-American Poet and Transmitter of German Culture to America." *German-American Studies* 5 (1972): 28–51.

Kühnhardt, Ludger. "Zwei Transatlantiker: Bezüge und Beziehungen zwischen Alexis de Tocqueville und Franz Lieber." *Franz Lieber und die deutsch-amerikanischen Beziehungen im 19. Jahrhundert.* Ed. Peter Schäfer and Karl Schmitt, 135–55. Jenaer Beiträge zur Politikwissenschaft no. 2. Weimar/Cologne/Vienna: Böhlau Verlag, 1993.

Lieber, Francis. *Letters to a Gentleman in Germany, Written After a Trip from Philadelphia to Niagara.* 1834. Reprint, New York/London: Johnson Reprint Co., 1971.

————. *The Miscellaneous Writings I: Reminiscences, Addresses, and Essays.* Ed. Daniel L. Gilman. Philadelphia/London: J. B. Lippincott, 1880.

_____. *The Miscellaneous Writings II: Contributions to Political Science.* Ed. Daniel L. Gilman. Philadelphia/London: J. B. Lippincott, 1880.

_____. *A Popular Essay on Subjects of Penal Law and on Uninterrupted Solitary Confinement at Night and Joint Labour by Day.* Philadelphia: Philadelphia Society for Alleviating the Miseries of Public Prisons, 1838.

_____. *Reminiscences of an Intercourse with George Berthold Niebuhr, the Historian of Rome.* London: Richard Bentley, 1835.

_____. *The Stranger in America.* Vol. 1. London: Richard Bentley, 1835.

Mack, Charles R. "Beauty in its Highest Degree: Francis Lieber and an 1844 Appreciation of Raphael." *Southeastern College Art Conference Review* 14, no. 1 (2001): 15–20.

Matthaei, Friedrich. *Verzeichniss der Königlich Sächsischen Gemälde-Galerie zu Dresden.* Dresden: Gästner'schen Buchdruckerei, 1835.

Murray, John. *Handbook for Travellers in Berks, Bucks, and Oxfordshire.* London: John Murray, 1860.

_____. *Handbook for Travellers in France: Being a Guide to Normandy, Brittany; the Rivers Seine, Loire, Rhone, and Garbonne; the French Alps, Dauphine, Provence, and the Pyrenees; their Railways and Roads.* 5th ed. London: John Murray, 1854.

_____. *Handbook for Travellers in Gloucestershire, Worcestershire, and Herfordshire.* London: John Murray, 1867.

_____. *Handbook for Travellers on the Continent: Being a Guide to Holland, Belgium, Prussia, Northern Germany, and the Rhine from Holland to Switzerland.* 9th ed. London: John Murray, 1853.

_____. *Handbook for Travellers in Southern Germany: Being a Guide to Bavaria, Austria, Tyrol, Salzburg, Styria, etc.* 3d ed. London: John Murray, 1843.

_____. *Handbook for Visitors to Paris.* 4th ed. London: John Murray, 1870.

_____. *Handbook to London as it is.* London: John Murray, 1868.

Perry, Thomas Sergeant. *The Life and Letters of Francis Lieber.* Boston: James R. Osgood, 1882.

Preuss, Hugo. *Franz Lieber: ein Bürger zweier Welten.* Hamburg: J. F. Richter, 1886.

Rook, Christian. "Lieber, Prescott, Schem, Zickel, and Schrader: Five 'German-American Encyclopedias.'" *Yearbook of German-American Studies* 32 (1997): 73–98.

Samson, Steven Alan. "Francis Lieber on the Sources of Civil Liberty." *Humanitas* 9, no. 2 (1996).

Schuette, Oswald F. "Franz Lieber und Alexander von Humboldt." *Franz Lieber und die deutsch-amerikanischen Beziehungen im 19. Jahrhundert.* Ed. Peter Schäfer and Karl Schmitt, 121–34. Jenaer Beiträge zur Politikwissenschaft no. 2. Weimar/Cologne/Vienna: Böhlau Verlag, 1993.

Vincent, John Martin. "Francis Lieber." *Dictionary of American Biography.* 1933 edition.

Index

This index includes names of persons and places. For subject access, see "Thematic References by Entry" on pages 115–16. Page numbers in italics refer to illustrations.